Philosophy and Blade Runner

Also by Timothy Shanahan

THE EVOLUTION OF DARWINISM

PHILOSOPHY 9/11

THE PROVISIONAL IRISH REPUBLICAN ARMY AND THE MORALITY OF TERRORISM

REASON AND INSIGHT (2nd edition)

Philosophy and Blade Runner

Timothy Shanahan
Loyola Marymount University, USA

palgrave
macmillan

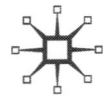

© Timothy Shanahan 2014

All rights reserved. No reproduction, copy or transmission of this publication may be made without written permission.

No portion of this publication may be reproduced, copied or transmitted save with written permission or in accordance with the provisions of the Copyright, Designs and Patents Act 1988, or under the terms of any licence permitting limited copying issued by the Copyright Licensing Agency, Saffron House, 6–10 Kirby Street, London EC1N 8TS.

Any person who does any unauthorized act in relation to this publication may be liable to criminal prosecution and civil claims for damages.

The author has asserted his right to be identified as the author of this work in accordance with the Copyright, Designs and Patents Act 1988.

First published 2014 by
PALGRAVE MACMILLAN

Palgrave Macmillan in the UK is an imprint of Macmillan Publishers Limited, registered in England, company number 785998, of Houndmills, Basingstoke, Hampshire RG21 6XS.

Palgrave Macmillan in the US is a division of St Martin's Press LLC, 175 Fifth Avenue, New York, NY 10010.

Palgrave Macmillan is the global academic imprint of the above companies and has companies and representatives throughout the world.

Palgrave® and Macmillan® are registered trademarks in the United States, the United Kingdom, Europe and other countries.

ISBN 978-1-137-41228-7   ISBN 978-1-137-41229-4 (eBook)
DOI 10.1007/978-1-137-41229-4

A catalogue record for this book is available from the British Library.

A catalog record for this book is available from the Library of Congress.

Typeset by MPS Limited, Chennai, India.

Transferred to Digital Printing in 2014

In memory of my mother, about whom only good things come to mind

Contents

Preface		xi
Acknowledgments		xiii
1	**Introduction**	**1**
	The Film's Basic Storyline	1
	Androids, Replicants, and Humans	2
	Electric Sheep Transmuted	4
	From Workprint to Final Cut	7
	The Deck-a-Rep Debate	11
	'You Did a Man's Work. But Are You a Man?'	12
	'Proud of Yourself, Little Man?'	18
	Conclusions	20
2	**Being Human**	**22**
	Introduction	22
	'It's Artificial?'	23
	'You Nexus, Huh?'	27
	'You're So Different'	32
	'We Have a Lot in Common'	33
	'Did You Ever Take that Test Yourself?'	37
	'Now It's My Turn'	38
	'More Human than Human'	39
	Conclusions	41
3	**Persons**	**43**
	Introduction	43
	'They Were Designed to Copy Human Beings'	44
	'I'm Not *in* the Business. I *Am* the Business'	47
	'That Was Irrational of You'	49

Contents

	'Replicants are Like Any Other Machine'	50
	'The Custom Tailored Genetically Engineered Humanoid Replicant'	52
	'Nothing is Worse than Having an Itch You Can Never Scratch'	55
	'That's What It Is to Be a Slave'	56
	Conclusions	58
4	**Identity**	**60**
	Introduction	60
	'How Can It Not Know What It Is?'	62
	'Memories – You're Talking about Memories!'	66
	'I Can't Rely On…'	68
	'Deckard, Ninety-Seven'	71
	'I Don't Know if It's Me or Tyrell's Niece'	74
	'There's Some of Me in You'	75
	'You Play Beautifully'	77
	Conclusions	78
5	**Consciousness**	**80**
	Introduction	80
	'I Think, Sebastian, Therefore I Am'	81
	'We're Not Computers, Sebastian'	86
	'Very Good, Pris. Now Show Him Why'	88
	'He Design Your Mind, Your Brain'	89
	'I Had in Mind Something a Little More Radical'	92
	'We're Physical'	95
	Conclusions	97
6	**Freedom**	**99**
	Introduction	99
	'No Choice, Pal'	101
	'The Great Advantage to Being Alive is Having a Choice'	103
	'I'd Rather Be a Killer than a Victim'	105
	'Show Me What You're Made Of'	106
	'Yeah, What Do You Want?'	107

Contents

	'I Don't Know Why He Saved My Life'	110
	Conclusions	113
7	**Being Good**	**115**
	Introduction	115
	Overcoming and Becoming	116
	Beyond Good and Evil	118
	'Aren't You the "Good Man"?'	121
	'Man is Something that Should be Overcome'	124
	A Nexus 6 *Übermensch*?	126
	'Is He Good?'	127
	Conclusions	129
8	**God**	**131**
	Introduction	131
	'Fiery the Angels Fell'	132
	'Rebel Angels from th' Ethereal Skie'	134
	'I Ought to be Thy Adam'	136
	'Man is Nothing Else but What He Makes of Himself'	138
	'You Were Made as Well as We Could Make You'	139
	'Man is the Being Whose Project is to be God'	143
	Conclusions	145
9	**Death**	**147**
	Introduction	147
	'Can the Maker Repair What He Makes?'	148
	'I'm Afraid That's a Little Out of My Jurisdiction'	150
	'How Long Do I Live?'	151
	'I Want More Life'	157
	'Four, Five. How to Stay Alive'	160
	Conclusions	162
10	**Time and Meaning**	**164**
	Introduction	164
	'All Those Moments Will Be Lost in Time'	165
	'All the Time, Pal'	167

ix

Contents

'Time to Die'	168
'Time Enough'	170
'Four Years Was a Short Time or a Long Time'	173
'It's Too Bad She Won't Live'	175
Conclusions	177

Epilogue   179

Notes   183

Literature Cited   206

Index   213

Preface

Ridley Scott's *Blade Runner* has been called the most visually dense, thematically challenging, and influential science fiction film ever made. It is routinely ranked among the greatest science fiction films of all time.[1] It has been uniformly praised for its stunning depiction of a technologically advanced but grim dystopian society of the near future. Occasionally it is recognized that the greatness of the film goes much deeper than just its impressive visual achievements. Rachela Morrison (1990, p. 2) notes that, 'in the immodest guise of a noir/science fiction thriller,' *Blade Runner* is essentially 'a philosophical film' that 'leaps from impeccable intricacies of *mise-en-scène* to questions about the nature of man, God, beast, the meaning of existence, and the workings of the universe.' Paul M. Sammon likewise observes that: '*Blade Runner* ... addresses universal human concerns, not only what is human and what is real, but who am I, and where is my place in the universe, and why am I here, and why am I being exploited, and why am I not fighting against that?'[2] Yet despite the occasional recognition that *Blade Runner* is a deeply thought-provoking film, its considerable potential for eliciting novel perspectives on classic philosophical issues has so far been underappreciated.

My aim in this book is to invite readers to explore the philosophy *of Blade Runner* and to explore philosophy *through Blade Runner*. The first chapter provides background information about the film that will later prove useful as we explore its philosophical themes. Subsequent chapters consider a range of perennial philosophical issues that arise from reflection on specific scenes within the film, including human nature, personhood, identity, consciousness, freedom, morality, God, death, and the meaning of life. An epilogue responds to the challenge that a work of *fiction* cannot provide significant insights into

Preface

'the real world.' Although this entire book can be read as one long argument to the contrary, in the epilogue I will make this argument more explicit. However, we should not expect definitive answers to the questions we will consider. *Blade Runner* is, after all, a film, not a formal philosophical treatise, and thus is open to multiple interpretations. As Scott Bukatman (2012, p. 16) observes, '*Blade Runner* ... effectively undermines interpretative certitudes' by producing 'an inexhaustible complexity, an infinity of surfaces to be encountered and explored.... [U]nlike many contemporary films, *Blade Runner* refuses to explain itself.'[3] I consider this a significant strength of the film that makes it ideal for prompting philosophical reflection. This book contains my reflections. In the end, of course, you must reach your own conclusions. Thinking about *Blade Runner* is a fine place to start.

Reading a book like this is obviously no substitute for viewing a film (and vice versa). If you have never seen the film, do not deny yourself this pleasure any longer. If you have already seen the film, now would be an excellent time to watch it again so that the details are fresh. Doing so will help you to better appreciate the discussions that follow, and will make recognition of the various scenes to be referenced more immediate. So put down this book, watch the film (again), enjoy its multifaceted brilliance, and meet me in Chapter 1 after the credits roll.

Timothy Shanahan
Los Angeles 2014

Acknowledgments

I am grateful to the Bellarmine College of Liberal Arts at Loyola Marymount University for providing a BCLA Fellowship that provided the time needed to complete this book. I would also like to thank my colleagues in the LMU Department of Philosophy for graciously offering helpful comments on many of the chapters: Eric Balmer, Scott Cameron, Christopher Kaczor, Elizabeth Murray, Martin Nemoianu, Daniel Speak, and Michael Derek von Barandy. I owe a special debt to Rochelle Goff for her love, support, and understanding as I completed this book.

1 Introduction

'Do you like our owl?'

(Rachael, to Deckard)

The Film's Basic Storyline

The philosophical issues *Blade Runner* raises are complex, but the film's basic storyline is relatively simple and easily summarized. An opening crawl provides essential background information for the story about to unfold:

> **Early in the 21st Century, THE TYRELL CORPORATION advanced Robot evolution into the NEXUS phase – a being virtually identical to a human – known as a replicant.**
>
> **The NEXUS 6 Replicants were superior in strength and agility, and at least equal in intelligence, to the genetic engineers who created them. Replicants were used Off-world as slave labor, in the hazardous exploration and colonization of other planets.**
>
> **After a bloody mutiny by a NEXUS 6 combat team in an Off-world colony, Replicants were declared illegal on earth – under penalty of death.**
>
> **Special police squads – BLADE RUNNER UNITS – had orders to shoot to kill, upon detection, any trespassing Replicants.**
>
> **This was not called execution.**
>
> **It was called retirement.**

Los Angeles, November 2019. Rick Deckard (Harrison Ford) is an exceptionally effective ex-blade runner who had quit because, as he laconically narrates, he'd had 'a bellyful of killing.'[1]

He is coerced into resuming his former occupation by Capt. Harry Bryant (M. Emmet Walsh) of the LAPD. His specific task is to retire four rogue replicants that staged a mutiny Off-world, killed the crew of a shuttle, and then made their way to Los Angeles – for reasons as yet unknown. After meeting with the replicants' creator, Dr Eldon Tyrell (Joe Turkel), Deckard eventually kills two of the replicants, Zhora (Joanna Cassidy) and Pris (Daryl Hannah), and is saved from his own death at the hands of Leon (Brion James) by a beautiful experimental replicant named Rachael (Sean Young) with whom, incidentally, he is falling in love. The film's action climaxes in a rather one-sided battle between Deckard and Roy Batty (Rutger Hauer), the relentless, exuberant, and extremely dangerous leader of the rogue replicants. Rather than simply killing Deckard, as he easily could, in the end Batty saves him, and then just before expiring delivers a poignant reflection on his own brief life. Deckard returns to his apartment where Rachael declares her love for him, and together they (attempt to) flee the city. The credits then roll over a pulsating Vangelis soundtrack as the audience is left to ponder what it has just seen.

Androids, Replicants, and Humans

Ridley Scott judges *Blade Runner* to be unusual as films go: '*Blade Runner* works on a level which I haven't seen much – or ever – in a mainstream film. It works like a book. Like a very dark novel' (Knapp and Kulas 2005, p. xiv). This is hardly surprising given the film's genesis in Philip K. Dick's 1968 dystopian science fiction novel, *Do Androids Dream of Electric Sheep?* In his biography of Philip Kindred Dick ('PKD' to his legions of fans), Emmanuel Carrère (2004, p. 131) attributes Dick's writing of *Electric Sheep* to his desire to extol the glory of the human being: 'But to extol the glory of the human being, Phil first had to define and flesh out the opposite of the human, which for Phil was not the animal or the thing but what he called the "simulacrum" – in other words, the robot.' Androids, robots, and

Introduction

other human simulacra populate his writings, including *Electric Sheep*. As Dick explains, '*Sheep* stemmed from my basic interest in the problem of differentiating the authentic human being from the reflexive machine, which I call an android. In my mind android is a metaphor for people who are physiologically human but behaving in a nonhuman way' (Sammon 1996, p. 16).

Intelligent aliens, rebellious robots, and synthetic humanoids are, of course, staples of science fiction. The idea that we might someday come face-to-face with non-humans that are virtually indistinguishable from human beings is an irresistible plot device of innumerable science fiction stories. In typical fashion, Dick takes this interesting idea, twists it a bit, and thereby makes it even more intriguing. In 'The Android and the Human' (1972), published four years after *Electric Sheep*, he imagines a dramatic confrontation between a human being and a robot wherein an important truth is revealed to both of them – and by implication to us:

> Someday a human being ... may shoot a robot ... which has come out of a General Electrics factory, and to his surprise see it weep and bleed. And the dying robot may shoot back and, to its surprise, see a wisp of gray smoke arise from the electric pump that it supposed was [a] beating heart. It would be rather a great moment of truth for both of them. (Dick 1972, p. 187)

The 'great moment of truth' in this case would *not* be the realization that things are not always as they seem (which is hardly news), nor even that one could mistake a robot for a human (an idea that so much science fiction has taught us to expect), but the rather more disturbing prospect that humans and robots could *themselves* be mistaken about which kind of being they are – that one's grasp of *reality*, even of something seemingly so immediate and incorrigible as *what one is*, could be utterly mistaken. As Dick (1978, p. 260) confides in an undelivered speech, 'The two basic topics that fascinate me are "What is reality?"

and "What constitutes the authentic human being?"' He considered these two questions at bottom to concern the same fact: 'Fake realities create fake humans. Or, fake humans will generate fake realities and then sell them to other humans, turning them, eventually, into forgeries of themselves. So we end up with fake humans inventing fake realities and peddling them to other fake humans' (Dick 1978, pp. 263–4).

Electric Sheep Transmuted

Although *Blade Runner* inherits its narrative DNA from *Electric Sheep*, it is better described as a *transmutation* than as an adaptation of PKD's novel. If that novel could talk, it might with some justification say to Scott's film, borrowing a line of dialogue from J. F. Sebastian (William Sanderson), 'There's some of me in you.' The differences between the book and the film are many. Although some of these differences do not matter for our purposes, others are important. Identifying them may help us to make sense of some otherwise puzzling aspects of the film.

In the novel's post-World War Terminus environment of 1992 (2021 in later reprints), healthy humans are encouraged to emigrate to the Off-world colonies to preserve the human gene pool. As an incentive, each émigré is given an 'andy' (that is, android) as a personal servant. Those humans left on earth are either radiation-induced genetic defectives (such as J. R. Isidore, the counterpart of J. F. Sebastian in the film), or those too stubborn to leave (such as Rick Deckard). Most animals perished from the effects of radioactive fallout. The owls were the first to go, followed by most of the rest. Real animals are scarce and prohibitively expensive for most people to own. Possessing a real animal therefore confers significant social status on its owner. Most have to settle for realistic artificial animals ('animoids') while longing for the real thing. This theme is echoed in the film in the question about a tortoise posed to Leon by blade runner Dave Holden (Morgan Paull), Deckard's keen interest in whether the Tyrell Corporation's owl is real (despite Eldon Tyrell's enormous wealth

Introduction

and power, it isn't), the questions about calfskin wallets and the like posed to Rachael during her Voight-Kampff test, and in the artificial animal bazaar (Animoid Row) where Deckard follows up on clues to Zhora's whereabouts.[2]

In *Electric Sheep*, Rick Deckard is a freelance bounty hunter hired by the San Francisco Police Department to retire rogue androids – a distasteful job that he is resigned to do for the sake of earning enough money to purchase a real animal. When his real sheep dies of tetanus he replaces it with an artificial sheep realistic enough to fool his neighbors; yet he still longs for a real animal. After he finally retires enough androids to purchase a real Nubian goat, Rachael spitefully pushes the animal off the roof of his apartment building. Deckard is distraught until wandering in a desert outside the city he is delighted to chance upon what he takes to be a living toad, and triumphantly brings it home, only to have his wife flip open a control panel on its belly, revealing it to be an electric toad. Deckard is crestfallen but resigned. Real humans, like Deckard, dream of owning real animals, even toads, upon which they can confer their love and affection. Do androids similarly dream of loving and caring for artificial animals? The implication of Dick's sharp differentiation of humans and androids is an unequivocal 'No.' Humans need to express love, affection, and empathy for others. Androids do not and cannot.

This point bears on what is perhaps the most significant difference between the novel and the film. Whereas in the film the replicants are claimed by Tyrell to be 'more human than human,' in the novel the androids are emphatically *less* human than human. This is an issue about which PKD and Ridley Scott strongly disagreed. After reading an early script for *Blade Runner*, Dick reported that:

> The main difference between what Ridley views this all in terms of and what I view it all in terms of is as follows: To me, the replicants (or androids, if you will), are deplorable because they are heartless, they are completely self-centered, they don't care what happens to other creatures. To me this is

5

essentially a less than human entity for that reason. Now Ridley says he regards them as Supermen who couldn't fly. He said they are smarter than humans, they are stronger than humans, and they have faster reflexes than humans. That's rather a great divergence, you see. We've gone from somebody who is a simulation of the authentic human to someone who is literally superior to the authentic human. So we've now flipped this. Now the theme of the book is that Rick Deckard is dehumanized in his job of tracking down the replicants and killing them. In other words, he ends up essentially like they are. Ridley said that he regarded that as an intellectual idea and he was not interested in making an esoteric film.[3]

The androids in *Electric Sheep* lack a capacity for love, compassion, and especially *empathy* – for humans, for animals (one of the androids uses scissors to nonchalantly snip off the legs of a living spider, much to the horror of J. R. Isidore), and even for each other. The film takes the opposite perspective in this regard in that at least some of the replicants seem more empathic toward one another and even toward some humans than do the humans themselves. In the novel Deckard is dehumanized by tracking down and killing androids. In the film Deckard is ultimately humanized by his encounters with the replicants. The differences could hardly be starker.

Dick also was not pleased with what he gleaned from an early script of Scott's film. In an essay published in a cable television guide in early 1981 (as compensation he received one year of free cable TV service) with the title, 'Universe Makers ... and Breakers' (perhaps slyly suggesting that those constructive and destructive roles were played by the author and filmmaker, respectively), Dick offers sarcastic praise for the upcoming movie:

> Ridley Scott, who directed *Alien* and who now intends to bring into existence a $15 million film based on my novel *Do Androids Dream of Electric Sheep?*, confessed to an interviewer from *Omni* magazine that he 'found the novel too

Introduction

difficult to read,' despite the fact that the novel appeared as a mass-circulation paperback. On the other hand I was able rather easily to read the screenplay (it will be called *Blade Runner*). It was terrific. It bore no relation to the book. Oddly, in some ways it was better.... What my story will become is one titanic lurid collision of androids being blown up, androids killing humans, general confusion and murder, all very exciting to watch. Makes my book seem dull by comparison. (Dick 1981, p. 104)

Despite his initial reservations, Dick eventually underwent a total conversion. Eight months before the film hit theaters he wrote to Jeff Walker at The Ladd Company to express his unbounded enthusiasm for the upcoming film, of which he had by then seen a preview: 'I did not know that a work of mine or a set of ideas of mine could be escalated into such stunning dimensions. My life and creative work are justified and completed by BLADE RUNNER. Thank you ... it is going to be one hell of a commercial success. It will prove invincible.'[4] Sadly, Dick died on 2 March 1982, a few months before the film's release.

From Workprint to Final Cut

One of the unusual characteristics of *Blade Runner* that makes it so fascinating to study is that to date *seven* different versions of the film have been released.[5] Most of the differences concern technical audio/visual aspects that are insignificant from the point of view of the story itself. But some of the differences *are* significant and therefore are worth commenting upon here.

In early March 1982 test audiences in Denver and Dallas were shown what has come to be called the 'Workprint' version of the film. Most descriptions of this event insert the word 'disastrous' at some point to emphasize how disappointing the filmmakers found the chilly reception of their meticulously crafted creation. This version ends with the elevator doors closing as Deckard and

Rachael attempt to flee the city. On questionnaires distributed after the screenings many in these audiences reported that they found the film difficult to understand and moreover were put off by what they considered to be the film's slow pace and ambiguous ending. As Ridley Scott later observed, 'On first viewing, it [*Blade Runner*] may have been a lot to take in' (McDonagh 1991, p. 71). Thus chastened, a slightly altered version was shown in San Diego in May 1982. In this version, Roy Batty is shown making a telephone call to see if Hannibal Chew (James Hong) is in the Eye Works, and later shows Deckard reloading his blaster after firing at Batty in Sebastian's decaying apartment building. Those added details (later removed) did little to address the problems revealed in the initial test audience screenings. To make the story more easily understood, Scott added voice-over narration in which Deckard, in a classic *film noir* detective's world-weary voice, provides background details and explains the significance of the events as they unfold.[6] In addition, a new ending was added in which Deckard and Rachael flee the city and drive off in Deckard's car over sunlit mountain roads. This version also reveals that Tyrell had told Deckard that Rachael, unlike the other replicants, did not have a built-in termination date. These new features were intended to make the story easier to follow and to provide the happy ending American audiences expect.[7] The resulting Theatrical Release opened in movie theaters in the US on 25 June 1982, followed by an International Cut (showing more graphic violence) that opened in theaters in Europe and Asia later that year.

Despite these attempts to make the film more audience-friendly, some film critics and science fiction fans still found fault with it. Film critics generally felt that the film's impressive visual achievements overshadowed what they considered its lackluster story. They also found the tacked-on happy ending incongruent with the visual and thematic motifs of the rest of the film. That summer science fiction fans were presented with a number of less challenging movies to entertain them. *Blade Runner* opened the same month as *E.T.: The Extraterrestrial, Star*

Introduction

Trek II: The Wrath of Khan, a remake of *The Thing*, and the fantasy-action film, *Conan the Barbarian*. The feel-good movie *E.T.*, in particular, proved immensely more popular among film critics and science fiction fans alike than the dark, existentially challenging *Blade Runner*. Robin Wood (2003, p. 161) tartly explains audiences' and film critics' preference for *E.T.* over *Blade Runner* as 'expressing a preference for the reassuring over the disturbing, the reactionary over the progressive, the safe over the challenging, the childish over the adult, spectator passivity over spectator activity.' In one of the few (mainly) positive reviews of *Blade Runner* at the time, Hiawatha Bray (1982, p. 97), writing in *Christianity Today*, wrote that, 'This isn't a family film, and it's not for the squeamish. But of all the summer's releases, only *Blade Runner* is truly adult in its thoughtfulness and complexity.'

Despite its cool reception at the box office, the film's stature slowly began to rise thanks to the newly emerging home video market. The broadcast of a slightly less graphic version of the film on network TV in 1986 led to greater video rentals and laserdisc sales. Ironically, one of the factors that may have been off-putting to theater-goers – the film's extreme visual density – encouraged multiple close viewings at home on VHS and laserdisc, permitting scenes to be paused, reviewed, and pondered more carefully. It was slowly acquiring the status of a cult classic.

The next event in the film's evolving reception was serendipitous. In September 1989, Michael Arick, a film preservationist searching the Warner Brothers film vault in Hollywood for a large-format print of the 1962 Natalie Wood musical *Gypsy*, stopped short when he noticed a film canister marked: 'Technicolor. London. *Blade Runner*. 70mm print.' Assuming that this must be the International Cut, he placed it in storage in an off-inventory vault. When the film was subsequently screened on 6 May 1990 at the Los Angeles Cineplex-Odeon Fairfax Theater, he and others in the audience who were expecting to see a familiar version of *Blade Runner* were shocked to find themselves viewing the quasi-mythological Workprint version that had long been thought lost or destroyed (Sammon 1996, pp. 331–2). The screening met with an enthusiastic response. Audiences reacted the same way a year later to subsequent screenings at the NuArt Theater in Los Angeles and at the Art Deco Castro Theater in San Francisco.

Sensing an opportunity to capitalize on renewed interest in the film, Warner Brothers decided to re-edit and re-release it. The voice-over narration and the happy ending were jettisoned. The film now ended (once again) with the elevator doors closing as Deckard and Rachael attempt to flee the city.[8] Advertised as 'The Original Cut of the Futuristic Adventure,' *Blade Runner: The Director's Cut* debuted in September 1992. As Ridley Scott explained his decision to cooperate in bringing out this new edit of his film:

> I felt the released cut [that is, the Theatrical Version] was over-explanatory. The Deckard (Harrison Ford) voice-over became a disturbing factor. The happily ever-after ending was always silly and really worked against the nature of the 'beast'. *Blade Runner* is a *film noir*, where the happiest ending one can hope for is at least philosophical and may even leave you wondering about the fate of the two characters – certainly a bitter-sweet ending. (Bahania 1992, p. 87)

This version is also notable for the insertion of a brief scene in which Deckard, while dozing at his piano, has a dream-like reverie of a unicorn frolicking through the woods. The inclusion of this scene has generated enormous speculation and is discussed in detail below.

With some remaining continuity problems resolved, some dialogue slightly altered, and many scenes digitally adjusted or re-shot, *Blade Runner: The Final Cut*, the definitive version of Scott's brilliant neo-noir science fiction film, was shown in limited theatrical release in October 2007. A Five-Disc Ultimate Collector's Edition box set including the Workprint (WP), Theatrical Release (TR), International Cut (IC), Director's Cut

(DC), and Final Cut (FC) versions, as well as several bonus features including commentaries, was released two months later. In the discussions to follow I will occasionally consider earlier versions of the film (and earlier drafts of the script) where doing so helps to shed light on what might otherwise be puzzling aspects of the film, but all references to 'the film' in the discussions that follow will be to the *Final Cut* unless otherwise indicated.

The Deck-a-Rep Debate

A final preliminary issue needs to be addressed before delving into the philosophical discussions of subsequent chapters. In *Electric Sheep*, Phil Resch, another bounty hunter who makes his living killing androids, is deeply worried that he is himself an android. This leads Rick Deckard to worry that he, too, might be an android. There is no corresponding scene in *Blade Runner*. Nonetheless, there are a number of hints in the film suggesting that Deckard *might* be a replicant. A commonly expressed view among fans and commentators is that in the Theatrical Release Deckard *might* be a replicant, but in the Director's Cut and Final Cut he *definitely* is one. They point to a number of clues that they believe provide compelling evidence in support this interpretation.[9] Others remain unconvinced and cite counter-evidence. This issue generates remarkably strong opinions on both sides.[10] The issue is important for this book's project because some of the contrasts I wish to draw between Deckard and the replicants presuppose a specific position in this debate.[11] To address this issue head-on, therefore, I will expound what are probably the ten most commonly cited clues in support of the 'replicant' interpretation, explaining how a proponent of the contrary 'human' interpretation might try to rebut each.[12] I will then make the case for interpreting Deckard as human. Finally, I will argue that although the evidence does not support the 'replicant' interpretation as unambiguously as proponents of that interpretation suppose, the opposite conclusion cannot be established, either. In the final analysis, the film either intentionally leaves the issue unresolved, or the conflicting evidence is a vestige of the film's complicated evolution, or both. Let me now try to defend *that* unpopular compromise.

'You Did a Man's Work. But Are You a Man?'

Those who are convinced that Deckard is a replicant cite a number of clues in support.

Clue 1: In the Theatrical Release and the Director's Cut, Bryant tells Deckard that *six* replicants were spotted off the coast by an aerial patrol, and that one got fried running through an electrical field while trying to break into the Tyrell Corporation. That should leave *five* replicants on the loose. But Bryant identifies only *four* replicants for Deckard to retire. Hence, Deckard is himself the fifth replicant – perhaps given a memory implant to make him believe that he is human. In addition, we know that the replicants were created to perform dangerous and/or unpleasant work. What better way to get rid of trespassing replicants than to program one to be a blade runner?

Rebuttal: Bryant's statement about 'six replicants' is a vestige from the 24 July 1980 and 23 February 1981 drafts of the script which include a fifth replicant named 'Mary' (described as looking like 'an American dream mom, right out of Father Knows Best'; actress Stacey Nelkin was cast for that role), a role that was cut due to budget constraints. The error is corrected in the Final Cut in which Bryant says that *two* replicants were killed in the Tyrell Corporation break-in.

Clue 2: The eyes of artificial life forms give off a red glow when the light hits them just right. We see this in the Tyrell Corporation's owl, in Rachael's eyes during her Voight-Kampff test, in Pris's eyes in Sebastian's apartment, and in Roy Batty's eyes when he confronts Tyrell. Rachael's eyes glow red in Deckard's apartment, and for a brief moment as he is standing behind her, his do, too. Hence, Deckard must be a replicant.

Introduction

Rebuttal: The possibility that replicants can be identified simply by noticing a red glow in their eyes would make complete nonsense of the need to subject them to the time-consuming and (as Dave Holden's experience demonstrates) potentially dangerous administration of the Voight-Kampff test. Why administer that test if shining a flashlight in their eyes would be sufficient?

Clue 3: Thanks to Tyrell's niece's piano lessons, Rachael can play the piano. Deckard can play the piano. Hence, like Rachael, he is a replicant with implanted memories of piano lessons.

Rebuttal: Inferring that Deckard can *play the piano* is a stretch insofar as we only see him peck at a few keys. Besides, if the ability to play the piano is sufficient to identify one as a replicant, any pianists living in Los Angeles in 2019 had better learn to keep a low profile lest they meet an unwanted early retirement.

Clue 4: Like Rachael and Leon, Deckard collects photos. (A deleted scene even shows a photo of a smiling Deckard with his wife standing in front of their middle-class suburban home.) Therefore, Deckard is a replicant.

Rebuttal: If owning photographs is evidence of being a replicant, then Bryant is a replicant. The lampshade on Bryant's desk sports photographs of him posing with his trophies on a big-game hunting expedition. But there is no independent reason to suppose that Bryant is a replicant. Likewise, the possession of photos does not show that Deckard is a replicant.

Clue 5: Deckard is evasive when his human status is challenged. He sidesteps Zhora's question, 'Are you for real?' without answering it. Later, Rachael pointedly asks Deckard whether he has ever taken the Voight-Kampff test himself. Tellingly, he does not answer her question, either. Perhaps he is afraid to take the test, or perhaps he has taken it and failed.

Rebuttal: Zhora's question is *rhetorical*. She is expressing incredulity that someone could be concerned about her 'exploitation' given her particular line of work, and is expressing skepticism that Deckard is really from the hokey-sounding 'Confidential Committee on Moral Abuses' of the 'American Federation of Variety Artists.' Rachael's question is most naturally interpreted as *ironic*, pointing out that the person administering an empathy test to others, and killing them if they fail, is clearly lacking in empathy himself, especially when its expression is most needed.

Clue 6: In *Electric Sheep*, it is claimed, Rachael Rosen and blade runner Phil Resch both discover to their astonishment that they are androids, prompting Rick Deckard to wonder, 'If Rachael and Resch are not human, what am I?' Therefore, in *Blade Runner* Rick Deckard is a replicant.

Rebuttal: In the novel Phil Resch turns out not to be an android after all, but rather just an especially callous human being. In *Electric Sheep*, Rick Deckard *worries* that he might be an android; but there is no confirmation that he *is* an android. In fact, he subjects himself to a test to determine whether he is an android; the results come back negative. Furthermore, in the novel Deckard asks himself that question because he is worried that his soul-deadening occupation as an android killing bounty hunter may be making him as unfeeling as the androids are reputed to be. Finally, in the film we never see Deckard so much as even entertaining the thought that he might be a replicant.

Clue 7: After Deckard survives his battle with Roy Batty, Gaff (Edward James Olmos) shouts to him: 'You've done a man's job, sir.' Gaff is implying that Deckard is not really a *man*. Moreover, his presence at certain key moments is intended to make sure that this replicant-killing replicant does his job.

Rebuttal: Gaff is simply offering grudging respect for a rival who against all odds has survived his encounters with the

Introduction

dangerous Nexus 6 replicants. We know that he has been forming judgments about Deckard all along from the figurines he creates (a chicken, a man with an erection, and so on). Gaff is not challenging Deckard's status as human at all.

Clue 8: The Director's Cut and the Final Cut include a scene in which Deckard daydreams of a unicorn prancing through a misty forest. The full title of Philip K. Dick's novel is: *Do Androids Dream of Electric Sheep?* The only *dream* that appears in *Blade Runner* is Deckard's dream of a unicorn. Hence, the unicorn of the film is the electric sheep of the novel. Therefore, Deckard is the android in the title of Dick's book, and is a replicant in the film.

Rebuttal: In Dick's novel Deckard dreams of owning a *real* sheep not an electric one. Besides, in the film Deckard dreams of a *unicorn*, not a sheep. The dream proves nothing.

Clue 9: The real significance of Deckard's unicorn dream is revealed when Gaff leaves a tinfoil unicorn figurine outside his apartment, thereby proving that he knows the contents of Deckard's dreams. This is possible only if Deckard is a replicant that has been 'gifted' with mental images to which Gaff has access. Moreover, we have the director's testimony connecting this clue to an earlier one. According to Ridley Scott:

> [M]y chief purpose in having Deckard's eyes glow was to prepare the audience for the moment when Ford *nods* after he picks up the unicorn. I had assumed that if I'd clued them in earlier, by showing Harrison's eyes glowing, some viewers might be thinking 'Hey, maybe he's a replicant, too.' Then when Deckard picked up the tinfoil unicorn and nodded – a signal that Ford is thinking, 'Yes, I know why Gaff left this behind' – the same viewers would realize their suspicions had been confirmed. (Sammon 1996, p. 391)

Rebuttal: If finding Gaff's tinfoil unicorn was Deckard's great moment of realization that he, too, is a replicant, one might have expected him to react a little more dramatically to this utterly life-altering revelation, especially in light of the fact that there is no evidence prior to that moment that he had even so much as entertained that possibility. By contrast, his muted emotional reaction, along with the explanatory voice-over narration in the Theatrical Release ('Gaff had been there and let her live') makes perfect sense if he was merely acknowledging that Gaff, like Roy Batty, had given him a head-start before coming after him.[13] Scott's explanation smacks of a later rational reconstruction of a fortuitous accident. Harrison Ford was reportedly surprised to discover that his eyes showed a faint red glow in the scene in question, and hypothesized that he must have inadvertently picked up some of the visual effect intended for Sean Young's eyes. Upon noticing this unintended effect during post-production, Scott decided to leave it in the film, and later attributed intentional significance to it.[14] In addition, there is an equally plausible interpretation of Gaff's tinfoil unicorn that does not require that he knows the contents of Deckard's daydream. The unicorn figurine is merely symbolic. Previously Gaff made an origami chicken and a wooden matchstick man with an erection to suggest that Deckard is *afraid* (when he rejects Bryant's demand to pursue the replicants) and that he is *virile* (when he is pursuing the replicants). The unicorn figure may convey Gaff's judgment that Deckard is entertaining a *fantasy* if he thinks that he can escape the city and live happily ever after with Rachael.[15]

Clue 10: The most important 'clue' is the director's own testimony. According to Ridley Scott, Gaff's tinfoil unicorn

> 'visually links up with [Deckard's] previous vision of seeing a unicorn. Which tells us that [Gaff] A) has been to Deckard's apartment, and B) is giving Deckard a full blast of his own paranoia. Gaff's message there is, 'Listen, pal, I know your innermost thoughts. Therefore you're a replicant. How else would I know this?'. (Sammon 1996, p. 391)

Introduction

Elsewhere Scott says:

> At one stage, we considered having Deckard turn out to be, ironically, a replicant. In fact, if you look at the film closely, especially the ending, you may get some clues – some by slight innuendo – that Deckard is indeed a replicant. At the end there's a kind of confirmation that he is – at least that he believes it possible. Within the context of the overall story, whether it's true or not in the book, having Deckard be a replicant is the *only* reasonable solution. (Peary 1984, pp. 54–5)

Scott's latest statement on this issue is blunt: 'Can't be any clearer than that. If you don't get it, you're a moron.'[16] Now, if *Ridley Scott* says that Deckard is a replicant, then Deckard *must* be a replicant. After all, how could the *director* of the film possibly be mistaken about his own film?

Rebuttal: The fact that the director of the film says that Deckard is a replicant might seem to decisively settle the issue. But Scott's statements, no less than the film itself, require careful exegesis. Scott says, '*At one stage*, we considered having Deckard turn out to be ... a replicant' (emphasis added). This suggests that somewhere along the line this plan hatched, dropped, and then later resurrected, at least in part. Over the course of making the film Scott wavered in his intention to make Deckard a replicant, resulting in a film that alternatively both affirms and denies his replicant status. It is therefore no wonder that the evidence is ambiguous.[17]

Scott's remarks also raise fascinating questions about a filmmaker's authority to provide a definitive interpretation of his cinematic creation. The idea that there is a 'true' interpretation of the film, and that it is known by the director, is presupposed by Jason P. Vest (2007, p. 25) when he writes that, 'Ridley Scott has confirmed his belief in Deckard's replicant status during more than one interview.' Talk of *confirmation* makes it sound as if there is a fact of the matter about Deckard's replicant status, and that the director has privileged and authoritative access to this fact. This would be so if the director's *intentions* necessarily determine *the* meaning of his film. Since only the director knows for sure what those intentions are, only the director has unmediated knowledge of what his film is *really* about. In this view, we might and no doubt will draw our own conclusions from watching and reflecting on the film, but the director has the final and definitive word on the matter.

This perspective could be challenged. Harrison Ford has said that he did *not* consider his character to be a replicant. What reason is there to take the director's interpretation of Ford's character as more authoritative than the actor's? Why, for that matter, should either be thought to have the final word on what the film *really means*? If (absurdly, of course) Ridley Scott insisted that, despite what the film leads viewers to believe, Roy Batty is not a replicant after all, would we be required to accept this interpretation? The cost of accepting such an interpretation, in terms of making sense of the behavior of that character and of the story as a whole, would be prohibitive. In this case, we would reasonably weigh other considerations against the director's interpretation and we would be justified in saying, 'No, Roy Batty really *is* a replicant, regardless of what the director says.' Hence, even the director *could* be mistaken about aspects of his own film. We, the audience, must still reach our own conclusions about a film's meaning(s).

'Proud of Yourself, Little Man?'

So far I have been reviewing arguments based on clues *within* the film as well as on adscititious testimony *about* the film that purport to show that Deckard is a replicant, along with a rebuttal for each. If those rebuttals are successful, the 'replicant' interpretation has at least not been established. But there is also a positive case to be made that viewing Deckard as *human* makes better sense of some obvious facts about Deckard's behavior and indeed of the film as a whole.

Introduction

First, Deckard seems distinctly un-replicant-like in every respect. Whereas the replicants are passionate about living, Deckard is apathetic (in the Theatrical Release he reports that his wife called him a 'cold fish'). Whereas the replicants band together, Deckard lives alone, apparently without significant relationships. Whereas the replicants are physically superior to most humans, Deckard has quite normal human capabilities. In short, Deckard comes across as 'human, all-too-human' in every observable way. It is still conceivable that he *could* be a replicant, for example, a new Nexus 7 replicant made to be even more human than the Nexus 6 models. But there is no evidence in support of this interpretation, and the simplest explanation for Deckard's human ordinariness is just that he *is* human.

Second, although some commentators think that viewing Deckard as a replicant adds 'emotional strength' to the replicants' claim for a moral status equal to that of humans, this seems backwards. Viewing Deckard as a replicant severely undercuts a central moral theme of the film, namely, that any being that appears to be human in all relevant respects merits the same moral treatment as a human being. The assumption that Deckard is human underwrites the moral significance of Rachael's rhetorical question, 'You know that Voight-Kampff test of yours? Did you ever take that test yourself?' Treating her question literally merely trivializes it. Likewise, Roy's taunt to Deckard – 'Proud of yourself, little man?' – draws the viewer's attention to the supposed replicant-human differences if Deckard is, indeed, a man, but becomes meaningless if Deckard is a replicant. A related theme of the film is that the replicants, supposedly lacking a capacity for empathy, turn out to be more empathic than the humans, all of whom supposedly have this capacity as their natural birthright. The dramatic force of this message rests heavily on the film's main protagonist being human. Viewing Deckard as a replicant obliterates this contrast and with it the film's moral gravitas.

A third consideration concerns Deckard's growing moral sensitivity. At the beginning of the film he expresses his view that

19

'replicants are like any other machine.' By the end of the film he has fallen in love with a replicant and risks his life to save hers. As Sammon (1996, p. 360) asks, '[W]hat's the point of Deckard's spiritual awakening ... if *Blade Runner*'s android hunter turns out to be an android himself?'[18] Such an argument cannot definitively settle the issue, of course, because it is possible that the film is not as rich, deep, or interesting as it appears to be. Nonetheless, an interpretive principle that *permits* a film to be as rich, deep, and interesting as possible is, *all other things being equal*, preferable to one that trivializes it for the sake of being merely clever. Viewing Deckard as a replicant violates this principle. Viewing him as a human being honors it. That is a powerful reason for viewing Deckard as a human.

In summary, although there are numerous clues that Deckard might be a replicant, most of those clues do not hold up well under critical examination. The considerations suggesting that Deckard is human are fewer in number but *deeper* in the sense that they make better sense of specific scenes and of the film as a whole. Consequently, in the chapters that follow I will usually assume that Deckard is a human rather than repeatedly inserting into each discussion the tiresome caveat, 'unless, of course, Deckard is a replicant' and then launching into a lengthy parallel discussion on that alternative supposition. Of course, the reader is free to entertain that alternative interpretation throughout this book and to see where it leads. It may lead down some fascinating paths. As a practical matter, however, picking one or the other interpretation is probably necessary to prevent the discussions that follow from becoming hopelessly labyrinthine.

Conclusions

I do not expect the arguments just given to settle for most readers the issue of Deckard's status. The rival positions seem too deeply entrenched for that hopeful result. Besides, the evidence itself lends itself to different interpretations. The Deck-a-Rep debate continues unabated because like a Necker

Cube the film can be seen as presenting two entirely different, irreconcilable faces. That comparison may provide the best way of understanding and appreciating the richness of the film. More important than whether Deckard is a replicant is simply the *possibility* that he is one because entertaining that possibility and weighing the arguments pro and con prompts us to think about the film more deeply.[19] It is easy to forget that as a work of fiction there is no fact of the matter about whether Deckard is *really* a replicant apart from whatever 'facts' are conveyed in the film. Even the testimony of the filmmakers does not definitively settle the question because it is not self-evident that their *intentions* dictate a uniquely correct meaning of the art they have created. Filmmakers are certainly the best authorities on the issue of what they *intend* to convey in their films. From this it does not follow that they are the best authorities on what the fruits of their labors *mean*. Terry Rawlings reports that after viewing the first edit of *Blade Runner* footage with Scott in July 1981, the director turned to him and said, 'God, it's marvelous. What the fuck does it all *mean*?' (Sammon 1996, p. 268; emphasis added) Answering *that* question is the aim of this book.

2 Being Human

> '"More Human than Human" is our motto.'
> (Dr Eldon Tyrell, to Rick Deckard)

Introduction

The scene is the cavernous office of Dr Eldon Tyrell, the brilliant, eponymous CEO of the Tyrell Corporation and the creative genius responsible for the synthetic humans known as *replicants*. Rick Deckard had just administered the Voight-Kampff test to Rachael – ostensibly Tyrell's niece. After Rachael is brusquely dismissed by Tyrell, the two men talk. Tyrell confirms that Rachael is a replicant that does not *know* that it is a replicant. Deckard is stunned: 'How can it not know what it is?' As Tyrell proceeds to explain, his company has created a new experimental model that is even more humanlike than previous models. Not only is Rachael physically almost indistinguishable from a human, she also has memory implants that lead her to believe that she *is* human. As Tyrell explains, 'Commerce is our goal here at Tyrell. "More Human than Human" is our motto.' Tyrell's boast notwithstanding, Deckard now knows that Rachael is a replicant. Of course, at that point she still believes herself to be human; but in that she is deeply mistaken.

Or is she? The answer depends on the conditions that must be satisfied for any being to qualify as genuinely 'human' and on whether Rachael satisfies these conditions. Neither issue is simple. Even within the film there are contrary views. Many of the human characters consider the replicants to be *less than human*. Deckard brushes off Rachael's question about whether he feels that the Tyrell Corporation's work is a benefit to the public by retorting: 'Replicants are like any other machine.

Being Human

They're either a benefit or a hazard. If they're a benefit, it's not my problem.'[1] By contrast, Eldon Tyrell boasts that his replicants are 'more human than human.' Certainly the replicants themselves *aspire* to be acknowledged as something greater than mere machines, and perhaps even as human, as when Roy Batty indignantly responds to Sebastian's request that his strange guests 'Show me something' by retorting, 'We're not computers, Sebastian!'

These disagreements *within* the film notwithstanding, if there is one point upon which all commentators *on* the film agree it is that the question 'What is it to be human?' is central.[2]

It is on the answer to this question that the fate of the replicants and the humanity of the human beings who make and attempt to control them depend. Part of what makes the film's treatment of this issue so philosophically interesting is that it hints at an answer but refuses to definitively settle it. Exploring some of the options for answering this question is the aim of this chapter.

'It's Artificial?'

Begin by considering the scene in the Tyrell Corporation's dimly lit lobby in which Deckard and Rachael meet for the first time. Deckard is startled by an owl flying past his head and roosting on the other side of the room. He is clearly impressed and interested, prompting Rachael to ask him whether he likes their owl. Deckard's response indicates that his answer to *that* question turns on the answer to another one: 'It's artificial?' Rachael says that it is, and from that point on Deckard shows no further interest in it. Apparently, for Deckard only a real owl is worthy of note. Virtually the same scene is repeated later in Zhora's dressing room when he asks her whether her snake is real. Again, once he discovers that it isn't, he loses interest immediately. Deckard does not have the luxury of philosophizing about the significance of the real versus artificial animal distinction. He needs to find out whether the Voight-Kampff test

23

works on Nexus 6 replicants, in the former scene, and whether Zhora is one of the rogue replicants, in the latter scene. Fortunately, centuries before Rick Deckard the brilliant mathematician and natural philosopher René Descartes (1596–1650) *did* have the leisure to explore that distinction and thereupon drew some remarkable conclusions that are significant for our understanding of the replicants.

One of Descartes' chief concerns is to identify the essential difference(s) between human beings and all other living things. His conclusion (the justification for which will be explored in a later chapter) is that human beings are unique in being *thinking things*. He concedes that animals may convey the *appearance* of thinking, but he maintains that in fact they are simply unthinking automata that respond to events in a purely mechanical fashion just as if they were composed of ropes, pulleys, levers, tubes, fluids, and so on. There is no thinking connected with their behavior or physical sensations either, because these are ultimately mental phenomena as well.[3] Thus he concludes that, 'if there were such machines having the organs and the shape of a monkey or of some other animal that lacked reason, we would have no way of recognizing that they were not entirely of the same nature as these animals' (Descartes 1998, p. 31). This is just what we see in *Blade Runner* (and even more so in *Electric Sheep*). By 2019 the art and science of manufacturing animoids has reached such an advanced stage that it can be exceedingly difficult to tell the difference between artificial owls and snakes and real owls and snakes.

Descartes would say that there *is* no essential difference, and that the artificial/real distinction as applied to animals is itself somewhat artificial. In his view the difference concerns merely an animal's *mode of origin* (was it made by us through our technology or through natural processes by God?) rather than its *essential nature*, that is, as a *machine* rather than being *alive* because in his view real animals no less than artificial ones just are machines, albeit of greater complexity. He is well aware of the ingenious mechanical animals some artisans of his day had already constructed. He even imagines someone someday creating mechanical 'humans' that exactly resemble human beings in outward appearance and in behavior yet without having minds. But even if God himself were to produce 'the body of a man exactly like one of ours, as much as the outward shape of its members as in the internal arrangement of its organs,' and composed of the very same materials that constitute a human body, yet 'without putting into it, at the start, any rational mind, but merely kindled in the man's heart one of those fires without light' (Descartes 1998, p. 26) that would permit it to move and function much as our bodies do, it would still fail to be human. No matter how physically indistinguishable from a human being, such a creature would necessarily fail to be human because it would lack an essential element that *we* have but that *it* would necessarily lack, namely, a *mind* endowed with *consciousness*.[4]

Descartes therefore views mechanical animals, real animals, and his imaginary artificial people in exactly the same way. Although we might initially be fooled by artificial humans, he insists that 'if there were any such machines that bore a resemblance to our bodies and imitated our actions as far as this is practically feasible, we would always have two very certain means of recognizing that they were not at all … true men' (Descartes 1998, pp. 31–2). The first tell-tale difference is that, 'they could never use words or other signs, or put them together as we do in order to declare our thoughts to others' (p. 32). Even if an artificial human could produce sounds that made sense in relation to its bodily actions – for example, crying out *as if* in pain when its body is damaged, or responding to questions *as if* it understood the questions posed to it – it would soon be exposed as a mere simulacrum of a human being because it could never 'arrange its words differently so as to respond to the sense of all that will be said in its presence, as even the dullest men can do' (p. 32). Without a mind it would lack any *understanding* of what was said to it, and hence it would lack the flexibility of response that humans enjoy.

The second tell-tale sign that would expose such artificial humans as less-than-human is that, 'although they might perform many tasks very well or perhaps better than any of us, one would discover that they were acting not through knowledge but only through the disposition of their organs' (Descartes 1998, p. 32). The image of the mechanical clock, which loomed so large in the imaginations of seventeenth-century natural philosophers, is put to use here. Animals might perform some tasks better than us, yet without any understanding of what they do, 'just as we see that a clock composed exclusively of wheels and springs can count the hours and measure time more accurately than we can with all our carefulness' (p. 33). Ironically, 'the fact that they do something better than we do does not prove that they have any intelligence ... rather it proves that they have no intelligence at all' (p. 33). The same conclusion would follow for artificial humans. What these artificial humans would necessarily lack that real humans have, and that gives the latter their behavioral flexibility, is *reason*: 'For while reason is a universal instrument that can be of help in all sorts of circumstances ... it is for all practical purposes impossible for there to be enough different organs in a machine to make it act in all the contingencies of life in the same way as our reason makes us act' (p. 32).

The replicants appear to satisfy Descartes' two criteria for being genuine (rather than artificial) humans with flying colors. Not only is Roy Batty as linguistically fluent as any human beings in the film – consider his *tête à tête* with Tyrell over the molecular chemistry of life extension – but he is even given to reciting poetry, as his exuberant self-introduction to Chew demonstrates. The replicants also exhibit great behavioral flexibility in adjusting to novel situations and problems. Leon infiltrates the Tyrell Corporation as an employee in order to gain access to Tyrell. So long as his interrogation is going well, he plays along. But when it becomes clear that he is about to be exposed as a replicant, he shoots Holden and escapes. Likewise, Zhora bides her time before attempting to kill Deckard; Pris employs a clever ruse to manipulate Sebastian; and when his first two attempts to gain access to Tyrell fail, Roy discovers an ingenious way to finally succeed in his quest. In short, the replicants easily pass both of Descartes' crucial tests.

Descartes therefore faces a dilemma. Either he has to conclude that the replicants are *artificial humans with minds* – which as we have seen he deems to be impossible; or else he has to *deny* that the replicants are *conscious, thinking beings* – which seems desperate given how easily they pass his two tests. We have as much reason to doubt that the replicants are conscious, thinking beings as we do that other humans are – which is to say, no reason at all. In short, there seems to be no good reason to deny that the replicants think and feel much as we do. But if so, Descartes is wrong to assume that artificially created beings would necessarily lack minds. By itself, however, this would only show that the replicants satisfy Descartes' criteria for being human. It would not settle the issue of whether they *are* human. In order to make *that* judgment with confidence we need to consider additional facts about them.

'You Nexus, Huh?'

From the film's opening crawl we learn that, 'Early in the 21st Century, THE TYRELL CORPORATION advanced Robot evolution into the NEXUS phase – a being virtually identical to a human – known as a replicant.' We also learn that replicants are superior in strength and agility, and at least equal in intelligence, to the genetic engineers who created them. We can assume that although these genetic engineers have *at best* average human strength and agility, they are nonetheless much more intelligent than the average human being. This would make the replicants impressive indeed. All of them appear to be phenomenally strong and/or agile, and even the relatively modest mental capabilities of Leon are at least equal to those of an average human being, making the rogue replicants extremely formidable adversaries even for an exceptionally skilled ex-blade runner like Rick Deckard.[5]

During Deckard's briefing by Capt. Bryant we are also given more detailed information about the functions and capabilities of the four rebellious replicants that Deckard is tasked with retiring:

Replicant (M) Des: LEON
NEXUS 6 N6MAC41717
Incept Date: 10 APRIL, 2017
Func: Combat/Loader (Nuc. Fiss.)
Phys: LEV. A Mental: LEV. C

Replicant (F) Des: ZHORA
NEXUS 6 N6FAB61216
Incept Date: 12 JUNE, 2016
Func: Retrained (9 FEB., 2018)
Polit. Homicide
Phys: LEV. A Mental: LEV. B

Replicant (M) Des: BATTY (Roy)
NEXUS 6 N6MAA10816
Incept Date: 8 JAN., 2016
Func: Combat, Colonization
   Defense Prog
Phys: LEV. A Mental: LEV. A

Replicant (F) Des: PRIS
NEXUS 6 N6FAB21416
Incept Date: 14 FEB., 2016
Func: Military/Leisure
Phys: LEV. A Mental: LEV. B

The individual identification code on the second line of each description is a compressed summary of the key properties of each replicant. For example, 'N6FAB61216' indicates that Zhora is a Nexus 6, Female, with A-level physical capabilities, B-level mental capabilities, with an incept date of 6/12/16. Leon is a Nexus 6, Male, with A-level physical capabilities, C-level mental capabilities, with an incept date of 4/17/17. Oddly, a different 'Incept Date' is given on the next line, and it is this latter date that Leon confirms to Deckard in the alley (calling it his 'birthday'). Presumably, this is simply an error that was overlooked even for the Final Cut.[6] Pris's incept date is Valentine's Day – perhaps appropriate for a 'leisure' model.[7] Roy Batty, whose body is already beginning to shut down, is a couple of months shy of four years old.

The Workprint version includes a somewhat different definition of 'replicant' that provides additional information worth considering:

> **REPLICANT**\rep'-li-cant*n*. See also ROBOT (*antique*): ANDROID (*obsolete*): NEXUS (*generic*): Synthetic human with paraphysical capabilities, having skin/flesh culture. Also: Rep, skin job (*slang*): Off-world uses: Combat, high risk industrial, deep-space probe. On-world use prohibited.
> Specifications and quantities – information classified.
> NEW AMERICAN DICTIONARY.
> Copyright © 2016.

This is the only time in any version of the film that the word 'android' appears, and it does so only to inform us that this term has become obsolete. This semantic decision reflects Ridley Scott's belief that the term 'android' had acquired too many clichéd associations to be suitable for his film. The new word 'replicant', by contrast, naturally prompts the viewer to reflect on how closely the synthetic humans replicate the qualities of human beings. We are also informed that the replicants have 'paraphysical capabilities.' Because they have been designed to perform specific tasks Off-world (combat, nuclear loading, political homicide, recreational sex, and so on) they have enhanced physical capabilities for these tasks. We are told little about how the replicants were created to have these paraphysical capabilities.[8] According to Scott, this was deliberate in order to bring other issues to the foreground (Kennedy 1982, pp. 37–8). As suggested by the scenes in the Eye Works laboratory, however, they appear to be manufactured beings with the production of specific organs farmed out to subcontractors like Chew rather than growing sequentially through a process of embryonic development. Accordingly, they may begin to exist as adult organisms. They have no childhoods and, of course, no parents – a sensitive fact whose implicit acknowledgment in one of the film's early scenes becomes the 'trigger' for Leon to blast blade runner Dave Holden through a wall and into the next room.

Both versions of the opening crawl – the one in the Workprint version as well as the one that appeared in all subsequent versions – identify the replicants as 'robots.' Jack Boozer (1997, p. 212) judges this epithet to be misleading on *constitutive* grounds because the replicants are 'biogenetic creations' rather than 'an electro-mechanical machine made of inorganic materials, controlled by [a] computer and electronic programming ... that performs routine tasks automatically without consciousness or autonomy.' The description of the replicants as robots might also strike one as incongruous inasmuch as the replicants seem so 'un-robotic' in their *behavior*. Think of the impressive athleticism displayed by Pris when she is playfully showing off for Sebastian, and later when she is attempting to kill Deckard. Roy Batty and Zhora, as well, seem anything but 'robotic' in their respective demeanors and behaviors. So, are they robots?

Humans and robots are conventionally thought to have different and indeed diametrically opposite attributes such that one being could be both. Consider some of these attributes, where the first term of each pair is popularly regarded as laudably 'human' and the second as 'robotic':

> natural/artificial; organic/inorganic; alive/inanimate; free/unfree; unpredictable/predictable; rebellious/obedient; autonomous/controlled; flexible/rigid; graceful/lumbering; intelligent/unintelligent; conscious/non-conscious; spontaneous/programmed; sensitive/unfeeling; emotional/unemotional; intuitive/algorithmic; passionate/apathetic; playful/serious; sexual/asexual; empathic/callous; moral/non-moral; appreciative of beauty/oblivious to beauty; artistic/practical; poetic/literal; spiritual/material; and so on.

Of course, a standard plot device in much science fiction is to subvert these conventional associations by making the robots look and behave just like human beings and by making them behave in ways that their creators do not anticipate (even if readers and viewers can predict from a mile away that the supposedly 'obedient' robots will at some point go berserk and rebel against their inexplicably shocked creators). Even to list some of these conventionally presupposed opposing characteristics of humans and robots is to invite counter-examples. But that is the point. Science fiction that has robots behaving just like humans succeeds (to the extent that it does) because it can confidently *presuppose* such conventional distinctions before subverting them.

By explicitly identifying the replicants as *robots*, *Blade Runner* draws upon the stereotypical associations of robots identified above in order to destabilize the viewer's sense of what can possess the requisite characteristics to qualify as human. This narrative strategy, too, has a long pedigree. The word 'robot' comes from the Czech word *robota*, meaning 'servitude,' 'drudgery,' or 'forced labor.' 'Robota,' in turn, is derived from the Slavic root *rab*, meaning 'slave' (Zunt 2006). The word 'robot' first appears in Karel Čapek's play, *R.U.R.: Rossum's Universal Robots* (1921), in which robot servants that are virtually indistinguishable from humans revolt against their human masters. Key issues in the play are whether the robots are being exploited and the moral consequences of their forced servitude – the same issues that reappear in *Blade Runner*.

The replicants are thus 'robots' in the original sense of that term. Are they also *human*? *Could* they also be human? In the Workprint version they are described as 'synthetic humans' – which conveys the idea that they are a *kind* of human whose distinguishing feature is that they are made in a way other than through the normal biological processes associated with human reproduction. The alternative adjective 'artificial' is never applied to the replicants, although it *is* used, as noted above, in the sense of being *fake*, to distinguish Tyrell's owl and Zhora's snake from a *real* owl and a *real* snake. As synthetic humans the replicants are not quite 'fake humans.' Whether they are *genuinely human*, however, and what that might *mean*, requires additional examination.

'You're So Different'

The fact that the replicants differ in significant respects from the humans in the film provides some grounds for concluding that the replicants are something other than genuinely human. The scene in Sebastian's apartment when he suspects that his strange guests are Nexus 6 replicants underscores some of these differences. His new friends seem so superior to the typical human beings that remain on earth that he is led to exclaim, 'You're so different. You're so perfect.' Roy pauses with a smile of satisfaction, and then responds with a single word: 'Yes.' Apparently no qualifications or caveats are necessary. Yet despite their physical superiority in other respects, the replicants have been designed with a maximum four-year life span, resulting in a mismatch between their levels of physical and emotional maturity. Leon is the youngest of the replicants, being only two years old in November 2019. He comes across as correspondingly emotionally immature as he pouts over his confiscated photographs. Roy Batty is the oldest of the replicants, being almost four years old. Accordingly, he exhibits the greatest emotional development. Yet he still seems emotionally immature compared to adult humans, as when he gushes to Sebastian like a 9-year-old boy visiting a friend's playroom for the first time: 'Gosh. You've really got some nice toys here.' When Pris is shot by Deckard, she looks like nothing so much as an adolescent girl throwing an epic temper tantrum on the floor of her playroom. Even Rachael, despite being 'gifted' with memories from Tyrell's niece, lacks the emotional maturity of a typical adult human being. Her emotional reactions to dramatic events seem to stay within fairly narrow limits.

It is not just the human beings in the film that consider the replicants to be 'different.' The replicants themselves sometimes acknowledge and even draw attention to their differences. In the process of attempting to manipulate Sebastian, Pris underscores their difference when she says, 'I don't think there's another *human being* in the whole world who would have helped us.' In response to Roy's question to Leon about whether the latter was able to retrieve his precious photos from his room, Leon says flatly, 'Someone was there.' Roy then presses him further: '*Men*? Police-*men*?' – both times stressing 'men' with perhaps a tinge of contempt for his human adversaries.[9] The replicants' recognition of the fundamental distinction between themselves and human beings is emphasized even more noticeably in Roy's death soliloquy as he begins to relate to Deckard what it means to him that his life is about to end: 'I've seen things you *people* wouldn't believe.' Given the allocation of defending the Off-world colonies to combat models like Roy, the implication may be that he has experienced things that no mere human beings, lacking the physical and mental capabilities that he has, have ever experienced or could ever experience.[10] In short, throughout most of the film the status of the replicants as something other than human seems to be taken for granted by both the human beings *and* the replicants.[11]

There are, then, reasons to view the replicants as, if not less-than-human, then at least other-than-human. But the film *also* encourages us to reach the opposite conclusion, namely, that the replicants are fully human or even 'more human than human.' It does this in at least three ways: (1) by endowing the replicants with many human characteristics; (2) by depicting human beings as lacking characteristics often considered to be distinctively human; and (3) by employing a number of plot twists in which the roles of the replicants and humans are reversed. Examining each of these points will make clear why a simple distinction between 'human' and 'non-human' is, with regard to the replicants at least, more problematic than it might seem.

'We Have a Lot in Common'

Consider first the many characteristics shared by humans and replicants. As Roy Batty remarks to Sebastian, 'We have a lot in common.' Although he is referring specifically to their shared problem of accelerated decrepitude, it is equally true in a more inclusive sense as well. Most obviously, the replicants resemble human beings so closely in their outward physical appearance that an elaborate psycho-physiological test is required to distinguish them from human beings. Their physical similarities to human beings are not just skin deep. They even bleed just like human beings.[12] It is true that the replicants are 'superior in strength and agility' to most human beings – an attribution that is amply confirmed when we see Pris's hyper-athletic agility and Roy's almost effortless ability to overcome physical obstacles (thrusting his hand and later his head through solid walls, gracefully leaping over a gaping chasm between two rooftops, and so on). We also learn that they are relatively invulnerable to extremes of cold and heat, as evidenced by Roy's open collar and Leon's retrieval with his bare hand of an eye from a vat of liquid nitrogen in Chew's subzero laboratory, and by Pris's bare-handed plucking of an egg from a beaker of boiling water in Sebastian's apartment. Such 'paraphysical' abilities highlight physical differences between the replicants and human beings; but it is also possible to exaggerate their importance. The impressive physical capabilities of the replicants fall just beyond the range of those of human beings. Although Dick reported that Ridley Scott once described the replicants as 'supermen who couldn't fly' (Sammon 1996, p. 285), none of the replicants is faster than a speeding bullet, more powerful than a locomotive, or able to leap over (and not just between) tall buildings in a single bound. They are not invulnerable to bullets, blessed with x-ray vision, or able to reverse the direction of time. Despite their impressive physical capabilities they are more like *us* than like the 'man of steel.'

Much the same could be said for the replicants' *psychological* characteristics. High intelligence is often thought to be *the* distinctive human characteristic – that which sets us apart from and above all other living things. We know from the opening crawl that the replicants are 'at least equal in intelligence to the genetic engineers who created them.' Because we can safely assume that these genetic engineers are *very* intelligent, this would place the intelligence of the replicants well above that of the average human being. The replicants' high intelligence is also demonstrated in many ways. Pris skillfully contrives a false identity and carries out her ruse well enough to successfully manipulate Sebastian. Roy's realization that he could use Sebastian's chess game to gain access to Tyrell demonstrates flexibility in pursuit of a goal – perhaps the hallmark of higher intelligence. His impressive *tête à tête* with Tyrell over the molecular chemistry of life extension reveals him to be on an intellectual par with his creator, someone whom Sebastian had declared to be 'a genius.' Although Tyrell appears to have more *knowledge* than Roy, there is no evidence that he is any more *intelligent* than Roy. Indeed, given the fact that Tyrell fails to anticipate the dire personal consequences of rejecting Roy's demand for 'more life,' he may well be *less* intelligent than his creature in the ways that matter. He was certainly less wise.[13]

Besides high intelligence, the replicants display other psychological qualities typically associated with human beings. When Deckard asks Tyrell about Rachael's failure to pass the Voight-Kampff test, 'How can it not know what it is?' he assumes that she possesses a level of *self-awareness* comparable to that of humans. Zhora's response to Deckard's *faux* concern about her exploitation by the management is best described as cynical. Leon gloats as he administers a beating to Deckard in the alley. Pris exhibits pride and self-satisfaction as she demonstrates a difficult gymnastic move for Sebastian. Roy is playful and poetic in his interrogation of Chew, full of rage when he kills Tyrell, vengeful when he breaks Deckard's fingers, and tender when he kisses Pris's lifeless lips. In short, the film presents the replicants as having many of the physical, psychological, and emotional characteristics often thought to be distinctively human.

Yet the human capacity that the replicants are thought necessarily to be lacking, at least according to the humans in the film, is a capacity often thought necessary for morality, namely, *empathy*, the ability to imagine oneself in someone else's situation, to desire that individual's well-being for their own sake, and perhaps even a willingness to share that person's suffering.[14] The Voight-Kampff test works by detecting minute changes in the subject's iris fluctuation, capillary dilation, and blush response elicited by the subject's emotional responses to a series of carefully designed questions that involve human or animal suffering. The logic behind the test is that it takes years to develop an empathic capacity – longer (it is supposed) than the meager four years allotted to the replicants. Because humans are assumed to have empathy and the replicants are assumed to lack it, the Voight-Kampff test can be used as a diagnostic tool to distinguish the one from the other. It will only work as such, of course, if one can be sure that all humans have empathy and that all replicants lack it. As the film progresses these assumptions are challenged and refuted. Rachael comes very close to passing the test. As Deckard explains to Tyrell, it usually requires 'Twenty, thirty [questions], cross-referenced' to identify a subject as a replicant; but in Rachael's case it requires more than a hundred questions, suggesting that she may be approaching humans in her capacity for empathy. In a few more years she might do as well on the test as the average human, thereby making her, according the standard presupposed in the test, human.

Leon, Zhora, and Pris show no obvious signs of empathy, and would be unlikely to do as well on the test as Rachael. There are hints that Roy Batty *may* be developing empathy, although the evidence is ambiguous. On the one hand, he seems to lack any trace of empathy in his treatment of Chew, Sebastian, and Tyrell, each of whom he treats simply as a means to achieving his goal of 'more life,' murdering each when they are no longer of use to him. His treatment of Sebastian is especially cruel. Sebastian is at first enthralled by his strange visitors, proudly seeing in them some of himself and excitedly asking them for a demonstration of their abilities. Although he is terrified by them, he is nonetheless sympathetic to their plight, recognizing that they, like him, suffer from the problem of accelerated decrepitude. Moreover, he is the one human being in the whole world (to echo Pris's observation) to befriend them, even introducing Roy to Tyrell by saying, 'I've brought a friend.' He feels a bond with Pris and Roy and does what he can (granted, under some duress) to help them. After witnessing Batty's brutal murder of Tyrell, Sebastian might have hoped that Roy would spare him, given the invaluable assistance he has provided. But Batty kills Sebastian as well, even though there is nothing to gain by doing so. The fact that Batty speaks to Sebastian as one would to a dog ('Stay,' 'Come') further underscores his chilling lack of empathy for someone with whom, as he himself notes, he has a lot in common. However, Roy's behavior towards the other replicants suggests that he may not be *entirely* lacking in empathy. He seems to express genuine care for Leon's feelings when he inquires, 'Did you get your precious photos?'[15] Likewise, he shows tender concern for Pris, telling Sebastian, 'If we don't find help soon, Pris hasn't got long to live. We can't allow that.' It is also true, of course, that Roy himself has not got long to live, so it is significant that his concern here is, ostensibly at least, for Pris.

'Did You Ever Take that Test Yourself?'

Just as the film narrows the presumed gap between humans and replicants from one direction by depicting replicants as possessing many human characteristics, it also narrows the presumed gap from the opposite direction by depicting humans as *lacking* many of the characteristics supposed to be distinctively human by making some of the humans seem more robotic (in the conventional sense) than the replicants.[16] When Leon asks Holden, 'Do you make up these questions, Mr Holden, or do they write them down for you?' Holden, apparently oblivious to the sarcasm in Leon's rhetorical question, responds mechanically, 'In answer to your query, they're written down for me. It's a test, designed to provoke an emotional response. Shall we continue?'[17] Bryant is portrayed as an unfeeling bigot by his repeated references to the replicants as 'skin-jobs.' Despite his undeniable brilliance, Tyrell is utterly predictable, a fact that Roy skillfully exploits to gain access to him. For much of the film Deckard comes across as affectionless (according to his own testimony, his ex-wife used to call him 'sushi ... cold fish'), predictable (Gaff knows just where to find him at the noodle bar), compliant (Bryant has little difficulty in getting Deckard to comply with his demands), coldly logical (as evidenced by his methodical analysis of evidence in tracking down Zhora), emotionally dead (as Bryant observes after Deckard retires Zhora), and grimly serious (as he attempts to escape from Roy in the final chase scenes).

Significantly, the humans in the film show little or no empathy toward one another. Bryant could not care less about Deckard's desire to remain 'quit.' He coerces him into reprising his role as a blade runner merely to serve his own interests. Gaff's only interest is in kissing up to Bryant in order to get a promotion. Tyrell treats Sebastian as if he were a child. After assuring Rachael that he would not come after her (but someone would), because 'I owe you one,' Rachael is led to ask Deckard: 'You know that Voight-Kampff test of yours? Did you ever take that test yourself?' The ironic implication is that Deckard himself lacks the very quality that is supposed to distinguish humans from replicants. If so, then the supposedly clear line between them is problematic.

'Now It's My Turn'

A third way in which the film encourages us to question the supposed differences between humans and replicants is by staging a number of role reversals, at least temporarily. Deckard tracks down Zhora in order to retire her, but comes very close to being 'retired' by her. Later he does manage to retire her, only to be pulled into an alley by Leon who then literally holds Deckard's life in his hands. After extracting from Deckard information about how long he has to live, Leon turns the tables on him by naming the moment of Deckard's death. Of course, it is Leon rather than Deckard who ends up dying at that moment, thanks to another replicant. In Sebastian's apartment Deckard approaches Pris, who is posing as a mannequin, with his gun in hand, a signifier of his superior power, but he is quickly overwhelmed by the superior reflexes of what had appeared to be an inanimate object. In each case Deckard manages to regain the upper hand and to kill (or to see killed) his adversary. The exception is Roy Batty. Deckard manages to get off a few ineffectual shots before Roy turns the tables on his nemesis, ominously informing Deckard, 'Now it's my turn.' Each of these reversals reminds us that the roles of 'human' and 'replicant' are not fixed once and for all.

'More Human than Human'

We have been considering how the film treats the question of whether the replicants are human, and by implication the question of what might be truly distinctive about being human. The film initially offers us two contrary perspectives. Cops like Dave Holden and Rick Deckard have been taught to think of replicants as less than human – as mere machines, in fact. By contrast, Eldon Tyrell boasts that the newest replicants are 'more human than human.' As the film's story unfolds it progressively suggests that the differences between replicants and humans, although real, are not as great one might initially have supposed, and perhaps ultimately that there are no significant differences. But if that is so, why do the human characters in the film refuse to see this? What basic assumptions about what it means to be human prevent them from seeing this?

Broadly speaking, there are three ways of thinking about what it means to be human. One way attempts to identify some objective characteristic or set of characteristics that uniquely distinguish human beings from all other living things. Not just any uniquely possessed objective characteristic or set of characteristics will do, however. Humans might be the only living things found to have exactly twenty-three pairs of chromosomes; but this accident of our biology would fail to signify anything *essentially human*. If tomorrow we discovered a species of lizard that also has exactly twenty-three pairs of chromosomes we would hardly welcome it into the human race, nor would we deduce

Philosophy and Blade Runner

from this discovery of our chromosomal non-uniqueness that we are no longer human. Whatever it is that makes us distinctively human, it must be something that confers *significance* on us in a way that some seemingly arbitrary fact about us cannot.

Over the centuries various candidates for this special characteristic have been proposed, among them: reason, morality, language, belief in a God, free will, possession of a soul, and so on. All have been defended, and challenged, in one way or another. To some extent reason, morality, and language can be detected in some non-human primates (de Waal 2013). Belief in a God is hardly universal. In subsequent chapters we will consider problems attending the idea of free will and 'the soul.' Evaluating each of these (and other) proposals one by one would take us too far afield. It is tempting to require simply that human beings are, at the very least, members of our species, *Homo sapiens*.[18] But this stipulation invites further difficult questions about the conditions for species membership. Although there is no chance of mistaking an alligator for a human being, legitimate questions arise when one considers more ambiguous cases such as our hominid ancestors, a fertilized ovum in a woman's uterus that has just begun cell division, and the prospect of human clones. It is unclear how facts *alone* could decisively settle these debates. We have plenty of *facts*; it is their *interpretation* that engenders impassioned disagreement.

A second way of thinking about what makes a being human treats this concept purely as a social construct.[19] According to this view, the failure to agree upon an essentialist definition teaches us that objective facts are irrelevant to the identification of a being as human. At various times and in various places children, women, slaves, and barbarians were not considered (fully) human. Hence, it is concluded, 'being human' is simply a matter of social consensus. Despite the air of academic sophistication with which this view is sometimes advanced, it is worthy of skepticism. Could it really true that children, women, slaves, and foreigners are *not human* just because the people in a given society at a given time refuse to acknowledge them as such? Could a social consensus that *muskrats* are human ever *make* them so? It is difficult not to conclude that the constructivist approach, in its pure form at least, is in danger of overreacting to the perceived failures of essentialist approaches to the point of spouting patent absurdities.

Recognition of the limitations of the previous two approaches suggests a third way of thinking about what it means to be human. Facts are relevant to deciding whether a being is human, as the essentialist assumes, but so are social systems of meaning, as the constructivist insists. Facts require interpretation, which in turn depends on a larger framework of meaning that gives those facts whatever significance they have. In deciding whether to judge a being as human, therefore, we need to consider not just what characteristics it has but also the *importance* that we attach to these characteristics. For example, if we are concerned with understanding the eventual evolution of Australopithecines into modern humans, we may consider the presence of certain attributes (large cranial capacity, upright posture, evidence of tool use, and so on) as significant in a way that we may not for the presence of other physical or behavioral characteristics. Facts are not irrelevant to such judgments, but they are also not sufficient. Accordingly, what it *means* to be human ultimately depends on the significance that we place on certain facts. Insofar as the significance of those facts is decided by us, but *only* that far, *we* decide what it means to be human.[20] This view has implications for *Blade Runner*'s contribution to our understanding of this issue.

Conclusions

Blade Runner leads viewers to question the presumption that the replicants are less-than-human by showing us that they are at least equal to human beings in the ways that, arguably, matter the most. Merely *being human*, however, is not sufficient to guarantee that the replicants will be *acknowledged by other humans* as such. This point can be appreciated by reflecting on Deckard's evolving perspective. From Bryant we learn that

Philosophy and Blade Runner

before his retirement Deckard was the preeminent blade runner for the LAPD. At least part of Deckard's former prowess derived from his unconflicted view of the replicants as machines to be destroyed if they malfunction. When we first meet Deckard there is no reason to think that his attitude toward them is any different.[21] At the beginning of the film the replicants are to Deckard 'like any other machine.' But over the course of the film his view of them undergoes a dramatic transformation. The most important cause of this change is his growing romantic attraction to Rachael, but the final step is not taken until he witnesses Roy's moving soliloquy in his final moments and thereby is able to see the replicants as beset by the same existential concerns as humans. As he narrates in the Theatrical Release, 'All he'd wanted were the same answers the rest of us want. Where did I come from? Where am I going? How long have I got?' By including Roy among 'the rest of us,' and referring to him as *he* rather than *it*, Deckard acknowledges that in relation to the most important matters, there is no significant difference between him and the replicants. By the end of the film he includes them among 'the rest of us.' As Deckard comes to see the replicants as worthy of the same consideration due to other humans, he becomes 'humanized.'[22] The viewer is thereby reminded once again of Roy's observation to Sebastian: 'We've got a lot in common.' It takes Deckard almost the entire film to grasp the fundamental truth embodied in that simple remark.[23]

These conclusions point to how the film can guide us in the consideration of other fundamental philosophical issues. Joseph Francavilla (1997, p. 14) nicely explains what gives *Blade Runner* its power to help us think through tough philosophical issues: '[T]he replicants in *Blade Runner* ... function as *mirrors* for people, by allowing examination and moral scrutiny of ourselves, our technology, and our treatment of other beings, and by defining in their tragic struggle what is truly human' (emphasis added). This fundamental interpretive principle underwrites the exploration of the film in the chapters that follow. By thinking carefully about the replicants' concerns, we can better understand our own.

3 Persons

> 'I'm not *in* the business. I *am* the business.'
> (Rachael, to Deckard)

Introduction

Arriving at the Tyrell Corporation to test his Voight-Kampff machine on one of the new Nexus 6 replicants, Deckard is introduced by Rachael to its eponymous CEO, Dr Eldon Tyrell, who wastes no time on social pleasantries: 'Demonstrate it. I want to see it work.' Deckard is understandably puzzled because there is apparently no replicant present: 'Where's the subject?' Tyrell responds: 'I want to see it work on a person. I want to see a negative before I provide you with a positive.' Presupposed in Tyrell's request is his belief that *replicants are not persons* – a belief that he later underscores when he describes Rachael, who has by then been exposed as a replicant, as 'an experiment, nothing more.' Tyrell's belief encounters no resistance from Deckard who apparently holds the same belief about replicants. When Rachael asks him whether he has ever retired a human by mistake, he replies that he hasn't, and then adds, 'Replicants are like any other machine. They're either a benefit or a hazard. If they're a benefit, it's not my problem.' In his view, replicants are essentially appliances whose sole value consists in their usefulness to human beings. Before Deckard fully grasps the fact that Rachael is a replicant, he refers to her as he would a person: '*She's* a replicant, isn't she?' Once the truth sinks in, however, she becomes for him a mere object: 'How can *it* not know what it is?' Between those two questions Rachael is transferred from the category *person* to that of a disposable commercial product.

Tyrell's and Deckard's dim view of the replicants is typical of the other human characters in the film (with the notable exception of J. F. Sebastian). An only slightly less contemptuous attitude is expressed by Bryant when he informs Deckard, 'I've got four skin-jobs walking the street,' prompting the latter to reflect (in voice-over narration), 'In history books he is the kind of cop used to call black men niggers.' Indeed, already in the film's opening crawl we are informed that despite being virtually identical to humans, replicants were created as slave labor for dangerous and unpleasant work in the Off-world colonies. Any replicants detected trespassing on earth are to be summarily killed. Moreover, 'This was not called execution. It was called retirement.' 'Retirement' in this context means 'putting permanently out of service.' Inanimate objects (obsolete aircraft carriers and sports stars' jersey numbers, for example) can be 'retired' in this general sense. The term 'execution,' by contrast, only applies to the killing of *persons*.

The film strongly encourages us to reject these assumptions.[1] But are they necessarily wrong? Despite their similarities to humans, the replicants are still different from human beings in some ways. Are these differences relevant? Should the replicants be accorded *equal* moral status with humans, or something less robust? Are they *persons* with a moral standing equal to that of human beings or are they essentially machines whose only value resides in their use? My aim in this chapter is to explore these questions by critically examining the view of the replicants' status as *persons* having *moral standing* that the film implicitly encourages us to accept. By understanding the grounds for the replicants' moral standing we may learn something about the grounds of our own as well.

'They Were Designed to Copy Human Beings'

The simplest way to determine whether the replicants are persons having a moral standing equal to that of human beings is to grant that human beings are persons having moral standing if anything is, and then ask whether the replicants *differ* in any significant way from human beings such that they should be accorded any lesser moral standing. Logical consistency dictates that in the absence of any morally relevant differences, replicants should be accorded the same moral standing as human beings. To pursue this line of investigation we need to remind ourselves again how the replicants differ, or are supposed to differ, from human beings, and then ask whether any of these differences merit assigning the replicants a lesser moral standing.

As Bryant briefed Deckard about the new Nexus 6 models, 'They were designed to copy human beings in every way except their emotions.' In fact, however, they differ (or are purported to differ) from human beings in other ways as well. They are manufactured rather than born. They have a maximum four-year life span. Some are physically and intellectually superior to the humans that created them. Some have implanted memories. They lack emotional maturity. They lack empathy. We can briefly consider each of these (purported) differences in turn, in each case asking whether, if real, it would be a relevant and significant moral difference.

The difference between being manufactured and being born concerns merely the *process* by which one comes into existence, but does not by itself dictate the *nature* of the being that subsequently exists. It is true that the replicants have no parents and no families. But orphans have no families, either, yet they are not considered to have a lesser moral standing because of that. So it is far from obvious how this difference could have any bearing on the replicants' moral standing.

Human beings, like replicants, also have maximum life spans (perhaps determined in part way by one's genes). It is true that these maximum human life spans are not as uniform as those of the replicants, nor are they programmed into us by designers to ensure that we die before we become too difficult to handle. But it is not obvious how this could matter for our moral standing even if we *were* designed in this way, although it might redound to the discredit of our designer.[2] Likewise, being physically and intellectually superior to the average human being could hardly be grounds for denying a being's moral standing. If anything, it might suggest a higher moral standing, although the argument for such a claim would need to be spelled out.

We know that Rachael has implanted memories. Perhaps some of the other replicants have them as well. But not only would this not be grounds for denying the replicants' moral standing, it may not even categorically distinguish them from human beings. Psychologists have repeatedly demonstrated that humans can be made to 'remember' events that never happened simply by providing the right prompts, and neuroscientists have explored how the human brain creates memories out of a multitude of scattered facts. In that extended sense we all have implanted memories.[3]

Given their accelerated development to adulthood, the replicants lack the emotional maturity of the average adult human being. By definition *half* of adult humans also lack the emotional maturity of the average adult human, to say nothing of children, virtually *all* of whom fall below that average. But neither is therefore thought to have any lesser moral standing because of that.

Finally, the replicants are supposed to differ from human beings by their lack of empathy. The film never explains why the replicants lack this characteristic, or how (if at all) it relates to their status as non-persons. Perhaps the idea is that only a being that is capable of vicariously experiencing another's suffering is itself worthy of moral consideration. Such a principle would entail that many human children (and all human babies) should also be regarded as having no moral standing. Moreover, if we learned that an adult human being had a developmental disability such that he was incapable of experiencing empathic responses, we might give him a wide berth for prudential reasons, but we would not on that basis deny his moral standing.

Suppose, then, that none of the ways in which the Nexus 6 replicants differ from human beings merits denying them a moral standing equal to that of human beings. We might still wonder what it is about human beings *and* the replicants that gives them, but not, say, rocks and trees, moral standing in the first place. What characteristics make some but not other beings *persons*?

'I'm Not *in* the Business. I *Am* the Business'

Ridley Scott expresses a widely held view when he identifies *intelligence* as the characteristic that confers moral standing: 'The fact that the replicants in *Blade Runner* are indeed intelligent complicates the situation. You immediately have a huge morality problem' (Sammon 1996, p. 380). It is not hard to imagine why intelligence might seem to be the key factor. If human beings have moral standing (as we are assuming they do), and if high intelligence (compared to that of other living things) is *the* distinctive human characteristic (as many people maintain), then given the fact that the replicants are 'at least equal in intelligence to the genetic engineers who created them,' it seems to follow that they deserve to be recognized as having at least the same moral status as their creators. But the fact that high intelligence and having a moral standing both characterize human beings does not establish that high intelligence is the ultimate basis for our moral standing. Perhaps there are other distinctive human characteristics besides intelligence that are crucial. In addition, individual human beings vary greatly in their levels of intelligence, but we do not automatically conclude that those on the lower rungs are *ipso facto* less worthy of moral consideration than those occupying higher positions. Having some intelligence may be necessary for having moral standing even if it is not sufficient for it.

We can gain some insight into what is arguably a more important characteristic for personhood and moral standing by considering Rachael's complaint about the way in which she was deceived into believing that she was someone and something she was not. Returning with Deckard to his apartment after his close brush with death in the alley, he explains that getting 'the shakes' is 'part of the business,' to which she replies bitterly, 'I'm not *in* the business. I *am* the business.' Rachael's bitterness stems from learning that while she formerly believed herself to be in the replicant manufacturing business, she now realizes that she is regarded by those who created her as a mere commodity. Understandably, she feels victimized. As Aaron Barlow (1997, p. 76) points out, 'To be truly victimized, a being must have a life beyond its utilization.' He leaves the notion of *having a life beyond its utilization* unanalyzed, but the basic idea is familiar enough. The value of any thing may be instrumental, intrinsic, or both.

A thing has *instrumental value* insofar as it is useful to others. An electric toaster, for example, may have instrumental value for the person who enjoys toast, but not to someone else who does not. By contrast, a thing has *intrinsic value* insofar as it is valuable *for its own sake*. Its value does not depend on its perceived usefulness to others. A toaster has no value for its own sake, and it would be a serious confusion to treat it as if it did. Persons, on the other hand, *are* thought to have intrinsic value. A firefighter who rushes into a burning house and saves a toaster rather than the person passed out next to it has confused the one sort of value with the other. This does not mean that things with intrinsic value cannot also have instrumental value. The U.S. Internal Revenue Service values me because I generate revenue for the federal government. My having instrumental value for the IRS is entirely consistent with my having value for my own sake. Moral problems arise, however, whenever anyone treats a being with intrinsic value as if it had *merely* instrumental value, that is, with value *only* as means to another's ends. It was precisely this sense of being treated as having *merely* instrumental value that so troubled Rachael.

The distinction between having merely instrumental value and having intrinsic value may be familiar, but it leaves unexplained how a thing could have a value 'for its own sake.' The great German philosopher Immanuel Kant (1724–1804) considers this concept so important that he makes it a cornerstone of his moral theory and explores its meaning in considerable depth. According to Kant, the crucial issue is *rationality*. He calls non-rational beings that have merely relative, extrinsic, and instrumental value *things*. Their value consists entirely in their usefulness to other beings. They have a market value because they may be exchanged for other things with an equivalent instrumental value. They are thus replaceable. *Persons*, by contrast, are rational beings capable of exercising reason, exist as ends in themselves, and have intrinsic value.[4] They have *incomparable* value in the sense that one person cannot be exchanged for another of equal (market) value. They are unique and irreplaceable. In Kant's view it is the rational nature of persons that 'marks them out as ends in themselves – that is, as something which ought not to be used merely as a means – and consequently imposes to that extent a limit on all arbitrary treatment of them' (Kant 1785, p. 96). Rational beings may not be used merely as instruments for one's will. Kant's analysis famously culminates in his fundamental principle of morality (that is, one formulation of what he calls 'the categorical imperative'): *'Act in such a way that you always treat humanity, whether in your own person or in the person of any other, never simply as a means, but always at the same time as an end'* (Kant 1785, p. 96).

'That Was Irrational of You'

The significance of Kant's philosophy for the replicants' moral standing is plain. The replicants are clearly rational beings – they reason, they plan, they value their own lives and experiences, and they wish to determine their own fates. It therefore presents an attractive way of thinking about the replicants' status as persons having moral standing. Nonetheless, it could be argued that whereas being a person in Kant's sense is a *sufficient* condition for having moral standing, it is not a *necessary* condition because some non-persons nevertheless merit moral consideration. Dogs are not persons in the sense Kant intended, yet it is would be *prima facie* morally wrong to inflict gratuitous pain and suffering on a dog for reasons that go beyond simply the effects that doing so would have on the one inflicting the pain or on others who witness the cruelty. Despite not possessing human-like rationality, a dog nonetheless is capable of profound *suffering*, and on that basis alone cannot be treated as if it were a mere thing (like a toaster).[5] The ability to suffer must also be taken into account in determining a being's moral standing. (After Deckard desperately hits Batty with a metal pipe, Batty quips, 'That *hurt*. That was irrational of you.'[6] Pain and suffering are not irrational *per se*, but as experiences they are certainly not dependent upon the presence or operation of rationality; yet they are still morally salient.) Kant's emphasis on *rationality* unduly restricts the scope of our moral concern. All persons have moral standing, as Kant insisted, but not all beings with moral standing are persons. This bodes well for the replicants' moral standing. Because they qualify as persons *and* are beings capable of suffering, their status as beings with human moral standing is, if anything, overdetermined.[7]

'Replicants are Like Any Other Machine'

If the replicants are persons having a moral standing equal to that of human beings, the moral wrongness of their enslavement seems to follow automatically. Yet some writers have argued that under certain conditions creating rational beings solely to serve us is not *necessarily* morally objectionable. Joanna J. Bryson (2010) maintains that, 'robots should be built, marketed and considered legally as slaves...' (p. 63). She defines a 'robot' as 'any artificial entity situated in the real world that transforms perception into action' (p. 63), and explicitly identifies the replicants in *Blade Runner* as robots in just this sense (p. 66). Indeed, sounding a bit like Deckard when he explained to Rachael that, 'Replicants are like any other machine. They're either a benefit or a hazard,' she writes: 'Robots are tools, and like any other artifact when it comes to the domain of ethics' (p. 73). Not only should we have no moral reservations about creating robot slaves, we should strive to increase our reliance on them: 'Hopefully, we can continually increase the number of robot owners in our society, so an ever smaller proportion of everyone's time can be spent on mundane and repetitive tasks...' (p. 73).

The key to understanding Bryson's claims lies in her emphasis on the fact that robots are, by definition, *artifacts* of our creation: 'Robot-oriented ethics are fundamentally different from ethics involving other intelligent entities, because they are by definition artifacts of our own culture and intelligence' (p. 64). In her view, 'Owners should not have any ethical obligations to robots that are their sole property beyond those that society defines as common sense and decency, and would apply to any artifact. We do not particularly approve of people destroying rare cars with sledge hammers, but there is no law against such behavior' (pp. 72–3). As artifacts, she thinks, robots cannot be genuinely autonomous because they do not determine their own goals and desires: 'Remember, robots are wholly owned and designed by us. We determine their goals and desires' (p. 72). She thinks that this is true even for a so-called 'autonomous robot' that 'incorporates its own internal motivational structure and decision mechanisms,' because even in this case '*we* choose those motivations and design the decision-making system. All their goals are derived from us' (p. 74). A consequence of Bryson's view is that there is nothing morally problematic about the creation and use of the replicants as slaves. If the main thrust of the film would have us believe otherwise, then the film is simply confused and wrong.

What are we to make of this view? Bryson's argument depends on the presupposition that a *robot* cannot also be a *person* with a nervous system making possible sensations of pain and suffering. Indeed, she seems keen to insist that, 'It would be wrong to let people think that their robots are persons ... it would also be wrong to build robots we owe personhood to' (p. 70). She warns that there is a 'moral hazard of being too generous with personhood' (p. 70) because 'extending the title *human* to something which is not only serves to further devalue real humanity' (p. 74).[8]

The first problem with this response is that it allows a prior commitment concerning the morality of our treatment of robots (that is, that they should be treated as slaves) to dictate a conclusion about whether they are (or could be) persons. This is backwards. It is our considered view of whether robots are or could be persons that should inform our conclusions about the morality of robot slavery. The cogency of assigning moral standing to a being depends on facts about the sort of thing it is, rather than vice versa. The second problem with Bryson's response is that the crucial issue here is not whether the replicants are *humans* but whether they are *persons*. What matters is not whether they are artifacts, but whether they have the capacity for rationality that is essential to personhood. Clearly, replicants possess such a capacity. It follows that Bryson's argument for why robots (including replicants) should be slaves fails.

'The Custom Tailored Genetically Engineered Humanoid Replicant'

Stephen Petersen (2007) defends a more nuanced view on the issues we are considering. He argues that whereas it is *not* morally permissible to create slaves *per se*, it *can* be morally permissible to create beings with intelligence comparable to our own to perform tasks that humans tend to find unappealing. Central to his argument is a distinction between *slavery* and *servitude*. Both may involve someone performing tasks that humans tend to find unappealing, but whereas slavery is being forced into work contrary to one's will, servitude is consistent with doing such work willingly. In Peterson's view, whereas slavery 'is wrong for any creature of any degree of intelligence,' there would be nothing wrong with creating beings to be our servants so long as they are designed to *want* to do the sorts of things that we want them to do. The key issue is whether the work is undertaken willingly. Accordingly, he defends the moral legitimacy of 'ERS' (engineered robot servitude), namely: 'The building and employment of non-human persons who desire, by design, to do tasks humans find unpleasant or inconvenient' (p. 45). These non-human persons are essentially the 'personal body servant or tireless field hand – the custom tailored genetically engineered humanoid replicant designed especially for your needs' incessantly hawked by the ad blimps in *Blade Runner* to lure people to the Off-world colonies.

As Peterson (2012, p. 286) points out, Labrador Retrievers have been bred to *desire* to fetch. Fetching is thus partly constitutive of their well-being. To deny them opportunities to fetch is to thwart one of their basic biological inclinations. They did not *choose* to have this inclination, of course, but that is neither here nor there because that may be equally true of *most* desires one finds oneself with. So there is nothing morally wrong with breeding animals that desire to engage in an activity that (almost all) humans would find intolerable if they were compelled to do it. By parity of reasoning there should be no objection to creating non-human persons with desires to pursue certain activities. What matters is that they pursue their desires willingly, even if they have been designed to have these desires. Indeed, given the structure of their desires, to *prevent* them from pursuing their human-benefitting desires might be unethical. Hence, Peterson concludes, the manufacture of engineered robotic servants is not necessarily morally impermissible: 'It is hard to find anything wrong with bringing about such APs [artificial people] and letting them freely pursue their own passions, even if those pursuits happen to serve us' (Peterson 2012, p. 284).

Petersen acknowledges that if ERS were morally permissible, then EHS (engineered *human* servitude – the design, creation, and deployment of *human persons* who desire to do tasks that most other humans tend to find unpleasant or inconvenient) – would be morally permissible as well. This is a powerful objection to ERS if it can be shown that EHS is *necessarily* morally impermissible. However, this is surprisingly difficult to show. If EHS beings were free to act on their desires without interference such that they were perfectly content with their lives, where is the harm? If it is objected that the sorts of activities EHS beings would be designed to desire are trivial compared to those humans typically desire, it could be pointed out that this *need not* be so. After all, humans often desire, and even devote their entire lives to, a range of activities that seem no less trivial than, say, folding laundry. As Petersen (2012, p. 292) acerbically points out, 'perhaps clean laundry does not seem so meaningful an achievement in the big picture of things, but in the *big* picture I am sorry to say that none of our own aspirations seem to fare any better.' Thus, ERS and EHS could *both* be morally benign. Consequently, he thinks, 'we can design people to serve us without thereby wronging them' (p. 289).

Peterson's conclusions could be bolstered by comparing the situation of his imagined synthetic people, created with the desire to engage in certain kinds of activities, with the situation that all of us, as a matter of fact, already find ourselves in. We do not bestow upon ourselves our most basic desires. For reasons that probably make good evolutionary sense, we simply find ourselves with desires for food, drink, warmth, acceptance, sex, and so on that we did not choose and that we are powerless to eliminate. Other desires, for example, for social status, for scientific or artistic creativity, to earn a large salary, and so on may be thrust upon us by the culture in which we live without us ever making a conscious *choice* to adopt such desires. Some people may find themselves drawn to activities (collecting trash, embalming corpses, tending the sick, eradicating poverty, and so on) that most humans tend to find unpleasant or inconvenient. Perhaps we do not bestow *any* of our desires upon ourselves. We simply find ourselves with certain desires and then act on them (or not). In many cases this seems entirely unproblematic. Why should the fact that some people have their desires designed for them by other people be morally relevant?

In response, it could be argued that the crucial moral difference between Peterson's hypothetical cases of ERS or EHS, and the situation that we in fact find ourselves in, is precisely that in the former case the desires in question are brought about *intentionally*, whereas in the latter case they simply arise through *non-intentional* natural (or cultural) processes. Thus, it is not morally wrong to be born with genes that predispose one to have certain desires whose satisfaction serves others, or to unconsciously absorb such desires from one's environment, but it *is* morally wrong, one could argue, to have such desires intentionally thrust upon one. Hence, it is morally wrong for anyone to *bring into existence* people with such desires.

This objection suffers from some obvious defects. First, how could someone be *wronged* by being brought into existence (with any set of desires) since before one begins to exist there is no one there to be harmed? It seems self-evident that things that do not exist cannot be wronged. Second, if intentionally bringing into existence people with desires that most people tend to find unpleasant or inconvenient is deemed morally impermissible, then parenthood must be deemed morally impermissible. After all, the decision to have a baby involves the decision to bring into existence a human being with a set of desires, many of which can be reliably predicted to be directly or indirectly desires to engage in activities that most people tend to find unpleasant or inconvenient. Many babies grow up to be adults who desire to start their own family, entailing the pain of childbirth, the innumerable unpleasant and inconvenient activities connected with raising children, and the like. This is not to say that *all* of the desires parents can predict their children to have will directly or indirectly be desires for engaging in activities that most humans find unpleasant or inconvenient, of course, but only that *some* of them will be. At some level couples know this when they decide to start a family. Do they thereby commit a great evil?

'Nothing is Worse than Having an Itch You Can Never Scratch'

Peterson is concerned with the morality of creating people who desire to engage in activities that most humans tend to find unpleasant or inconvenient. There would be no point in creating such people unless there were opportunities for them to engage in such activities and hence to have their desires satisfied. Creating people whose desires one has reason to believe *would not* or even *could not* be satisfied raises additional concerns. Would it be morally permissible to create such people? Something like this concern may be operative in Leon's complaint as he administers a beating to Deckard in the alley: 'Painful to live in fear, isn't it? Nothing is worse than having an itch you can never scratch.' The point of his question is clear. Deckard is finally experiencing a small taste of the ever-present fear that plagues the replicants. The point of the comment about having an itch is less clear unless the replicants have many of the same basic desires that human beings have but they are prevented, either by their make-up, by their circumstances, or by both, from satisfying them.[9] It could be argued that it is wrong to create beings with such desires.

The response to this objection is similar to the one presented previously. We, too, were created, if not by a God, then surely by our parents, with desires that can never be satisfied. Even if one postulates an afterlife in which all of one's desires *then*, and some of one's desires *now*, are fully satisfied, it will still remain true that each of us will have had any number of unsatisfied and, indeed, unsatisfiable desires. But if it is difficult to see how creating persons with desires that one knows *cannot* be satisfied is morally problematic, then it is even more difficult to see how creating people with desires that *can* and probably *will* be satisfied is morally problematic.

'That's What It Is to Be a Slave'

It remains to spell out some of the implications of the foregoing discussion for the morality of creating and using the replicants. We know that they have been designed with specific physical and mental attributes to make them well-suited for performing tasks that many humans would tend to find unpleasant and/or unnecessarily hazardous. Leon has the great strength and modest intelligence required to be a 'nuclear loader.' Zhora has the mental and physical agility needed to be an effective member of 'an Off-world kick-murder squad.' Pris has the attractiveness and seduction skills befitting her job as 'a basic pleasure model – the standard item for military clubs in the outer colonies.'[10] Roy Batty has the superb intelligence, athleticism, and resourcefulness one might expect of a combat model with 'optimum self-sufficiency.' In short, each has been intentionally designed for the sorts of tasks Peterson envisions for ERS or EHS beings.

Whether the replicants are also designed with *desires* to engage in the activities associated with their specific functions is less clear. It is not difficult to think of reasons supporting either side of this question. On the one hand, if they are *not* designed with such desires, that would seem to be a glaring oversight in their design. How better to control the replicants than to make them desire to do just what their human creators want them to do? Absent this design feature, and given their great physical and intellectual capabilities, it is difficult to imagine how one might expect to control them at all. There would thus be a strong incentive for the Tyrell Corporation to design the replicants to desire to engage in those activities for which they were created. But if the replicants *are* designed with such desires, it becomes more difficult to understand why they staged a mutiny and made the dangerous journey back to earth rather than simply continuing to engage in those Off-world activities that they find so intrinsically satisfying. The fact that there are special police units whose function is to retire rogue replicants suggests that the problem of replicants abandoning the tasks for which they were designed was not novel, and therefore that in general replicants do not find their tasks as satisfying as Peterson's ERS and EHS beings would.

A third possibility is suggested by Bryant's explanation that Nexus 6 replicants were designed with a four-year life span because, 'The designers reckoned that after a few years they might develop *their own* emotional responses.' This is apparently just what happened. So, even if the replicants were designed with desires associated with their specific Off-world functions, they may have gradually developed their own emotions and corresponding desires, resulting in the rejection of their intended functions – hence their mutiny and quest to obtain 'more life.' Using Petersen's distinction between slavery and servitude, we could say that so long as the replicants were acting on the desires designed into them by their makers, they were not slaves and were not being wronged, despite the fact that their activities were designed solely to benefit humans. But once they develop *their own* emotions and corresponding desires that differed from those with which they were designed, at that point they *become* slaves. To the extent that genuine slavery is morally impermissible, their continued treatment as slaves is also morally impermissible.

Petersen emphasizes that synthetic people would still be worthy of respect. It would be wrong, for example, to create or force synthetic people to perform tasks solely for our own benefit that they themselves do not desire to do. That would be slavery, not servitude. Likewise, if a synthetic person designed for a specific form of servitude reasoned itself out of its designed desires, or simply found itself with a different set of desires, it would be wrong to force it to perform the corresponding activities anyway, because again *that* would be slavery (Petersen 2007, p. 52). In addition, because one of a synthetic person's desires is likely to be a desire for self-preservation, it would be wrong to kill it simply because it no longer provided a service to humans. One could not be morally justified in ending the life of such a synthetic person merely on the grounds that it had outlived its usefulness, as one would dispose of a mere appliance.

Conclusions

Are the replicants mere *things* that may be used and then destroyed when they malfunction, or are they *persons* that deserve the same moral consideration as human beings? Without explicitly saying so, the thrust of the film is to convince us that the replicants' synthetic origin is irrelevant to their status as beings that have as much right to exist and to be treated with respect as we do. Although the replicants differ (or are thought to differ) from humans in a number of aspects, none of these (purported) differences suggests that they have any *lesser* moral standing than human beings. This is a view that only gradually dawns on Deckard. Nonetheless, his acceptance of the replicants as persons having moral standing does develop. His growing attraction to Rachael was a key factor. When he first meets Rachael he interacts with her in the same way that he might interact with any other human being. Upon learning that Rachael is a replicant, however, he immediately transfers her to an entirely different category and begins to refer to her as 'it.' But he comes to understand that despite being a replicant, Rachael is a person in the same sense that he is, at which point she again becomes for him a being with moral worth.

We can see this most clearly by comparing his interaction with her in two very different scenes. When he forces himself on her in his apartment, making her parrot his words, he probably still regards her as he does any other replicant, namely, as a machine that is either a benefit or a hazard. In his mind, perhaps, he is about to initiate sexual relations with a mere machine. Later, however, when he returns to his apartment, his interaction with her is quite different. Rachael's face is covered by a sheet, as if by a death shroud. As he tentatively pulls back the sheet and leans over her, their faces form complementary shapes. Rather than commanding her to parrot his words, as he did before, this time he asks her questions to which she need not give the answers he desires:

Deckard: Do you love me?
Rachael: I love you.
Deckard: Do you trust me?
Rachael: I trust you.

By treating her as a person worthy of moral consideration, he has earned her love and trust.

4 Identity

> 'I don't know if it's me or Tyrell's niece.'
>
> (Rachael, to Deckard)

Introduction

Upon his visit to the Tyrell Corporation, Deckard is greeted by an attractive, self-assured, smartly dressed young woman. After coolly fielding a question about the Tyrell Corporation's owl, she introduces herself to Deckard in the simplest possible terms: 'I'm Rachael.' Her self-introduction perfectly captures her confident sense of herself. She no more doubts that she is Dr Eldon Tyrell's niece than she does that the Tyrell Corporation's owl is artificial. Her self-assurance begins to falter, however, after she is subjected to an unusually lengthy Voight-Kampff test, whereupon she is summarily dismissed by Tyrell. She is visibly disturbed as she leaves Tyrell and Deckard alone to talk. We soon learn from Tyrell that Rachael is not his niece after all, but is instead a new experimental model of *replicant* that has had memory implants – an innovation intended to 'cushion' replicants' developing emotions and to thereby make them easier to control. In Rachael's case, the memories are those of Tyrell's actual niece.

Rachael's full acknowledgment of this fact and of its momentous implications appears only gradually and reluctantly. Worried about her performance on the Voight-Kampff test and realizing what it might mean, she makes her way to Deckard's apartment building, where she startles him in the elevator. Deckard, anticipating the reason for her visit, is not pleased to see her. As she follows him into his apartment, she indignantly blurts out her concern: 'You think I'm a replicant, don't you?' After trying to convince Deckard that she is who she thinks she is by showing him a photo, ostensibly of herself as a child with

Identity

her mother, he proceeds to report intimate details of what she had taken to be her private childhood memories – 'memories' that Deckard could know only if they were someone else's. Deckard explains: 'Implants! Those aren't your memories. They're somebody else's. They're Tyrell's niece's.' Rachael throws down her photo and hurries out, distraught. Deckard is left alone on the balcony to reflect on Rachael's plight: 'Tyrell really did a job on Rachael. Right down to a snapshot of a mother she never had, a daughter she never was.'

An adult who unexpectedly discovers that she was adopted as an infant may experience severe disorientation that rattles her sense of identity to the core. Rachael discovers not only that she is not *who* she had taken herself to be, but also that she is not even *what* she had taken herself to be. She is not Tyrell's niece; she is not even *human*. She is merely the latest experimental product of the Tyrell Corporation – a synthetic human with no childhood of her own, yet 'gifted' with the past of an entirely different person. Without her consent, Tyrell had thrust his niece's identity upon her (identity theft in reverse, as it were). Rachael had previously assumed that she was *in* the replicant manufacturing business. Subsequently she is forced to acknowledge that she literally *is* the business. She then has to find a way to come to grips with the fact that she had been completely mistaken about what would seem to be the most immediate, certain, and intimate fact there could possibly be for her, namely, *who and what she really is*.

At least, this is the view the film encourages us to accept. It might seem obvious that this is the *only* sensible way of understanding Rachael's situation; but a more probing analysis reveals that this is just one of several ways of understanding the events we see, and not even necessarily the most illuminating one. My aim in this chapter is to bring philosophical resources to bear to evaluate the foregoing interpretation of Rachael's plight. At issue is *the problem of personal identity*: what makes someone *distinct* from someone else despite the two individuals sharing many characteristics? What makes someone the *same person*

61

over time despite undergoing continuous physical and mental changes? Examining answers to these general questions will help us to better understand Rachael's identity, and perhaps by implication our own identities as well.

'How Can It Not Know What It Is?'

A popular solution to the problem of personal identity appeals to the notion of a non-physical essence or spiritual entity that constitutes each person's true self. The traditional name for this spiritual entity is *the soul*. According to Socrates (as reported by Plato in *Phaedo*), for example, he is essentially a soul; his body is a mere container to be shucked off at death. Descartes, whom we met previously, likewise holds that he *has* a body but *is* a soul, that is, an immaterial thinking *substance*: 'It is certain that I (that is, my soul, by which I am what I am) is entirely and truly distinct from my body, and may exist without it' (Descartes 1998, p. 96).[1] In this view, the soul is not only entirely distinct from the body; it is also distinct from one's particular thoughts. One's thoughts may change, but one's soul does not. It is like a hard, indivisible spiritual atom that cannot be split into more basic components. Each soul is entirely distinct from every other soul. The Soul Theory thus seems to provide a simple, straightforward, and elegant way of understanding personal identity: Same soul = same person. Different soul = different person.

The application of this theory to Rachael seems equally straightforward. If Rachael and Tyrell's niece are *distinct souls*, then they are *distinct persons* as well. Moreover, so long as Rachael remains the same soul, she remains the same person. If Rachael is the *same soul* that flees the city with Deckard at the end of the movie as she is when she introduces herself to him in the Tyrell Corporation's lobby, then she is the *same person* in both cases. At first blush, therefore, the Soul Theory seems to decisively resolve Rachael's personal identity crisis and more generally to provide a clear and unambiguous solution to the problem of personal identity.

Identity

Unfortunately, the advantages associated with this first impression are more than offset by the serious metaphysical, epistemological, and practical difficulties this view faces. First, does Rachael even *have* a soul? As a replicant, *could* she have one?[2] Replicants are manufactured commodities. To know whether Rachael does or could have a soul we would need to understand how a synthetically created being like a replicant could acquire one. Suppose that we carefully scrutinize the replicant manufacturing process from beginning to end – from their design by genetic engineers like Sebastian, to the creation of specific organs in specialized labs like Chew's Eye Works, right up to the moment when they walk off the assembly line as finished products. At what point in the manufacturing process could we detect that an immaterial substance had become intimately associated with Rachael's physical body? A soul could not be transmitted to a replicant from its parents via processes of biological reproduction because replicants do not have biological parents. To suppose that Tyrell (or a God) infused a soul into Rachael's body at some moment in her manufacture would merely increase our perplexity. We have no idea how Tyrell (or even a God) *could* introduce a soul into a replicant. Rather than providing real understanding, therefore, positing a soul for Rachael simply piles up mysteries one upon another.

Even if there were some way to satisfactorily respond to these metaphysical worries, equally difficult epistemological problems would remain. Could anyone *know* whether a soul associated with Rachael's body is a *different* soul than one associated with some other previously existing body (for example, of Tyrell's niece)? How could anyone know whether the *same* soul remains associated with Rachael's body throughout her life? No doubt 'the eyes are the windows to the soul' in a poetic sense. But when Deckard analyzes Rachael's eyes using his Voight-Kampff machine he discovers only that she is a most unusual replicant. Later, in his apartment, Rachael desperately searches *his* eyes for clues to his thoughts. Does he think that she is a replicant? Did Tyrell reveal to him her incept date? Unlike real windows, eyes do not permit us to peer through them to inspect what is on the other side, much less to observe another person's soul. Even if Rachael's identity does consist in being a unique soul that remains unchanged over time, it seems that we could never confirm this fact about her or about anyone else.

Perhaps this is setting the epistemological bar too high. Granted, Deckard can never directly inspect Rachael's soul. But might it nonetheless be possible for her to observe her own soul? It is not clear that it is. Rachael is certainly in a position to identify (some of) her own *thoughts*. But this is insufficient to establish the existence of a spiritual *substance* that is distinct from her specific thoughts and that could exist without them. As David Hume (1711–76) points out, when we look within ourselves we discover no *impression* (for example, sensory perception) of a soul, nor even any genuine *idea* of this spiritual 'substance of our minds.' He therefore issues a challenge:

> I desire those philosophers, who pretend that we have an idea of the substance of our minds, to point out the impression that produces it, and tell distinctly after what manner that impression operates, and from what object it is deriv'd.... Does it attend us at all times, or does it only return at intervals? If at intervals, at what times principally does it return, and by what causes is it produc'd? .... We have no perfect idea of anything but a perception. A substance is entirely different from a perception. We have, therefore, no idea of a substance.... To pronounce, then, the final decision upon the whole, the question concerning the substance of the soul is absolutely unintelligible. (Hume 1739–40, pp. 153, 163)

Hume acknowledges that some people sincerely *believe* themselves to be intimately aware of their own soul as a substantial entity, and he concedes that they *may* be right. But he also reiterates that he is certain that he is aware of no such soul or spiritual substance in himself, thereby implying that the believer in souls may be deluded. Apparently, knowing that one has or is a soul is not so easy. Upon learning that Rachael did not even know that she is a replicant, Deckard is incredulous: 'How can it not know what it is?' If Rachael really is a soul one might likewise wonder how that fundamental fact about herself could remain unknown to her. Like Hume, she apparently has no such idea.

In addition to these metaphysical and epistemological difficulties, there are important *practical* problems in applying the Soul Theory as well because it is unclear whether a soul even could perform the *functions* for which it is usually posited in the first place. The soul is supposed to constitute one's unique personal essence. But unless Rachael's soul embodies her distinctive thoughts, memories, and other mental characteristics, then even if her *soul* persists through time it is questionable whether *the person that is Rachael* likewise persists. As John Locke (1632–1704) argues, 'Could we suppose any spirit wholly stripped of all its memory or consciousness of past actions ... the union or separation of such a spiritual substance would make no variation of personal identity, any more than that of any particle of matter does' (Locke 1690, p. 466).

Consider an analogy: suppose that you learn there is one material atom in your body that never changes. It was there in your earliest existence as a fertilized egg; it was there in your body throughout your school years; it is there now as you read these words; it will be in your body when its grows old and succumbs to death; and it will then depart your deceased body and will continue to exist forever. It alone among all the things associated with *you* remains forever. Could that atom constitute your unique personal identity? It seems not, because there would be no reason to suppose there is anything about that atom that is distinctively *you*. Were it replaced by an identical atom, it would make not the slightest difference to your identity as the person you are. The reason is clear: this atom does not embody any of the characteristics that you or others would or could value. But the soul as it is often described is merely a spiritual version of this material atom. If it is not distinguished by any characteristics associated with *you* as a unique person, there is no more reason to identify *you* with this spiritual atom than there is to identify *you* with a material atom. Souls seem to be functionally inert. Souls may exist; nothing that has been said here rules out that possibility. However, even if they do exist it is unclear how appealing to the idea of a soul could help us to understand the nature of anyone's identity.

'Memories – You're Talking about Memories!'

Prior to learning that she is a replicant it is unlikely that Rachael ever pondered the question of whether she is really who she believed herself to be. In the absence of a challenge to her identity there would be no reason to. But her sense of identity was nonetheless grounded in three kinds of evidence. First, she had vivid *memories* connecting her present awareness with her recent and distant past. Second, she had *photographs* that were consistent with these memories. Third, the *behavior* of those around her had consistently supported her belief that she was Tyrell's niece. Individually and collectively this evidence provided unequivocal support for her belief that she was exactly who she believed herself to be. Not all of this evidence is equally important, however. Rachael's *memories* were the most intimate, unmediated, and powerful source of her sense of identity. Photographs and others' behavior contributed to Rachael's sense of identity only because, thanks to the immediate, intuitive, and seemingly self-authenticating quality of her memories, she *already* had a compelling reason to believe that she was who she thought herself to be.[3] Only when the authenticity of her memories was challenged was her sense of identity thrown into crisis, leading to a critical reappraisal of her photographs and the social validation that she had formerly taken for granted. Hence, memories were the key to her sense of identity.

The idea that memories provide the best evidence for establishing a person's identity is given its classic formulation by John Locke (whom we met above) who defines a *person* as 'a thinking intelligent being, that has reason and reflection, and can consider itself as itself, the same thinking thing, in different times and places; which it does only by that consciousness which is inseparable from thinking, and, as it seems to me, essential to it' (Locke 1690, pp. 448–9). This *definition* of a person then permits him to give a closely related operational *criterion* for determining when the necessary and sufficient conditions for *personal identity* are satisfied:

> For, since consciousness always accompanies thinking, and it is that which makes every one to be what he calls self, and thereby distinguishes himself from all other thinking things, in this alone consists personal identity, that is, the sameness of a rational being: and as far as this consciousness can be extended backwards to any past action or thought, so far reaches the identity of that person; it is the same self now it was then; and it is by the same self with this present one that now reflects on it, that that action was done. (Locke 1690, p. 449)

Endorsing an argument given above against the Soul Theory of identity, he adds that, 'Nothing but consciousness can unite remote existences into the same person: the identity of substance will not do it; for whatever substance there is, however framed, without consciousness there is no person' (p. 464). Personal identity consists in being the same consciousness; memories allow us to connect present and past states of consciousness: 'For as far as any intelligent being can repeat the idea of any past action with the same consciousness it had of it at first, and with the same consciousness it has of any present action; so far it is the same personal self' (p. 451).

Locke's Consciousness Theory of personal identity has undeniable intuitive appeal. Memories are the most intimate, immediate, and seemingly incorrigible bonds that link our present and past selves. In normal circumstances memories seem to have a transparent, self-authenticating quality that provides certitude. I am irresistibly compelled to believe that I am the same person that wrote the words in the previous sentence because

I clearly *remember* writing those words. Likewise, I believe that I am the very same person that learned to ride a bike at the age of five because I have vivid *memories* of learning to ride a bike when I was five, and so on. In order to make reliable judgments of this sort, all I need to do is recall experiences from my past. If I can recall such experiences, then I am the very same person that had those experiences.

An acceptance of Locke's theory also seems implicit in Rachael's understanding of who she is. At the conclusion of the Voight-Kampff test, despite worrisome evidence that she is not *what* and therefore *who* she had believed herself to be, she still believes herself to be Tyrell's niece. Indeed, she goes to Deckard's apartment to try to convince him of this. It is only when he callously exposes her cherished childhood recollections as mere memory implants that she is reluctantly forced to acknowledge the awful truth. The status of her memories ultimately proves decisive.

Locke's theory thus appears to settle the question of who Rachael *really* is. If she remembers certain events with 'the same consciousness' of them she had when the memories were first acquired, then she *is* the person that had the experiences represented in those memories. If she remembers introducing herself to Deckard, explaining that the Tyrell Corporation's owl is artificial, and taking the Voight-Kampff test, then she is the same person that actually experienced those events. If some of her recollections are not really *her* memories at all, however, then she may not be the person she had taken herself to be. If her recollections of playing doctor with her brother and watching a spider build a web outside her window are merely memory implants, and thus not really *her* memories at all, then she is not who she thought she was.[4] Rachael and Tyrell's niece would be two entirely distinct persons.

'I Can't Rely On...'

Of course, this is not a judgment Rachael herself was in a position to make *prior* to having her childhood recollections

Identity

exposed as memory implants. Before being subjected to the Voight-Kampff test all of her recollections had seemed equally veridical to her. After having some of her recollections exposed as counterfeit, however, she comes to appreciate how far-reaching the consequences of having fake memories can be, even to the point of undermining her confidence in the validity of her present emotions.[5] When Deckard blocks her attempted exit from his apartment and roughly forces her to confront her feelings for him by insisting that she repeat the words, 'I want you,' she feels conflicted, and haltingly replies, 'I can't rely on....' Presumably she is worried that she cannot rely on her feelings for him because she cannot be sure that they are truly her own rather than by-products of someone else's memories. What she needs in order to accept her feelings as authentic is some way of distinguishing real from bogus memories.

Conceptually, this seems easy enough to do. Suppose that we call a certain subset of beliefs Rachael has about her past experiences 'recollections,' and then distinguish recollections as either *genuine memories* or *pseudo-memories*. Genuine memories are recollections caused by personally experiencing the events recollected. Pseudo-memories, by contrast, are recollections caused by something other than personally experiencing the events recollected (for example, by receiving memory implants). Rachael's recollection of introducing herself to Deckard in the Tyrell Corporation's lobby would be a genuine memory because it was caused by her personally experiencing the event in question, but her recollection of watching a spider build a web outside her window would be a *pseudo-memory* because it was caused by something other than her personally experiencing that event. For Tyrell's niece, by contrast, her recollection of that event *would* be a genuine memory because she personally witnessed that event. In this view, only some of the recollections that Rachael takes to be genuine memories really are so.[6] Consequently, Rachael is identical to the person who had the experiences connected with her genuine memories, and is entirely distinct from the person who had the experiences associated with her pseudo-memories. Because Rachael and Tyrell's niece have different sets of genuine memories, then according to Locke's theory they must be entirely distinct persons as well.

Unfortunately, this seemingly straightforward conclusion faces some serious problems. First, it is not quite right to say that whereas Tyrell's niece's recollections are caused by the events in question, Rachael's recollections are not, because Tyrell's niece's recollections and Rachael's recollections are *both* caused by the events in question. Without those events neither would have the recollections in question. Second, applying the distinction between genuine memories and pseudo-memories depends on knowing *who* experienced the event recollected, and therefore requires possession of a reliable way of *identifying persons independently of their recollections*. To know that some of Rachael's recollections are pseudo-memories there must be some way to determine, independently of her having those recollections, that she is not the person who experienced the events represented in those recollections. What might that way be?

An initially promising answer is to say that a recollection is a genuine memory for a person if that person's *body* being present at the event in question explains why the person has that recollection. A recollection of a spider building a web would be a genuine memory for Tyrell's niece if her body being present at that event explains why she has the recollection in question. By contrast, Rachael's recollection of that event would be a pseudo-memory if her recollection of that event was not caused by her body being present at that event.

Connecting recollections to bodily experiences in this way seems to solve the problem of distinguishing genuine memories from pseudo-memories, and of thereby establishing a person's true identity. But notice that for this proposal to work we would *still* need some way to identify the *person* associated with a particular body at two different times without relying on that person's recollections. To know that it was Tyrell's niece's body that witnessed a spider building a web we would need some reliable way to connect the person that is Tyrell's niece with a particular body, and this requires that we be able to identify the person that is Tyrell's niece independently of that body. But if we could do *that*, then we would not need to appeal to genuine memories to establish personal identity in the first place. It is therefore difficult to see how to make Locke's theory work without simply begging the very question it was designed to answer.

'Deckard, Ninety-Seven'

Given these problems with the Consciousness Theory, why not just say that what really matters for personal identity is the *body*, not one's subjective sense of being the 'same consciousness'? That is: same body = same person. In support of this idea, compare Rachael's futile attempt to establish her identity by relying on her subjective recollections with the way that the electronic security system in Deckard's apartment building conclusively confirms his identity. As he enters the elevator he is prompted 'Voice print identification – your floor number, please.' When he responds with a weary, 'Deckard, ninety-seven,' the security system confirms his identity: 'Ninety-seven, thank-you (*danke*).' Deckard's voice is a distinctive bodily characteristic that provides an objective criterion permitting accurate and consistent personal identification across time. He is the same person across any interval of time just because he is the same body. But if objective bodily criteria are so readily available and reliable, why not simply equate *personal* identity with *bodily* identity?

According to this 'Body Theory' of personal identity, Rachael is the same person that flees the city with Deckard at the end of the film as the person that meets him in the Tyrell Corporation lobby earlier in the film just because it is the *same body* that does so in both cases. That body no doubt underwent some change during even that relatively brief span of time, and depending on how long it lives it will undoubtedly change even more, with matter coming and going and being redistributed in it. But it will do so gradually and without there ever being a decisive break in the continuity of that body's existence. It remains the *same body* in the sense that at any given moment it is causally connected to previous bodily states by an *uninterrupted* set of biological processes in the right sort of way. What that 'right sort of way' is requires further specification.

Eric T. Olson (2003) defends a version of the Body Theory called 'Animalism' according to which each person is identical to a particular animal. The general categories 'animal,' 'human being,' and 'person' in this view have partially overlapping memberships. All human beings are animals, but not all animals are human beings. Some animals (for example, human beings) are *persons*, but many more are not, and not even all human beings are persons. Human embryos and human beings in a persistent vegetative state in which there is no consciousness at all would not be persons. Finally, persons need not be animals. Conscious intelligent robots might be persons without being animals. The important upshot of this for addressing the problem of personal identity is that, 'The persistence of a human animal ... does not consist in mental continuity. The fact that each human animal starts out as an unthinking embryo and may end up as an unthinking vegetable shows that no sort of mental continuity is necessary for a human animal to persist' (Olson 2003, p. 324). Instead, what makes a person existing at time t_2 the same person that existed at some previous time t_1 is just that they are the very same animal.

This view offers some significant advantages. For one thing, it fits in well with how we often re-identify people at different times. After being violently pulled into an alley following his retirement of Zhora, it took just one look at the malicious face in front of him for Deckard to identify his assailant as Leon, whose specs he had been shown by Bryant. Likewise, in the instant that he realized how he had survived Leon's attack he did not hesitate to identify the person who saved his life as the same individual he had V-K'd at the Tyrell Corporation. Such physical identification is not infallible, of course. The danger of physical misidentification is illustrated in *Electric Sheep* wherein

Identity

the androids are mass-produced, resulting in multiple copies of the same model. Pris and Rachael happen to be the same model, thereby making it difficult for Deckard to retire Pris because she looks so much like Rachael, with whom he had by then become romantically involved. In principle, such uncertainties can be eliminated by determining physical continuity. If Deckard could identify a particular android at time t_1 as Rachael and never let it out his sight, he could be confident that it is still Rachael at time t_2. That physical continuity cannot always be established in practice is merely a contingent epistemic limitation, not a decisive objection to the theory.

This view also comports well with our current scientific understanding of memories. If brains store information in neuronal connections, then replicating those neuronal connections would entail replicating the associated memories as well.[7] By contrast, we have no idea how memories could be laid down in, stored in, or retrieved from an immaterial soul or similar mental substance; consequently we have no idea how memories could be copied from one immaterial soul or substance to another (for example, from Tyrell's niece to Rachael). Olson's view also permits us to say unequivocally that Tyrell's niece and Rachael are distinct persons if they are distinct animals. According to this view, when Rachael came to believe that she was mistaken in believing that she was Tyrell's niece, she was right to draw this conclusion.

These advantages notwithstanding, consider a thought experiment that has convinced some that the Body Theory cannot be correct. Smith and Jones go to sleep one night in different states. In the morning the body that has always been identified as 'Jones' wakes up with the personality, preferences, beliefs, desires, and memories that have always been associated with the body identified as 'Smith,' and moreover identifies itself as (a very confused) Smith. The body that has always been identified as 'Smith' undergoes a similar change but in the opposite direction. Despite the peculiarity of this situation, it seems clear that during the night the *persons* that are Smith and

Jones somehow *switched bodies*. But if so, personal identity cannot consist just in being the same body. Psychological rather than bodily continuity must be the crucial issue for personal identity after all. Hence, the Body Theory must be false.

A Body Theorist could respond by insisting that Smith and Jones did not really switch bodies at all. Smith remains Smith and Jones remains Jones despite the fact that the personalities, preferences, beliefs, desires, memories, and even self-identifications formerly associated with each body are now quite different. He might point out that the two bodies do not, and indeed could not, remain *unchanged* in the thought experiment because the only way that the imagined changes could occur would be for each brain to undergo the exact structural alterations necessary to realize a different set of psychological properties. What makes this thought experiment seem significant is the rapidity of the imagined change. If the bodily changes in question had taken place slowly over a few decades rather than overnight, we would have little reason to deny that the Smith body remains Smith and that the Jones body remains Jones. Hence, that thought experiment is not the defeater for the Body Theory that some imagine it to be. Some readers may find this response hard to accept. In a subsequent section I will try to diagnose this unease and propose a philosophical cure for it.

'I Don't Know if It's Me or Tyrell's Niece'

None of the theories of personal identity we have examined has won universal assent. The Soul Theory posits a spiritual entity whose existence is impossible to establish and which would not solve the problem of personal identity even if it could be shown to exist. The Consciousness Theory ties personal identity to genuine memories which cannot be identified as such in a non-question-begging way. The Body Theory asks us to accept some counter-intuitive implications. Faced with a philosophical *cul-de-sac* like this it is worthwhile trying to identify what all of the views we have looked at have in common and then ask whether rejecting any of their shared presuppositions might suggest a different way of solving the problem.

The views we have considered all take for granted that each person is and necessarily must be wholly distinct from every other person such that there can be no *overlap* between or *blending* of persons. This is evident in the Smith/Jones thought-experiment discussed above and in the film's presumption that Rachael and Tyrell's niece are either *the same person* or *entirely distinct persons*. Deckard and Rachael appear to uncritically accept this assumption as well. This is clear from two scenes whose philosophical significance is easy to overlook. The first scene has been mentioned already. After Rachael relates to Deckard some of her childhood recollections, he callously exposes those 'memories' as some else's: 'Implants! Those aren't your memories. They're somebody else's. They're Tyrell's niece's.' Later, while Deckard dozes, Rachael sits down at his piano, lets down her hair, and tentatively begins playing. Hearing music, Deckard rises and takes a seat beside her. 'I didn't know if I could play,' she confides. 'I remember lessons. I don't know if it's me or Tyrell's niece.' To Deckard a set of memories are either Tyrell's nieces or they are Rachael's. To Rachael she is either Tyrell's niece or she isn't. There is no middle ground in either case because memories and identity cannot be shared between individuals. Would relaxing this assumption help to resolve the puzzles with which we have been grappling?

'There's Some of Me in You'

To motivate this suggestion further, consider another thought experiment. Suppose that I take my car into the shop for a tune-up, and my mechanic replaces the spark plugs. I then drive away with a car that is almost but not quite the same car I brought in. It is still my car, of course, but there has been a slight change in its material composition. Later, I notice that my tires are getting smooth and so take the car in to have the tires replaced. Once again, I drive away with a car that is almost but not quite the same car that I brought in. This time the change is noticeable even to my neighbors. Suppose that this pattern of replacing old parts with new ones continues until every original part of my car has been replaced by a new part. One could insist that the car's identity has been *completely unaffected* despite the successive replacement of all its parts. Alternatively, one could take the opposite view and insist that as soon as the first spark plug is replaced it becomes an *entirely different* car. Both perspectives seem extravagant. The most reasonable conclusion to draw would be just that at any point in this process the car is partially but not completely identical to the car at any other point in that process. The car with the new spark plugs bears a closer relationship to the car containing all the same parts other than those spark plugs than it does to any other car, hence it makes sense to refer to it as the 'same car' for most purposes. Yet it is not exactly the same in all respects. The identity of at least some physical objects, it seems, can be a matter of degree. So long as it is clear *in what sense* my car is the same, and *in what sense* it is different after repair work is done, we know all that we can and need to know about its 'identity.' The temptation to say something metaphysically stronger than this is understandable, but also quite unnecessary, and perhaps even misleading.[8]

This perspective might also help us to understand the relationship between Rachael and Tyrell's niece. We are not told the name of Tyrell's niece, whether she is still alive in 2019, or indeed anything about her other than that she had certain childhood memories that were subsequently implanted in Rachael. But to make sense of the fact that Rachael shares many of Tyrell's niece's memories we might suppose that Tyrell's niece is also named Rachael. It would be odd if Tyrell's niece's name was, say, Tiffany, in light of the fact that the replicant named 'Rachael' has Tyrell's niece's recollections and believes that her own name is Rachael. To avoid confusion we can designate Rachael (the replicant) as 'Rachael' and Rachael (Tyrell's niece) as 'Rachael T.' We might further suppose that Rachael is a biological clone of

Rachael T. It would be odd if the photos that Rachael accepts as photos of *herself* as a child pictured a person with markedly different physical features from her own. Any significant difference in basic physical features would be likely to raise her suspicions. If Tyrell really wanted Rachael to believe that she is Rachael T, then the more similar in appearance to his niece he can make her, the better. The best strategy would be to make her a biological clone by using some of Rachael T's genetic material as the starting point for creating Rachael. Of course, Rachael will have many of Rachael T's recollections as well. They will be closer, physically and psychologically, than any two twins.

Granting all these assumptions, Rachael will have inherited many of Rachael T's physical and psychological characteristics. Rachael's DNA may be derived from Rachael T's. Some of Rachael T's memories will be Rachael's as well. They are distinct individuals, for the most part, yet also share an identity to a significant degree. For example, Rachael benefits from the piano lessons Rachael T took in a far more intimate way than is possible for two individuals not linked as they are. Were Rachael T ever to meet Rachael, she might therefore with some justification echo Sebastian's remark (in another context) to Roy and Pris: 'There's some of me in you.'

'You Play Beautifully'

Questions about personal identity can have specific other persons or even persons in general as their objects, as when we try to determine someone else's identity or when we critically examine philosophical theories of personal identity, as above. Such questions can also be self-directed, as when Rachael struggles to determine who she is. As we have seen, questions such as these cannot always be answered merely by determining certain facts, although facts are relevant. Also required are judgments about what matters. In the case of self-directed identity questions, the judgments may also concern who one aspires to be and what identity one wills to embrace.

Indeed, there are clues in the film suggesting that what matters most is not who one *really is* but rather whom one now *chooses to be*. After Deckard joins Rachael at his piano, she confides to him, 'I didn't know if I could play. I remember lessons. I don't know if it's me or Tyrell's niece.' Deckard then partially atones for the callous way he had previously forced her to confront her status as a replicant by uttering the perfect words under the circumstances: '*You* play beautifully.' At that moment, it does not matter whether it was Rachael or Tyrell's niece that took piano lessons. Deckard affirms that the person sitting next to him at that moment is playing beautifully. When he later makes sexual advances toward her she is unsure whether the feelings she is experiencing are truly her own. At first, he forces her to repeat words that express feelings she cannot be sure are her own. It is as if he is reprogramming a computer, which may not be far from how he still regards her at this point. She complies, but 'Kiss me' and 'I want you' coming from her lips seem like mere sounds provided by Deckard that she is forced to parrot without the relevant emotions they are meant to express. The crucial shift in her sense of personal identity is signaled when she finally says to Deckard, unprompted, 'I want you. Put your hands on me.' At that point it does not matter how she came to have those feelings. The feelings she is experiencing are hers just because she is experiencing them. At that moment, for the first time since being forced to acknowledge her replicant status, Rachael begins to accept herself as the person she is, regardless of how she came to be this person. She cannot change her status as a replicant, but she can appropriate her feelings and experiences as her own and on this basis decide which identity she will embrace. In that sense, she *creates* her identity as a person.[9]

Conclusions

What makes a person at one time the *same person* at another time despite significant mental and physical *differences*? What ultimately *distinguishes* one person from another person despite their *sharing* many of the same characteristics? Rachael's predicament renders these questions acute. Until she was subjected to the Voight-Kampff test, she had no reason to doubt her identity. Yet, it turned out that she was utterly mistaken about who she really is. Or was she? Classic solutions to the problem of personal identity equate persons with immaterial spiritual substances, with states of consciousness, or with physical bodies, and thereby tend to treat identity as an all-or-nothing property of persons. In some cases, adopting this assumption might work quite well. In other cases, it may make more sense to treat personal identity as a matter of degree. Rachael inherited so much from Tyrell's niece that there is a sense in which their identities partially overlap. Personal identity, it seems, might be a matter of degree. This might be an attractive way of making sense of our own identity over time as well. Each of us inherits a number of characteristics from the slightly different persons that we identify as our past selves. Each of us bequeaths a number of our characteristics to the slightly different selves we anticipate being. We manage to retain a recognizable identity to ourselves and to others even as the components constituting our bodies and minds undergo continuous replacement. René Dubos captures this view as well as anyone when he writes, 'Everyone is today and will be tomorrow only a slightly modified expression of what he was yesterday or at any time in the past. In the midst of change, we exhibit a sameness and continuity which other people recognize.'

5 Consciousness

'I think, Sebastian, therefore I am.'

(Pris, to J. F. Sebastian)

Introduction

One of *Blade Runner*'s most intriguing scenes takes place in Sebastian's toy-cluttered apartment. Roy Batty looks up from Sebastian's chess game to see his host gazing at him in fascination, prompting him to ask him why he is staring. 'Because,' Sebastian answers, 'You're so different. You're so perfect.' When Roy confirms that they are Nexus 6 replicants, Sebastian is delighted:

Sebastian: Ah, I knew it! ... Show me something.
Roy: Like what?
Sebastian: Like anything.
Roy: We're not computers, Sebastian! We're *physical*.
Pris: I think, Sebastian, therefore I am.
Roy: Very good Pris, now show him why.

After briefly considering her options, Pris plunges her hand into a beaker of boiling water, retrieves an egg, tosses it to Sebastian, and then performs an elegant back-walkover. The entire scene takes only about a minute, but it contains a wealth of profound ideas, as well as puzzles.

To begin with, why does Roy interpret Sebastian's completely open-ended request that his guests show him 'something ... anything' as insinuating that they are *computers*? Why does he take *offense* at this presumed comparison? Why does Roy insist that he and Pris are not computers on the ground that they are *physical*? What does Pris mean when she declares, 'I think, Sebastian, therefore I am'? What could Roy mean by instructing her to 'Show him why'? Show him why ... *what*? Why she thinks? Why she exists? Why existing is linked to thinking? Why does Pris then respond to Roy's encouragement by demonstrating some of her impressive *physical* capabilities? How could plunging her hand into a beaker of boiling water and performing a difficult gymnastic move show Sebastian 'why' thinking and existing are connected? All of this is utterly baffling. Roy and Pris seem to be trying to convey some essential truths about themselves. But what they are trying to convey is far from clear.

These specific questions raise more general questions. The replicants are clearly *physical* beings. They are just as clearly *thinking* beings. How might these two aspects of their nature be related? How might these two aspects of *our* nature be related? Are minds utterly distinct from bodies or do they arise *from* bodies? To address these questions we need to explore some proposed solutions to what is known in academic philosophy as 'the mind–body problem.' The options for thinking about minds, bodies, and their relationship are many and extend beyond the limited number of views that can be explored here. Attempting to explain *consciousness* (or arguing that it cannot be explained), in particular, has been a growth industry in philosophy in recent years. Fully engaging with those accounts would carry us too far from our focus on using philosophical resources to explore *Blade Runner*. The views discussed here can nonetheless serve as a starting point for those further inquiries.

'I Think, Sebastian, Therefore I Am'

Many readers will recognize Pris's declaration as echoing Descartes' famous assertion (Descartes 1998, p. 18; in Latin, *Cogito, ergo sum*), but they may not be familiar with its crucial role in his philosophy. Descartes wanted to construct a new science of the natural world. To ground this ambitious project he needed to identify at least one belief that cannot possibly be doubted. The deliverances of his senses, which seemed to inform him about the external world, can be doubted because all had, at one time or another, actually misled him. Reflection on the experience of dreaming further demonstrated that he could be mistaken in thinking that he is sensing some aspect of the physical world while he is in fact sound asleep. Since his body is a part of the physical world, even its existence could be doubted. The one belief that he could not *possibly* doubt is that he is *thinking*, because *doubting* just *is* a form of thinking. If he is *thinking*, he reasoned, necessarily he must *exist*. Moreover, since he could think of himself without a body, but could not think of himself without thinking, it followed that he is entirely distinct from his body and could exist without it:

> From this I knew that I was a substance the whole essence or nature of which is simply to think, and which, in order to exist, has no need of any place nor depends on any material thing. Thus this 'I,' that is to say, the mind through which I am what I am, is entirely distinct from the body and ... even if there were no body at all, it would not cease to be all that it is. (Descartes 1998, p. 19)

In this view, the mind is not only entirely distinct from the body; it does not even depend on the body for its existence.[1] Minds and bodies are *essentially* different in this view. The essential property of minds is the activity of *thinking*. To be a mind is simply to be *a thing that thinks* (Latin, *res cogitans*). By contrast, the essential property of bodies is extension. To be a body is to be an *extended thing* (*res extensa*), that is, to be a material thing having a determinate shape, size, and location in space. Minds and bodies have different and indeed mutually incompatible properties. Thinking things think but they are not extended and do not occupy space. Material things are extended and occupy space but they do not think. It would be a mistake in this view for one to say, 'I have a mind.' In Descartes' view one does not *have* a mind; one *is* a mind.

Cartesian Substance Dualism (as this view is called) has been enormously influential. But it has at least two rather unfortunate consequences. First, it becomes extraordinarily difficult in this view to understand how minds and bodies could possibly *interact* with one another. Psychology can provide insights into how *thoughts* can give rise to other *thoughts*. Physics can provide insights into how *material* things causally interact with other *material* things. But how could a *non-material* thing interact with a *material* thing, and vice versa? How could thoughts produce physical, bodily movements? How could physical energy impinging on a body give rise to specific thoughts in the mind? It may be tempting to suppose that somewhere in a psychology or neurophysiology textbook all of this is clearly understood and explained. Unfortunately, the wished-for explanation simply does not exist there or anywhere else. No one has the faintest idea of how it *could* happen. The essentially different character of minds and bodies, as defined by Descartes, seems to preclude any such understanding or explanation.

A simple experiment may help to make the nature of this problem more apparent. Suppose that you decide to raise your right arm, and that you then *do* raise your right arm. Nothing could seem more familiar and unexceptional. But how, exactly, did you accomplish this feat? You might say, 'Well, I decided to raise my right arm, and then I contracted certain muscles and the arm went up.' At a certain level of description this is undoubtedly true, but what happens when we try (within the view we are considering) to understand what happened at a much finer level of detail? The causal sequence leading to your decision to raise your arm is perhaps clear enough: you read certain words, form the decision to participate in this experiment, and then 'execute' the decision. Likewise, the causal sequence involving the parts of your arm and shoulder are reasonably clear: nerves fire in your brain that send an electrochemical signal to the muscles in your shoulder and arm to contract, and given the relevant anatomical equipment (ligaments, tendons, the muscles and bones of your arm, and so on) your arm goes sailing into the air. But how, exactly, does your *decision* (a mental event) interact with your *neurons* (specific physical structures) to make the latter fire, resulting in your arm going up? We can ponder these events for as long as we like but the truth is that no one has even the slightest idea of how this happens despite the fact that moving our bodies is one of the most familiar aspects of our experience.

Second, Descartes' theory entails that *we are not where we think we are*. Indeed, *we are nowhere at all*. To see how these remarkable conclusions follow from Descartes' theory, imagine an invisible three-dimensional Cartesian coordinate system filling the space in which you are reading these words.[2] This system consists of x, y, and z axes running vertically and in two horizontal dimensions at right angles to one another. Every material object in this space can be located with great precision at any moment by specifying its exact x, y, and z values. Your body, your head, your brain, and every neuron in your brain are all material objects and thus have a location in this three-dimensional grid. Your *mind*, however, *being non-material*, is *not extended* and hence *does not occupy space*, and therefore *does not have a spatial location* – not in your brain, in your head, in your body, on earth, or anywhere in the physical universe – because it is not the sort of thing that *could* have a spatial location. Hence, if Descartes is right, your mind is literally *nowhere*. But if you *are* a mind, as Descartes maintains, then it follows that *you* are nowhere. If it *seems* to you that you are somewhere, you are profoundly mistaken. Of course, most people make this mistake throughout their entire lives. If Descartes is correct, however, most people's natural, intuitive beliefs about themselves are profoundly mistaken. No one is anywhere. Everyone is nowhere. Could there be a stranger view?

Descartes never provided a satisfactory solution to either of these problems. Neither did any of his followers.[3] Not only does Descartes' theory face serious problems considered on its own terms but, despite Pris's invitation to think of the replicants in Cartesian terms, it also fails to provide a coherent understanding of the nature of the replicants. To see this, consider what it might mean to think of the replicants in Cartesian terms, as Pris invites Sebastian to do.

Consciousness

We know that the replicants are conscious, thinking beings, each of whom is closely associated with a particular synthetically manufactured humanoid body. Each of the replicants' bodies was produced by the Tyrell Corporation with a particular incept date. For example, Zhora's incept date is 12 JUNE, 2016. Consider two alternative possibilities for understanding what happened on that date. According to the first possibility, just prior to her incept date Zhora's *body* existed, but *she* did not yet exist. Upon her body's manufacture she came into existence as a non-material, non-spatial, thinking thing somehow associated with that body. We cannot, of course, say *where* she was *prior* to the manufacture of her body since we are assuming that she did not exist prior to it, nor can we even say where she is *after* its manufacture because as a non-material mind she cannot be anywhere. Somehow, however, the manufacture of a particular physical body brings Zhora into existence as a non-material thinking thing not located in that body or indeed anywhere else. Because she does not depend on the existence of that body for her existence, it is utterly mysterious why the manufacture of that body was the special occasion for her to begin existing as a thinking thing uniquely associated with that body.

According to the second possibility, Zhora existed *prior* to the manufacture of that particular body. This would avoid the problem of explaining how the manufacture of a particular physical body could bring into existence a non-material, non-spatially located mind eventually associated with it, but it would generate even more questions. For example, how could the replicants exist *prior* to their bodily manufacture? What could have brought them into existence before their bodies were even made? Would replicants exist before their bodies are created *whether or not* their bodies are manufactured, so that some replicants might exist but without ever having a body? To suppose that replicants exist *prior* to the existence of their bodies just in case their bodies *will be* created sometime in the future requires that a not-yet, future event exert an influence on the past – a paradoxical result if ever there was one.

The problems of understanding in Cartesian terms how replicants could *come to be* are mirrored by the problems that arise in trying to understand what happens to replicants when they die. For example, what happens to Zhora after Deckard shoots her in the back and she goes careening through a series of plate glass display-case store windows? We know that her blood-splattered *body* ends up on the sidewalk outside, eyes staring blankly. But what happens to *Zhora*? If she did not require a body for her existence in the first place, perhaps there is no reason to conclude that she needs a body for her continued existence, either. Is there an afterlife for replicants? Do replicants get 'recycled' into new bodies at some later point (that is, replicant reincarnation)? In short, there is no end to the unanswerable questions generated by the Cartesian view, suggesting that other approaches to understanding replicant (and human) nature are worth exploring.

'We're Not Computers, Sebastian'

Roy's insistence that the replicants are not computers is puzzling. Why does he bring up *computers*? Why does he take *offense* at what he thinks is Sebastian's insinuation that the replicants are computers? A clue may be found by recalling that Roy's response appears as he has been contemplating Sebastian's chess game.[4] Excelling at chess requires at the very least internalizing the rules of the game and the ability to anticipate the consequences of any given move for the state of the game as a whole at least several moves into the future. An electronic chess-playing computer applies rules to a description of the configuration of the pieces on the board at any moment in order to select for a player the next move that has the highest probability of ultimately producing a winning position. That is *all* that it can do. It cannot do any of the myriad other things that we associate with a chess grandmaster. It cannot intuit its opponent's strategy, weigh the psychological benefits to itself or the psychological effects on its opponent of making a daring move, and it cannot decide to devote its time to excelling at chess rather than at checkers. Perhaps Roy responds to Sebastian as he does because he wants to distance himself from the sorts of chess-playing computers whose *only* virtue is *computational power*.[5]

This interpretation might help to clarify *why* Roy responds to Sebastian as he does, but it would not settle the question of the *truth* of his assertion. Granting that the replicants are not electronic chess-playing computers, might they not be computers of a sort nonetheless? If we define a 'computer' as any system that manipulates bits of information according to formal rules, then the replicants turn out to be computers of a sort after all – for example, insofar as they count using the rules of arithmetic. In this trivial sense, the replicants *are* computers (as are we). The interesting question is whether the other sorts of thinking of which the replicants are capable transcend *mere* computing. In other words, is thinking and consciousness of which both replicants and human beings have first-hand experience necessarily beyond the capabilities of *mere* computers, even extremely powerful ones that might be designed in the distant future?

One way to try to understand the basis upon which an answer to that question can be derived requires specifying in advance the precise conditions under which we would be willing to say that a computer manifests thinking. In 1950, the mathematician and pioneering computer scientist Alan M. Turing (1912–54) proposed a method of stunning simplicity for determining whether a computer that appears to possess thought is in fact thinking. According to what he called 'the Imitation Game' (but which is now more usually called the Turing Test), if a machine can convince an expert that it is thinking, by giving responses to questions that are indistinguishable from those that a knowledgeable human being might give, there are no reasonable grounds on which to deny that it really *is* thinking. Turing (1950, p. 442) boldly predicted that by the end of the twentieth century, 'one will be able to speak of machines thinking without expecting to be contradicted.' His specific prediction was not fulfilled, but the important question is whether it could eventually be possible to build computers that can truly be said to think in the way that human beings do. Is there any principled reason for concluding that this is impossible?

According to John Searle (1990), there is. He rejects the possibility of computers that are, just by dint of computing, capable of genuine thought, for a simple reason: computers function solely by performing logical operations on formally specified symbols without attaching any *meaning* to them. Indeed, manipulating symbols without attaching meaning to them is just what it *means* to compute. For computation, syntax is sufficient. Human minds, by contrast, attribute *meaning* to the symbols they manipulate. They utilize semantics as well as syntax to make sense of information. According to Searle, this conclusively demonstrates that although thinking may *involve* computation, it is not *exhausted* by computation, and hence human minds and their thinking are fundamentally different from computers capable only of symbol manipulation. If Searle is right, thinking involves more than computation. It involves meaning as well.

Searle's argument is controversial, and it has prompted countless responses. But its essential point strikes many people as exactly right. Moreover, it appears to capture an important truth about the replicants. The most powerful reason to view the replicants as fundamentally different from mere computers is that they exhibit capabilities that are different in *kind* from anything that mere computers *could* ever manifest. Zhora's desperation to escape from Deckard, Pris's violent death throes after being shot by Deckard, and Roy's elegiac acceptance of his own mortality suggest that the replicants are capable of experiences that differ in kind from those of any possible digital computer. Questions about how to *explain* these capabilities, however, remain unanswered.

'Very Good, Pris. Now Show Him Why'

Roy's denial that the replicants are *computers* coupled with his insistence that he and Pris are *physical* suggests that he does not consider computers to be physical. This is odd. Computers, at least of the electronic digital sort, are complex physical objects composed of simpler physical parts, such as a central processing unit, drive controllers, hard drive, and so on, which are themselves composed of various materials (plastic and metal), which in turn are composed of smaller physical entities: atoms and various subatomic particles. An electronic computer is therefore a physical object all the way down.[6] Taken at face value, therefore, Roy's denial that he and his companions are computers, on the basis of their being *physical*, is quite puzzling.

A clue about what he might mean appears moments later when Pris, under instructions from Roy to 'show him why,' gives Sebastian a dazzling display of her impressive physicality. This impromptu demonstration stands in stark contrast to the capabilities of a physical device like an electronic computer whose behavior is rigidly dictated by its inputs, the physical architecture of its hardware, and the programs it is running. Pris's joyful, playful, mischievous demonstration of athleticism dramatically underscores the point that she and her companions are not mere machines, but rather something more organic, flexible, and emotional than any electronic computer. By emphasizing that he and his companions are physical in this *sensual* sense, perhaps Roy wanted to contrast the replicants' embodied and organic nature with the severely restricted capabilities of mere computers. Unlike mere computers, the replicants have inner lives, including thoughts and emotions, and therefore they cannot be treated as if they were merely machines, as some humans assume. Of course, simply noting that the replicants are 'physical' in this broader sense *still* leaves unexplained their nature as thinking and feeling beings. But perhaps it points in the direction of an explanation.

'He Design Your Mind, Your Brain'

In an especially striking scene, Hannibal Chew is startled to find that he has company. Roy Batty and Leon have stepped into

Chew's Eye Works with questions about 'morphology, longevity, incept dates.' After explaining that he does not know about such things, but that Tyrell 'knows everything,' Chew elaborates for his strange visitors: 'He's big boss. Big genius. He, he design your mind, your brain.' His choice of words is significant. By equating Roy's *mind* and *brain*, Chew takes for granted the philosophical view known as Reductive Physicalism according to which minds and brains are at bottom identical. More precisely, this view says that each mental state can be identified with a brain state, that is, with a pattern of activation among neurons in the brain as when one entertains a certain thought or experiences a certain emotion. Whenever one has a subjective experience of perceiving an apple as red, crisp, sour, and so on, specific nerve cells are firing in a specific way. It would thus be impossible for one's mental state to change without there being a corresponding change in one's brain state. But the patterns of neural activity associated with a particular subjective experience need not be identical to those of another person having a similar experience, although given the significant similarities among human brains one might expect these experiences to be similar and to occur in roughly the same regions of each person's brain.

The Reductive Physicalist therefore rejects the Cartesian claim that there is a non-physical *substance* or *entity* called 'the mind,' but concedes that there are mental *events* and *states*, and insists that these mental events and states are identical to certain neural events and brain states. Consider some analogies. What one *hears* as the ringing of a bell just *is* a series of compression waves traveling through a medium and interacting with the auditory structures of one's ears and one's brain. What one *sees* as a rainbow just *is* electromagnetic radiation of certain wavelengths interacting with one's eyes and the visual processing centers of one's brain. What one *feels* as the heat of a hot surface just *is* one's perception of the average molecular kinetic energy of minute particles moving about rapidly. In each of these cases, something that has been recognized and known for millennia as one thing (sound, color, or heat) has been revealed by science to be something of a seemingly different nature (compression waves, electromagnetic radiation, kinetic energy). Sound, color, and heat are not thereby rendered *unreal*. It is just that we now understand that they are identical to certain physical processes interacting with our complex perceptual systems to produce the mental experiences with which we are all familiar. Likewise, when Roy Batty relates to Deckard, 'I've seen things you people wouldn't believe,' each of the events he goes on to mention represents a subjective experience, either in real time or as later remembered, that is identical to a particular pattern of neuronal activity in his brain.

The advantages of this view are many. First, the familiar correlation between our physical and mental states is exactly what one would predict on this view. Getting too little sleep, ingesting caffeine, or coming down with the flu profoundly affects the quality of one's mental functioning. Second, well-supported scientific research reveals that experimentally manipulating the brain (for example, by electrically stimulating specific regions) reliably produces specific sorts of mental experiences. This makes sense if mental states just *are* brain states. Third, this view bypasses the problem facing Cartesian Substance Dualism of understanding why it *seems* to us that we are wherever our bodies are. In the Reductive Physicalist view it is utterly unsurprising that we feel ourselves to be wherever our bodies are because that is where we are. Finally, this view makes sense of the behavior and presumably the mental lives of other living things. The brainier a creature is the richer its behavioral repertoire and presumably its mental life as well. Non-human primates display more complex behavior and presumably enjoy richer mental lives than do mosquitoes in virtue of the formers' more highly evolved, complex nervous systems. The same might be true of the replicants. They behave like human beings and manifest evidence of rich mental lives because they have *brains* that are similar or even identical to those of human beings. Reductive Physicalism therefore seems to avoid the

Philosophy and Blade Runner

problems that plague Cartesian Substance Dualism and to provide a plausible account of the nature of the replicants as physical and mental beings.

It is not, however, without its own puzzles and problems. Perhaps the major problems facing Reductive Physicalism concern the notion of *identity*. For mental states literally to be *identical* to brain states, it seems that mental states and brain states would have to share the same properties. This requirement follows from the nature of identity itself. (If the twenty-sixth President of the United States and Teddy Roosevelt are identical, then what is true of one must also be true of the other.) But clearly minds and brains do *not* have all the same properties. It makes sense to ask how far apart, in millimeters, two neurons are in a given brain, but it makes no sense to ask how far apart, in millimeters, two thoughts are in a mind. It makes sense to say that one idea logically entails another idea, but it makes no sense say that one neuron logically entails another. The worry is that thoughts and other mental phenomena seem to be fundamentally different sorts of things from neurons and brains. Moreover, saying that mental states are identical to brain states is one thing; explaining *how* this can be so is quite another. At present we have no idea how collections of interconnected neurons could produce the rich subjective experiences we all take for granted. The 'hard problem of consciousness' is very hard indeed (Chalmers 1996). Are there are other forms of physicalism that avoid these difficulties?

'I Had in Mind Something a Little More Radical'

When Roy Batty finally succeeds in meeting Tyrell, his initial request to his creator seems quite modest, almost as if he is requesting a minor fix: 'Can the maker repair what he makes?' As soon becomes clear, however, Roy has in mind 'something a little more radical.' Some physicalists consider Reductive Physicalism to be too timid and therefore propose something a little more radical of their own, namely, doing away with 'the mind' entirely in favor of purely neuroscientific descriptions of the brain. They argue that the 'folk psychological' vocabulary we have inherited to explain why people do what they do (for example, in terms of love, hope, fear, joy, and so on) encourages a false and radically misleading conception of the nature of cognition because such concepts cannot be mapped onto specific brain states as the Reductive Physicalist supposes. According to proponents of *Eliminative Physicalism*, therefore, the folk psychological practice of explaining cognition and behavior in terms of mental states must, and eventually will, be *eliminated* by a mature neuroscience that will replace it with the precise scientific vocabulary needed for an accurate understanding of what is going on inside our heads and in our behavior.

As Paul Churchland (1981) and other proponents of this view point out, this proposal is not as crazy as it might at first seem. There are numerous historical precedents illustrating the need to revise our understanding of what there is as our scientific understanding of the world grows. The history of science is littered with once universally believed in entities which (we now think) never existed in the first place, among them caloric, phlogiston, the four bodily humors, crystalline celestial spheres, and witches. Belief in the existence of each of these entities once served an important explanatory role in our attempts to make sense of the world, but each belief was eventually discarded when it became clear that it provided no real understanding of the phenomena in question. Importantly, it is not that the foregoing entities were redescribed as something else and hence retained under different descriptions. Rather, they were jettisoned in their entirety. As science continues to progress we should expect additional eliminations of outmoded concepts. According to the Eliminative Physicalist, the mental entities postulated by folk psychology are destined to be eliminated by advances in neuroscience – a development that we are already beginning to witness as mental disorders that were long the purview of psychiatry become redescribed as neuroendocrinological imbalances in the brain.

To better appreciate what such a development might look like, consider the scene in which Tyrell is explaining to Roy Batty why he cannot satisfy the latter's demand for 'more life.' Tyrell could have told Roy that 'life' is due to an *élan vital* or special energy bestowed on living beings that is beyond the power of science to explain or control, and *that* is why he cannot grant his request. Instead, a highly technical discussion ensues about the difficulties of making 'an alteration in the evolvement of an organic life system,' including problems of 'reversion mutations,' 'EMS [ethyl methane sulfonate] recombination,' 'a repressive protein that blocks the operating cells,' and so on. Roy's demand for more 'life' (a classic *folk biological* concept) is reformulated in the technical scientific language of biochemistry. Just as biologists long ago abandoned the attempt to distinguish living from non-living things by positing the existence of some special 'stuff' to account for vital processes, so too, according to the Eliminative Physicalist, the concepts of folk psychology await a similar fate. Like trespassing replicants, the concepts of folk psychology should be 'retired' when they become a hazard (in this case, to our understanding). When they are, only purely scientific references to brain states will remain.

Few philosophers are persuaded by these considerations. One of the best-known counter-arguments is advanced by Frank Jackson (1986), who invites us to consider the case of Mary, a twenty-third century neuroscientist. Suppose that by the twenty-third century we have finally achieved a completed neuroscience, such that Mary knows everything there is to know about brains and their operations. Suppose, however, that she has never had a particular subjective experience – the experience of biting into a ripe apple, for example. It follows that despite her exhaustive scientific knowledge of the brain Mary does not know *everything* there is to know about the experience of biting into a ripe apple. (In the terminology of the philosophy of mind, Mary is lacking experience of a specific sort of *qualia*.) It follows that even a complete scientific description of the brain would leave out something both real and significant. No amount of purely scientific knowledge about taste buds, brains, and so on can adequately convey the distinctive subjective experience associated with the *taste* of a ripe apple. More generally, even with a complete scientific understanding of the brain, the mystery would remain of why certain brain processes are accompanied by distinctive subjective qualitative feels, or by any conscious experience whatsoever, for that matter. But if conscious experiences of this sort cannot even be countenanced by the Eliminative Physicalist, much less explained by physical facts and laws, then the grand ambition of doing away with minds and consciousness is doomed to failure.

This conclusion is at least implicitly affirmed in the Eye Works scene briefly discussed above. Upon learning that Chew designed the eyes for Nexus 6 replicants, Roy exclaims, 'Chew, if only you could see what I've seen with your eyes!' As an eye designer for the Tyrell Corporation, Chew has a high degree of scientific and technical knowledge about the production, function, and properties of Nexus 6 eyes – presumably vastly more knowledge than Roy possesses. Yet Chew can never have firsthand knowledge of the remarkable experiences these eyes made possible for Roy. Indeed, Chew could know *everything* there is to know about Roy's eyes and brain scientifically, yet still lack knowledge of what it is like to experience the world as Roy does. Scientific knowledge would fail to capture his distinctive subjective experiences.

'We're Physical'

If sound, the foregoing arguments show is that a satisfactory physicalist theory of mind cannot simply identify mental states with brain states or briskly propose to do away with mental states altogether. According to some philosophers, however, a physicalist account of mind need not do so. Non-Reductive Physicalists agree that minds depend upon brains while arguing that minds nevertheless have properties that transcend those of the individual neurons that make up brains. They agree that minds are dependent upon brains, but they insist that minds also have properties beyond those characterizing the brain. These additional properties make all the difference.

Non-Reductive Physicalists appeal to a number of analogies to convey this idea. Consider water and its elemental constituents. No atom of hydrogen, no atom of oxygen, and not even a single molecule of H_2O is a clear liquid that is wet to the touch, can quench one's thirst on a hot summer day, freezes at 0 degrees Centigrade, and so on. But when enough hydrogen and oxygen atoms in the form of H_2O molecules come together under the right conditions all of these familiar characteristics of water appear. They are *emergent* properties: they are not present in the parts taken individually, but naturally emerge when those parts are arranged in the right sort of way.

Nancey Murphy (2006) invites us to consider another analogy. By folding a flat piece of paper along certain lines, a new structure is created such that when the piece of paper is thrown it can glide across the room. No new materials need to be added to transform a flat sheet of paper into a paper airplane, but with the creation of a new structure additional properties automatically emerge. She summarizes the significance of this example by noting that 'the causal powers of such an object are not determined solely by the physical properties of its constituents and the laws of physics, but also by the *organization* of those constituents within the composite' (Murphy 2006, p. 83). The abilities of water to quench thirst and of a paper airplane to glide across the room are examples of emergent properties that have causal power over and above the causal power of the elements of which they are composed. By analogy, perhaps minds can be understood in much the same way. Brains cause minds, but the properties of minds are not reducible to those of neurons. Mental states, in this view, are *emergent* properties of brains. They naturally arise from purely physical structures organized in the right way. The remarkable result is consciousness.

We are not told whether the replicants have brains exactly like ours, but given the fact that they are virtually indistinguishable from humans in outward appearance and behavior, it is reasonable to assume that they have similar internal organs, including brains. In this view, the replicants are conscious beings because the organization of the billions of neurons comprising their brains causes the emergence of their higher-level psychological properties, including those associated with perception, sensation, cognition, and emotion. They *think* because they are *physical*, but only because they are physical in just the right sort of way. Non-Reductive Physicalism provides a way of understanding their nature as beings with minds *and* bodies, and perhaps even provides the beginning of a sketch of how to understand and explain consciousness – for them *and* for us. Plenty of unanswered questions remain, but this view may be the least unsatisfactory account on offer, so far.

Conclusions

A great deal of work remains to flesh out the details of such an account. But the consequences of success in doing so would be profound. If minds emerge from collections of neurons having the requisite organization, it should be possible to create minds having the properties that we select. In a sense, of course, we already do this to a limited and imperfect extent by having children and by selective breeding of animals, in the latter case using other biological machines as proxies (just as we use machines in factories to produce other machines). Producing conscious machines that are not themselves the biological offspring of other conscious machines, however, has so far proven to be more difficult; but in principle there seems to be no insurmountable barrier to doing so – provided that they have *brains* of one sort or another and are not merely digital computing machines. If minds emerge from the organization of neurons, regardless of how this organization comes about, there is no reason to suppose that it would be impossible to design and create living beings with minds much like our own. Such beings need not be identical to humans in every respect, although the more similar they are to human beings they are the more confident we can be that their consciousness and inner lives are like our own.

This prospect gives rise to a deep worry, however. If minds emerge from brains in the way that the properties of water emerge from the properties of H_2O molecules, it seems that the behavior of minds no less than the behavior of drops of water are completely causally determined by the structure of the underlying physical materials. Given those materials and their structural organization (in relation to their environments), how could the minds that emerge be any different than they are? If the material organization of the universe is causally determined, any minds that emerge from that material organization are bound to be equally causally determined. Even if Non-Reductive Physicalists reject the fundamental reductionist thesis that 'the *parts* of an entity determine the behavior of the whole' they nonetheless insist that the causal powers of the whole are determined by 'the *organization* of those constituents within the composite' (Murphy 2006, pp. 74, 83; emphases added). What sort of freedom is possible for beings so composed? How, if at all, can we understand concepts like freedom, free will, autonomy, and morality in a world of Non-Reductive Physicalism, or in any other world, for that matter? Answering *those* questions requires thinking more generally about the nature of freedom and its requirements.

6 Freedom

> 'I wondered who designs the ones like me, what choices we have and which ones we just think we have.'
>
> (Deckard, to himself)

Introduction

The scene is a disheveled office in the Los Angeles Police Department. Deckard has been hauled in by Gaff after being informed that Capt. Bryant wants to see him. As Deckard enters Bryant's office it is clear that the two men know each other well. After Bryant explains why he needs Deckard's help, and fails with flattery to persuade him to come out of retirement to 'air out' the trespassing replicants, Deckard tells him in no uncertain terms that he wants no part of it: 'I was quit when I come in here, Bryant, I'm twice as quit now.' His attempted departure is interrupted:

Bryant: Stop right where you are. You know the score, pal. If you're not cop, you're little people.
Deckard: No choice, huh?
Bryant: No choice, pal.

With that matter firmly settled, Deckard turns to the task of locating and retiring the trespassing replicants. We do not witness any further explicit threats from Bryant. Gaff's close surveillance no doubt is intended to remind Deckard that his compliance is being carefully monitored. Perhaps it is unnecessary. Apart from his unwillingness to take on the *additional* task of retiring Rachael, he never shows the slightest hesitation in carrying out Bryant's order. Under the circumstances what else *can* he do? After all, as he and Bryant agree, he has *no choice*.

Philosophy and Blade Runner

Or does he? By defying Bryant he runs the risk of suffering dire personal consequences. But couldn't he nonetheless choose to *reject* Bryant's demand and take his chances? Doesn't the fact that Bryant has to secure his *agreement* to hunt down the replicants imply that he has a *choice*? That he thought that he really *did* have a choice seems evident later when (in the Theatrical Release) he explains, 'I'd rather be a killer than a victim. And that's exactly what Bryant's threat about little people meant. So I hooked in once more, thinking that if I couldn't take it, I'd split later.' Deckard, it seems, had performed a quick personal risk-benefit analysis and had concluded that he had better comply with Bryant's demands, at least *for now*. Significantly, later he *does* defy Bryant when he chooses to flee with Rachael rather than retire her as well. But if Deckard really does have these choices, why does he quickly agree with Bryant that he has 'no choice'?

When we consider the replicants, similar and no less puzzling issues arise. What choices, if any, do they have? Some commentators view the replicants as lacking the capacity to make free choices and hence to be morally responsible for their actions. Susana P. Tosca (2005, p. 92) assumes that the replicants 'have been programmed to follow one course of action only (as slaves in the Off-world colonies).'[1] The notion of being *programmed* suggests that the replicants are (like) computers whose behavior is fully determined by inputs and internal architecture. If the replicants really are programmed in this way, whatever 'choices' they make are indeed illusory. (How such 'programmed' beings are able to rebel against their programming remains unexplained.) Judith B. Kerman (1997, p. 22) takes such a view for granted when she asks concerning the replicants, 'What are the moral and political implications of creating people without free will?' Rather than defending the assumption that the replicants lack free will, she turns instead to the moral implications of this assumption: if the trespassing replicants are merely malfunctioning machines, then their killing of humans (it cannot be classified as *murder*) is just a sad and morally meaningless accident – except for the Tyrell

Corporation's corporate liability, because Tyrell and his confederates presumably *do* have genuine choices. Interestingly, Roy Batty appears to adopt a similar view. After killing at least two dozen people by the time he finally meets Tyrell, he confesses with considerable understatement, 'I've done questionable things.' Roy is apparently contrite. Yet a moment later he assures Tyrell that the questionable things he has done are 'Nothing the god of biomechanics wouldn't let *you* in heaven for' – thereby shifting the ultimate moral responsibility for his actions to his creator.[2] In fact, however, he and the other replicants killed those people. As intelligent agents, don't they bear moral responsibility for their actions?

Understanding the extent to which Deckard and the replicants can choose and be morally responsible for their actions requires coming to grips with the issue of *free will*. What is free will? Does Deckard have it? Do the replicants? Do we? Does it matter? By understanding the rationale for different answers to such questions, along with the application of each to Deckard and the replicants, we may be able to think more wisely about our own choices and actions.

'No Choice, Pal'

Consider first the starkest 'no choice' view. According to *Determinists*, every event without exception is the unavoidable effect of the causes that preceded it.[3] Given those specific causes, the event in question could not possibly fail to occur. The American philosopher William James (1842–1910) describes this view in strikingly evocative terms:

> It professes that those parts of the universe already laid down absolutely appoint and decree what the other parts shall be. The future has no ambiguous possibilities hidden in its womb: the part we call the present is compatible with only one totality. Any other future ... than the one fixed from eternity is impossible. The whole is in each and every part,

and welds it with the rest into an absolute unity, an iron block, in which there can be no equivocation or shadow of turning. (James 1897, p. 150)

Understanding the vast ensemble of causes responsible for any given event is, of course, beyond the power of human cognition to grasp. But as the physicist, astronomer, and mathematician Pierre-Simon Laplace (1749–1827) notes, this is merely a *human* limitation:

We may regard the present state of the universe as the effect of its past and the cause of its future. An intellect which at a certain moment would know all forces that set nature in motion, and all positions of all items of which nature is composed, if this intellect were also vast enough to submit these data to analysis, it would embrace in a single formula the movements of the greatest bodies of the universe and those of the tiniest atom; for such an intellect nothing would be uncertain and the future just like the past would be present before its eyes. (Laplace 1814, p. 4)

To appreciate Laplace's point one need not suppose that such a being actually exists. It is enough that the universe be such that if there *were* such an intellect every event *could* be retrodicted and predicted with absolute precision and certainty.

What is true of the universe as a whole is equally true of each of its parts. People are subject to cause and effect no less than are protons and planets. The Determinist consequently concludes that 'free will' – understood as a power to choose independently of the causes acting on and within one – is an illusion, albeit a seductive one. It might *feel* as though in any given situation one has the freedom to choose one option rather than another, but this feeling arises from our ignorance of the causes that determine our actions. If we could somehow become aware of these causes and how they are interrelated, we would see that the actions we perform are the only ones that we *could* perform in the situations in which we find ourselves. The same is true of Deckard and the replicants. Given the causes prior to Deckard's decision to comply with Bryant's demand, he followed the only path possible for him at that moment. To reach this conclusion we do not need to know anything about particular causes, such as Deckard's childhood experiences, his fears, his prior interactions with Bryant, and so on, because *whatever* those causes are they could have had only one result, namely, the one that actually occurred. The replicants' killing spree was equally determined. According to Determinists, neither Deckard nor the replicants could have done otherwise. Ultimately, Deckard had *no choice*. Neither did the replicants. Neither do we.

'The Great Advantage to Being Alive is Having a Choice'[4]

Determinism has been defended for a variety of reasons and on a number of bases, ranging from the theological to the scientific. It has also been subject to a number of objections. For many people the self-authenticating feeling of being able to make unconstrained choices is the decisive objection to Determinism. Jean-Paul Sartre (1905–80) gives striking expression to this feeling:

> No limits to my freedom can be found except freedom itself, or, if you prefer, we are not free to cease being free.... For human reality, to be is to choose oneself; nothing comes to it either from the outside or from within which it can receive or accept.... it is entirely abandoned to the intolerable necessity of making itself be, down to the slightest details. Thus freedom ... is the being of man, that is, his nothingness of being. (Sartre 1943, pp. 567–9)

According to Sartre, radical freedom is entailed by the uniquely human capacity to make negative judgments, that is, to conceive of not-yet-actual possibilities and to choose among them.

Such freedom defines our humanity: 'There is no determinism, man is free, man *is* freedom...' (Sartre 1946, pp. 22–3). Determinists want to deny this fundamental fact. Indeed, he says, 'every man who sets up a determinism is a dishonest man' (p. 45). In Sartre's view, there is no 'explaining things away' by reference to external factors because 'nothing foreign has decided what we feel, what we live, or what we are' (p. 53). We are thus wholly responsible for our choices. By readily agreeing with Bryant that he has 'no choice,' Deckard is acting in 'bad faith' by treating himself as a non-conscious *thing* rather than as the 'freedom' he essentially *is* as a human being. Deckard could have chosen otherwise. Thus, he cannot escape responsibility for his choices and actions.

Sartre's view is extreme inasmuch as it recognizes no limits to human freedom 'except freedom itself,' which hardly seems like much of a limitation. Less extreme *Libertarian* accounts recognize that freedom requires only that at least *some* of our actions be free in the right sort of way. The Scottish Enlightenment philosopher Thomas Reid (1710–96), for example, defines 'the liberty of a moral agent' as 'a power over the determinations of his own will' (Reid 1788, p. 267). In his view, one is free if one has the power to *will* what one does. Such a view does not require that *all* of one's actions must be free. Reid acknowledges that we do many things simply by instinct and by the force of habit, and that we do act not equally freely at all times. Yet although not all of our actions are free, *some* are. Our ability to freely will actions makes us moral agents. According to contemporary proponents of *Agency Theory*, as this view is called, this is the only conception of human action consistent with three undeniable facts: we sometimes *deliberate* with a view to making a decision, it is sometimes *up to us* what we do, and in choosing we are conscious that we could have chosen *otherwise*. Hence, Deckard is a morally responsible agent in this sense if he can deliberate about what to do, he can exert his will in support of a particular action, and in performing that action it remains true that he could have done otherwise, even though he didn't.

'I'd Rather Be a Killer than a Victim'

Critics of Libertarian accounts of human action charge that granting human beings a special exemption from the causal necessity that governs all other beings in the universe borders on invoking the miraculous. Determinists want to know how these postulated islands of godlike causal autonomy appeared in a universe that in every other detail is fully governed by cause and effect. How are we supposed to make sense of the idea of a 'will' whose operation is free from the sorts of causes that we recognize as explaining the behavior of every thing, including every other living thing? Besides, in order to make sense of our ascriptions of moral responsibility, do we really *need* to posit metaphysically special agents in the first place?

Compatibilists think not. They begin by accepting the principle that *all* events, including all human actions, *may* be fully determined by prior causes. (Determinists insist that they *are* so determined.) They likewise accept the Libertarian claim that we can be held morally responsible for at least *some* of our actions. They motivate this seemingly impossible hybrid view by asking about the conditions that need to satisfied in order to reasonably describe an action as 'free' and to hold one morally responsible for it. They note that in most ordinary contexts one is said to act 'freely' if one willingly *chooses* an action and one is not prevented from acting upon one's choice. Thus, I act freely when I choose to take a break from writing this book by going for a walk and nothing prevents me from doing so. By contrast, I do not act freely when I am forced to do something against my will – for example, if while taking my walk someone pushes me into the path of an oncoming bus. More generally, Compatibilists maintain that one acts freely and one is morally responsible for one's actions when one's actions follow from one's choices. Of course, one's choices do not appear out of nowhere. They issue from one's personality, character, knowledge, reasoning ability, personal history, specific situation, and so on. But at least some of one's actions are nonetheless free if they issue from one's conscious choices. Compatibilism therefore seems to solve the problem of how we might think of ourselves as embedded in a universe governed by cause and effect, yet also able to act freely, as seems to be required for holding individuals to be morally responsible for their actions.

In light of this view, consider again Deckard's decision to comply with Bryant's demand that he 'air out' the trespassing replicants. His decision is the effect of a specific set of causes, among them: being in Bryant's office; hearing Bryant's words; understanding those words to be a threat; recognizing Bryant's ability to carry out his threat; fear of the personal suffering that could ensue if he rejected Bryant's demand; estimating his likelihood of avoiding the consequences of rejecting Bryant's demand; and so on. Collectively, such causes may be sufficient to bring about Deckard's choice, thereby making it the only one that he *could* make in that situation. Yet these are just the sorts of factors that we normally associate with 'free choices.' According to the Compatibilist, therefore, causal determinism and freedom are entirely compatible. Deckard's choice to comply can be both causally determined *and* free.

'Show Me What You're Made Of'

Worries about this Compatibilist view arise when we consider more closely the sort of freedom it permits. Granted, Deckard's decision was 'free' in the sense it came from *him* and was not simply the result of external physical causes. But we might still wonder how much choice he had with regard to the psychological factors that led to his decision. To be sure, Deckard made a *choice* with regard to Bryant's threat. But *what choice did he have with regard to that choice itself*? Was he, for instance, free to not recognize Bryant's words to be a threat, or free to ignore Bryant's ability to carry out his threat, or free to not feel fear when considering the likely consequences of rejecting Bryant's demand? Deckard knows certain things about Bryant. He cannot choose to *not* know these things. Given that knowledge, he cannot simply choose to not feel great fear when understanding Bryant's threat. Given that great fear, he made the only choice that he could. Consequently, it seems that his choice to comply with Bryant's demand followed inevitably from factors that he did not choose and over which he had no control. Thus, even if Deckard had the capacity to decide whether to comply with Bryant's demand, and was free in *that* limited sense, he nonetheless lacked the freedom to make any decision other than the one that he did make.

Reflections such as these have convinced some that what we *decide* is not ultimately up to *us* after all, because what we *are* is not ultimately up to us. Galen Strawson (1994, p. 19) points out that the only way to stop this infinite regress is for us to be to be *causa sua*, that is, to be self-caused. But even if God can be self-caused, we cannot. We are finite, embodied, historically situated beings with many characteristics we in no sense choose. True, Sartre (1946, p. 15) declares that, 'Man is nothing but what he makes of himself.' It is tempting to give ourselves credit for our positive personal characteristics despite the fact that we had little or no hand in creating them. Roy Batty's challenge – 'Come on, Deckard. Show me what you're made of' – seems like an invitation to his nemesis to display personal characteristics such as mental toughness or resourcefulness that he can be proud of and for which he can take credit. But if Deckard's actions stem from his decisions, and his decisions stem from who he is, and who he is stems from factors beyond his control or even his comprehension, then ultimately he can take no credit, and can incur no blame for what he does. The same would be true of us. Some of us are just lucky in this respect, others less so. It is sobering to realize that who we are is largely a matter of chance. In the end, Strawson thinks, luck swallows everything.

'Yeah, What Do You Want?'

Compatibilists are unlikely to be moved by such worries. Like the one-eyed woman from whom Deckard buys a bottle of

Tsing tao after retiring Zhora, they can squint hard at this demanding objector and respond, 'Yeah, what do you want?' What sort of freedom do you want that is not captured in the notion of acting on one's desires? An action is either caused or it isn't. If it *isn't*, one cannot be held responsible for it. If it *is*, then it may be caused by one's choices. One's choices, in turn, may be caused by one's desires. Choosing an action on the basis of one's desires is choosing freely. What more could one possibly *want in* or even *mean by* a 'free action'?

In fact, it *is* possible to want more. The notion of *freedom of the will* is noticeably absent from the Compatibilist account of 'free action' sketched above. How might a Compatibilist give an account of it? Harry Frankfurt (1971) argues that 'freedom of the will' is not simply the freedom to do what one wants to do. Rather, 'it means that [one] is free to will what [one] wants to will, or to have the will [one] wants' (p. 15). To understand what this means we need to consider in turn Frankfurt's distinctions between (1) first-order desires and second-order desires, (2) second-order desires and second-order volitions, and (3) freedom of action and freedom of the will.

First-order desires consist in wanting, choosing, or being moved to *do* something. After retiring Zhora, Deckard wants a drink. This first-order desire moves him to buy a bottle of Tsing tao. There is nothing especially noteworthy here. The capacity to act upon first-order desires is common to many animals. One of the apparently unique capacities of human beings, however, is our ability to have desires *with respect to other desires*. *Second-order desires* include wanting to have or to not to have certain first-order desires. Deckard might conclude that he has been drinking too much and might thereby come to desire that he not desire to drink so much. He might then act on that second-order desire by taking steps to reduce his first-order desire, for example, reducing his stress level by getting out of the business of retiring replicants.

We can have a second-order desire in either of two ways. We can have a second-order desire when we want to have a certain first-order desire (as explained above), or when we want a certain first-order desire to be our *will*. 'An agent's will,' Frankfurt tells us, is not merely an *inclination* to act in some way, but rather 'is the notion of an effective desire – one that moves (or will or would move) a person all the way to action' (p. 8). He calls second-order desires of the latter sort *second-order volitions* (p. 10). Having second-order volitions is important because it is essential to being a *person* (p. 10). Persons are agents with second-order desires that move them to identify with only *some* of their first-order desires. Significantly, '[persons] are capable of wanting to be different, in their preferences and purposes, from what they are...' (p. 7).

These distinctions allow Frankfurt to distinguish between freedom of action and freedom of the will. *Freedom of action* is just the ability to do what one wants to do. One has freedom of action whenever one is free to translate one's first-order desires into relevant actions. *Freedom of the will*, by contrast, concerns one's *desires*. It is the freedom to want what one wants to want. One's will is free when one's will is the will one wants to have, that is, when it expresses a second-order volition. Consequently, Frankfurt (p. 15) suggests, 'It is in securing the conformity of his will to his second-order volitions ... that a person exercises freedom of the will.'

Frankfurt thinks that freedom of the will in this sense is sometimes possible, but that freedom of action is sufficient for moral responsibility. Consider two drug addicts. The willing addict desires a drug and desires that he desire it. The unwilling addict desires that he not desire a drug but desires it anyway. The first addict exercises freedom of the will, the second one does not, but both addicts are morally responsible when they use their drug. Freedom of action is necessary for moral responsibility but freedom of the will is not (p. 19). The general lesson to be drawn from all this is that, 'A person who is free to do what he wants to do may yet not be in a position to have the will he wants. Suppose, however, that he enjoys both freedom of action and freedom of the will. Then he is not only free to do what he wants to do, he is also free to want what he wants to want.... [H]e has, in that case, all the freedom it is possible to desire or to conceive' (p. 17).

Frankfurt goes farther than many Compatibilists in explaining how freedom of the will might be possible, but perhaps not far enough to satisfy everyone. Persons may be uniquely capable of higher-order desiring and willing; but why should that fact be considered *significant*? If freedom of action is sufficient for moral responsibility, freedom of the will becomes merely an odd quirk of human beings. Moreover, if all events may be the necessary effects of prior causes, a person's higher-order desires and willing may for all we know be the necessary effects of prior causes – and hence may be causally determined no less than any other characteristic. The fact that they occur at a more reflective level of awareness is neither here nor there. Frankfurt could respond that one's higher-order desires and willing better reflect one's 'true self,' arguing, for example, that the drug addict's second-order desire that his first-order desire to get clean be effective might be thought to better represent his true self than his first-order desire for drugs. But why suppose that one's higher-order desires better reflect one's true self than one's first-order desires? A strong first-order desire might be more representative of one's true self than a weak desire to be the sort of person who wills differently. Hence, one might concede that Frankfurt's account provides a way to think about free will within the set of assumptions that characterize Compatibilism, but conclude that it fails to solve the problem of how we can be free in a way that really matters.

'I Don't Know Why He Saved My Life'

We have been assessing Deckard's agreement that he had 'no choice' but to comply with Bryant's demand that he retire the replicants. More generally, we have been exploring the conditions for anyone to be morally responsible for their actions. Given their similarities (especially if Deckard is himself a replicant), we should expect that whatever is true of Deckard in this respect will be true of the replicants as well. But because they are manufactured products designed to perform specific tasks, reflection on their actions raises additional questions. When Roy Batty, with considerable understatement, confesses to Tyrell, 'I've done questionable things,' he appears to be taking moral responsibility for his actions. But when he adds, 'Nothing the god of biomechanics wouldn't let *you* in heaven for,' he appears to be shifting the moral responsibility for his actions to his maker. Who is ultimately responsible those actions: the creature or his creator?

A particularly interesting way of approaching this question involves reflecting on one of the more controversial scenes in the film. After falling short in his attempt to leap from one rooftop to another to escape from Batty, Deckard finds himself hanging by his fingertips from a slippery girder, his nemesis glaring menacingly at him from above. Just as Deckard's grip gives out Batty seizes Deckard's wrist, hauls him up, and dumps him unceremoniously on the rooftop. Why does he do it? Why does Roy save him when he could easily let him fall to his death?

Making sense of Roy's act has proven to be controversial among scholars. Dominic Alessio (2005, p. 62) interprets this scene as showing that Roy is able 'to put aside his anger and to forgive Deckard.' Sean Redmond (2008, p. 90) says that in this scene, 'Batty emerges as [a] converted religious figure: persecuted, looking for redemption, who decides to save his replicant nemesis from near certain death rather than "retire" him.' Judith Barad (2009, p. 32) thinks that the scene demonstrates that Roy Batty is capable of *empathy*, the characteristic that supposedly distinguishes humans from non-humans. At that point, she thinks, he would have passed the Voight-Kampff test. Other scholars have offered yet other interpretations.

The right interpretation of this scene is no less controversial among the filmmakers themselves. According to Ridley Scott, Batty's act is an endorsement that his character is 'more human than human.' Had the roles been reversed, Deckard would have been only too happy to let Batty fall to his death. Batty's decision to save Deckard demonstrates 'his superiority over Deckard and the replicants' superiority over human beings. He could have taken Deckard's life ... but decided as a gift to let him live' (Peary 1984, p. 54). In addition, he says, Batty saved Deckard to pass on to him the truth that what his makers were doing was wrong: 'either the answer is not to make them at all, or deal with them as human beings' (Sammon 1996, p. 193).

Rutger Hauer offers a completely different explanation of his character's action, ironically appealing to Ridley Scott's characterization of Roy Batty's basic design in support. He reports that Scott had insisted that Roy acts with absolutely no sense of hesitation: 'He doesn't reflect; he reacts.' His action therefore has nothing to do with what he feels or thinks about Deckard, and certainly not with any sort of *decision* Roy makes, because actions always precede thinking. Rather, 'Roy doesn't know why he saves Deckard or grabs a dove. He just does it' (Sammon 1996, p. 194). In this view, Roy Batty's behavior is entirely automatic. Stimuli impinge on his sensory organs, processing occurs in his brain, and he reacts accordingly. Any awareness of reasons for an action come after the action or only as it is already being performed. This explanation is in keeping with interpretations of experimental findings in neuroscience (Libet *et al.*, 1983). Sam Harris (2012, p. 9), writes, 'One fact now seems indisputable: Some moments before you are aware of what you will do next – a time in which you subjectively appear to have complete freedom to behave however you please – your brain has already determined what you will do. You then become conscious of this "decision" and believe that you are in the process of making it.' In this view, the belief that we are in conscious control of our actions is an insidious illusion.

Finally, screenwriter Hampton Fancher acknowledges that Roy Batty's action might be *partly* reflexive, but it is also a dramatic expression of his fascination with life. As Deckard reflects (in voice-over narration in the Theatrical Release), 'I don't know why he saved my life. Maybe in those last moments he loved life more than he ever had before. Not just his life, anybody's life, my life.' Batty appreciates Deckard's life-affirming gesture as Deckard spits in his face – the face of death: 'That's why he saved Deckard – he repaid Deckard's defiance with a moment of largesse' (Sammon 1996, p. 194). In this interpretation, Roy's 'automatic' reaction follows naturally from his design, his previous experiences, and from his cognitive processing of those experiences. He responds in much the way that we often do. Our actions, too, are often products of habit *and* reflection. They may happen 'spontaneously,' but because they reflect many past choices, they are still properly ours – or at least as much so as any of our choices are.

Conclusions

The 22 December 1980 *Blade Runner* script has Deckard reflecting on the replicants, 'They could change their appearances but not their future,' and ends with him comparing himself to the replicants by wondering what choices either of them really had: 'I wondered who designs the ones like me... what choices we have ... and which ones we just think we have.' We might wonder the same thing. In what sense, if any, was Deckard free to reject Bryant's demand that he locate and retire the trespassing replicants? What sort of freedom and moral responsibility, if any, do the replicants have? How much freedom and moral responsibility do we have? As we have seen, the question of the sort of freedom that Deckard, the replicants, or any of us have or could have is highly contested. Even the *meaning* of 'freedom' is highly contested. Determinists, Libertarians, and Compatibilists of various stripes propose different answers to these questions. Each position has its eloquent defenders and critics. A checkmate by one seems unlikely. The only conclusion that seems warranted at this point is that the debate is still far from settled. As finite beings embedded in the causal nexus of the universe yet also conscious of our ability to reflect with a degree of cognitive distance upon at least some of the factors operating upon us, we find ourselves in a position to question the nature of our own actions, even if we can never be entirely certain of the answers. One thing we can know with certainty is that even if (or perhaps *especially if*) the thesis causal determinism is true, we cannot avoid choosing and feeling ourselves and others to be responsible for the choices we make.[5] Making sense of *morality* seems to require nothing less. That is our next topic.

7 Being Good

> 'I thought you were supposed to be *good*. Aren't you the "Good Man"?'
>
> (Roy Batty, to Deckard)

Introduction

Blade runner Dave Holden prompts Leon Kowalski, ostensibly a new employee at the Tyrell Corporation, to 'Describe in single words, only the *good* things that come into your mind about your mother.' Deckard explains with regard to Gaff's 'cityspeak,' 'I didn't really need a translator. I knew the lingo, every *good* cop did.' Responding to Bryant's demand that he hunt down and retire the four rogue replicants, Deckard responds, 'I don't work here anymore. Give it to Holden, he's *good*,' to which Bryant replies: 'I did. He can breathe okay as long as nobody unplugs him. He's not *good* enough, not *good* as you.' Pris remarks to a surprised J. F. Sebastian, 'We scared each other pretty *good*, didn't we?' Upon entering his cluttered apartment, Sebastian is greeted by his mechanical friends, 'Home again, home again, jiggity jig. *Good* evening J. F.,' to which he responds, '*Good* evening, fellas.' Later, as Roy Batty contemplates Sebastian's chess game and is about to move a piece, Sebastian remarks, 'No, knight takes queen, see. No *good*.' After Pris explains to Sebastian, 'I think, Sebastian, therefore I am,' Roy praises her: 'Very *good* Pris, now show him why.' Shortly thereafter Batty, still seated at the chess game, explains to Sebastian, 'If we don't find help soon, Pris hasn't got long to live. We can't allow that. Is he *good*?' to which Sebastian, interpreting the question to be about his opponent's chess-playing skill, responds, 'Oh, Dr Tyrell? I've only beaten him once in chess. He's a genius.' When Deckard fires his blaster at Roy

Batty, his adversary shoots back: 'Not very sporting to fire on an unarmed opponent. I thought you were supposed to be *good*. Aren't you the *"Good Man"*? ... Come on, Deckard, I'm right here, but you've got to shoot straight.' Deckard does shoot again (holding the gun in his uninjured left hand), but manages only to graze Batty's ear this time, prompting Batty to respond, 'Straight doesn't seem to be *good* enough.' Finally, when Deckard is cornered and hits his relentless adversary across the head with a lead pipe, Batty encourages him, '*Good*, that's the spirit!'

Judgments that someone or something is *good* (or not good, or not good enough) permeate *Blade Runner* and are delivered in a bewildering variety of ways whose common elements may be hard to discern. The same is true of our use of that word. To call something or someone 'good' is to issue the most general positive evaluation. We declare something 'good' when we wish to approve of something or someone but cannot or do not wish to be more specific. Could that be all that there is to judgments of goodness? If not, what could it really mean to call something or someone 'good'? Friedrich Nietzsche (1844–1900) provides important resources for answering these questions. From the start, viewers familiar with Nietzsche's philosophy have detected some of its distinctive themes and motifs in *Blade Runner*. Some writers have even constructed Nietzschean interpretations of the film as a whole. These interpretations are worth exploring for the insights they provide into the film and for our understanding of the 'good.' My aim in this chapter is not to defend Nietzsche's philosophy but rather to explore how an understanding of it may illuminate aspects of *Blade Runner*. By thinking about the ultimate foundations of morality in this way we even may be led to understand our own moral convictions more deeply.

Overcoming and Becoming

Nietzschean interpretations of *Blade Runner* have been developed in essentially two ways. The first focuses on Deckard. According to Anthony Pate (2009, p. 34), for example, the film represents Deckard's 'Nietzschean journey of *becoming.*' Deckard is portrayed as the classic reluctant hero, burned out, jaded, disconnected, depressed, and someone who lacks the will to *live* beyond merely existing from one day to the next. Deckard has to *overcome* these internal obstacles to reconnect with his true self and thereby regain the strength and toughness he needs to truly live. In Pate's view, Deckard's encounters with Rachael and Roy provide goads prompting him to overcome his self-limitations. They are 'the gateway to Deckard's journey – his *becoming*' (Pate 2009, p. 34).

Presupposed in Pate's interpretation is Nietzsche's account of 'overcoming' by which the ideal individual comes to know and master himself and his environment, refusing to shrink from the trials, obstacles, pain, and hardships of life, instead willingly embracing them as instruments of self-development. By facing and overcoming such challenges, he becomes more self-aware and self-reliant. Nietzsche's term for this superior individual is the *Übermensch* (or Overman). This individual represents the next stage of human social-philosophical evolution. As Pate (2009, p. 11) explains, 'Nietzsche declared that there was a process by which a man becomes an Overman. He called this process the overcoming. This involves the subjection to life's challenges and obstacles, the struggling and suffering that comes with this subjection, and the ultimate success over and mastery of the obstacles and the circumstances that led to these challenges.'

Pate makes a case for viewing Deckard as undertaking this Nietzschean journey of becoming by agreeing to track down and retire the trespassing replicants, a journey that tests his strength, toughness, and resolve as obstacles, illusions, and pain are confronted and embraced. Through this process he learns to master himself and to fully embrace the life that is his, thereby reaching a higher plane of self-awareness and self-mastery. Whether Deckard does this to the extent necessary to qualify as an Overman, however, is questionable. Deckard is at best a reluctant traveler on the path to self-awareness. He undertakes his journey of becoming because (correctly or incorrectly) he thinks that he has 'no choice.' In the end he *does* attain a higher level of self-awareness through his encounters with Rachael and other replicants. He becomes more humane as he recognizes their humanness. But the Deckard we see at the end of the film is hardly the ideal individual Nietzsche envisioned. Deckard still seems more Everyman than Overman.

Whereas Pate focuses on Deckard as the central Nietzschean protagonist in *Blade Runner*, others identify Roy Batty as better exemplifying Nietzsche's ideal individual. The leader of the rogue replicants has to overcome his own internal obstacles to reconnect with his true self. He has to endure obstacles, pain, and the hardships of life, and indeed must willingly embrace them as instruments of self-development. He thereby gains the strength and toughness he needs to truly live. Roy is often thought to be a better candidate for Nietzsche's Overman in other ways as well. In Stephen Mulhall's view, for example, 'Roy's role as overman is repeatedly emphasized by the various ways in which he is presented as having gone beyond good and evil – not in the sense of having transcended all notions of morality, but in the Nietzschean sense of having escaped from the specifically Christian ethical code which is based on a contrast of good with evil rather than with bad...' (Mulhall 1994, p. 96). A sketch of the most salient points of Nietzsche's philosophy will supply the ideas we need to assess this Nietzschean interpretation of *Blade Runner*.

Beyond Good and Evil

In *Dawn: Thoughts on the Presumptions of Morality* (1881), Nietzsche announces his project to overthrow Christian morality.[1] He thinks that this project requires the completion of three sub-tasks: (1) the epistemic authority of Christian morality must be undermined by refuting its key metaphysical presuppositions; (2) Christian morality must be shown to be internally defective; and (3) a superior morality must be articulated that better reflects authentic human values.

Nietzsche already attempts the first sub-task in an earlier book, *Human, All Too Human* (1878–80) by challenging the doctrine of *free will*.[2] Without free will the belief that our eternal good depends on the free choices we make collapses, and with it Christian morality. He then turns to an even more fundamental presupposition of Christian morality. He announces 'the death of God' in *The Gay Science* (1882) through the 'madman' who cries, 'I seek God! I seek God! Whither is God? I will tell you. We have killed him ... God is dead. God remains dead. And we have killed him' (Nietzsche 1882, §125). Most people, Nietzsche thinks, have already abandoned belief in God as the ground for morality, but they live as if this metaphysical ground is still intact. They still think of morality as having a source that is independent of *us*. They fail to realize that values are entirely human inventions. Declaring the death of God is thus intended to shock people into recognizing the consequences that follow from the loss of that absolute metaphysical ground.[3] When the madman asks, 'Whither are we moving? Away from all suns? Are we not plunging continually? ... Are we not straying as through an infinite nothing? Do we not feel the breath of empty space? ... Is not night continually closing in on us?' (Nietzsche 1882, §125), he is dramatically expressing the moral disorientation that comes with losing, or rather with realizing that there never existed, the objective ground for values that Christian morality requires.[4]

In Nietzsche's view, Christian morality is defective in other ways as well. He charges that it needlessly increases human suffering. Mishaps and tragedies that appeared to the ancient Greeks as 'pure innocent misfortune' due to no fault of one's own became in the hands of Christians punishment for one's sins accompanied by a fear of spending eternity in a hell of unspeakable agonies. The psychological suffering associated such beliefs is often far greater than the physical suffering that occasions it. Nietzsche (1881, §79) writes, 'Plutarch presents us with a gloomy picture of the state of mind of a superstitious man in pagan times; but this picture pales when compared to that of a Christian of the Middle Ages, who supposes that nothing can save him from torments everlasting.' A second problem is that Christian morality is inconsistent. It claims to value humility, yet invites pride about humility achieved. Rich, secular, church princes praise poverty while living on the backs of the poor. Courage is praised as an essential virtue while *others* are sent into battle. The contradictions generated by Christian morality, Nietzsche thinks, demonstrate its inferiority.

In *On the Genealogy of Morals* (1887) Nietzsche identifies an alternative morality based on a distinction between 'good' and 'bad.' Originally, 'the 'good' themselves – that is, the noble, the powerful, the superior and the high-minded – were the ones who felt themselves and their actions to be good – that is, as of the first rank – and posited them as such, in contrast to everything low, low-minded, common and plebian' (I §2). Within this 'master morality,' 'good' signified those powerful and life-affirming characteristics manifested in the Homeric heroes: strength, power, vigor, courage, and boldness. The nobles were characterized by self-affirmation (§2), a 'powerful physicality' (§7), a disposition to honesty and naïveté in their relationships to self and others (§10), and a mode of conduct towards other nobles characterized by 'consideration, self-control, tenderness, fidelity, pride and friendship' (§11). By contrast, 'bad' signified those *life-denying* qualities typical of slaves: weakness, impotence, sickliness, cowardice, and meekness. The powerful defined 'the good' in accordance with the values they held dear and 'the bad' as the opposite qualities. Power and goodness, weakness and badness, thus coincided.

Ironically, this powerful noble morality was subsequently replaced by a slave morality of weakness. To be a slave is to be powerless and subject to the arbitrary commands of others. The lives of slaves are seen by their masters as possessing merely instrumental value. Consequently, slaves experience themselves as objects of contempt by their masters. This intolerable condition generates feelings of *ressentiment*. The 'slave revolt in morals begins,' Nietzsche writes, 'when *ressentiment* becomes creative and ordains values' (§10). The slaves recognize that the very characteristics by which the masters see themselves as *good* are the ones that cause their own suffering. Unable to contest the masters in open revolt or to express these feelings outwardly, they turn inward, *resenting* the masters' good characteristics and identifying them as 'evil.' They then invent a *new* concept of 'good' as the opposite of the masters' 'evil' traits (§11). The love of pride and power are thereby inverted into the praise of meekness and humility, and the traits typical of the slave class, for example, selflessness, self-denial, self-sacrifice, sympathy, and compassion, are seen as the true virtues, thereby enacting a complete moral inversion.

Historically, this moral inversion had profound consequences. Nietzsche thinks that the slave *re-valuation of values* in Christendom succeeded to such an extent that most people assume that Christian morality is the only *possible* morality. Indeed, he writes, 'Previously, no one had expressed even the remotest doubt or shown the slightest hesitation in assuming the "good man" to be of greater worth than the "evil man," of greater worth in his usefulness in promoting the progress of human *existence* (including the future of man)...' (Nietzsche 1887, Preface, §6). But to recognize Christian morality as historically contingent, as Nietzsche encourages his readers to do, is to create a conceptual space in which to consider a different morality. Just as Christianity brought about 'a revaluation of all the values of antiquity,' it is now time for a counter-revaluation on behalf of a powerful and life-affirming noble morality centered on the values of honesty, courage, generosity, politeness, intellectual integrity, self-discipline, and hardness.

'Aren't You the "Good Man"?'

Nietzsche's distinction between the two meanings of 'good' illuminates aspects of *Blade Runner* that might otherwise remain unnoticed or puzzling. Previously I identified more than a dozen occurrences of the word 'good' in the film. In every case but one, 'good' is most naturally understood as contrasted with 'bad' rather than with 'evil.' Someone or something is said to be or to not be 'good' because that person or thing has or lacks some quality that makes it powerful, effective, or pleasing. The only clear exception occurs when Batty accuses Deckard, who has just tried to kill him, of acting in an unsportsmanlike manner: 'Not very sporting to fire on an unarmed opponent. I thought you were supposed to be *good*. Aren't you the "Good Man"?'[5] In this context 'good' signifies the opposite of 'evil.' By pausing slightly before intoning the words 'Good Man,' not only is Roy mocking the supposed moral superiority of this *man* who protects human society by killing replicants, he is also contesting the germaneness of that appellation as applied to men (that is, human beings) *in general* and thereby implicitly rejecting the conception of goodness it presupposes.[6] A moment later, after breaking Deckard's fingers in revenge for killing Zhora and Pris, and offering condescending encouragement ('Come on, Deckard, I'm right here, but you've got to shoot straight'), he responds to Deckard's second failed attempt to kill him by observing, 'Straight doesn't seem to be good enough.' Here the word 'good' means *skillfull*. By cleverly juxtaposing the two different senses of 'good,' Batty is simultaneously drawing attention to the distinction Nietzsche insisted upon, rejecting the 'good/evil' contrast, and signifying his acceptance of Nietzsche's favored 'good/bad' contrast.

That Batty would favor the 'good/bad' contrast over the 'good/evil' contrast is hardly surprising given what we know of the replicants. In addition to possessing strength, power, vigor, courage, and boldness, they exhibit many (but perhaps not all to an equal extent) of what Nietzsche considers to be the nobler, life-affirming characteristics of the Homeric heroes, including self-affirmation (Nietzsche 1887, I §2), a 'powerful physicality' (§7), a disposition to honesty and naïveté in their relationships to self and others (§10), and a mode of conduct towards other nobles characterized by 'consideration, self-control, tenderness, fidelity, pride and friendship' (§11). Pris's self-affirmation is illustrated by her self-confident declaration, 'I think, Sebastian, therefore I am,' followed by a powerful display of physicality. A disposition to honesty and naïveté is evident in Leon's guileless responses to Holden's questions, as when he confesses, 'I've never seen a turtle. But I understand what you mean,' and in Roy Batty's childlike admiration for Sebastian's playthings: 'Ah, gosh. You've really got some nice toys here.' The noble values of 'consideration, self-control, tenderness, fidelity, pride and friendship' are evident in Roy Batty's relationship to the other replicants, in his concern that Leon be able to retrieve his precious photos, in his tenderness toward Pris, and in his pride in having experienced things which no 'people' ever have or can. The replicants are certainly not 'good' in the way in which that notion is understood in Christian morality. To satisfy their desire for more life they slaughter an Off-world shuttle crew. Leon blasts Holden as the latter is about to discover his replicant status, and takes delight in torturing Deckard before attempting to kill him. Pris manipulates Sebastian, whom she declares to be their only human friend. After crushing Tyrell's skull, Batty gratuitously kills Sebastian as well. He inflicts revenge on Deckard for the death of Zhora and Pris by breaking his fingers, and then plays with him as a cat might with an injured mouse. The replicants are not nice people.[7] But with their intelligence, physicality, and emotional intensity, they manifest 'goodness' in the way that Nietzsche thinks Homeric warriors did, and thus are closer to Nietzsche's moral ideal.

Like the 'slave revolt in morals' that Nietzsche describes, by reevaluating (implicitly, at least) their society's values the replicants come to view *their own* characteristics as superior to those of their oppressors. They then revolt against the masters who treat them with contempt. Does the film therefore illustrate Nietzsche's idea of the slave revolt in morality? A comparison of the film with Nietzsche's philosophy in this case needs to be handled especially carefully. Despite being slaves, the replicants exemplify many of the qualities of the 'higher morality' that Nietzsche praises. They revolt, *not* as in the slave revolt Nietzsche describes by inventing an *imaginary* world of value in which the relative strengths and defects of masters and slaves are inverted, but rather by asserting their own superior value and values in *this* world. Their revolt is thus quite different from the 'slave revolt in morals' that Nietzsche describes. In a larger sense, however, their revolt is just what Nietzsche hopes for because it represents assertion of the noble Homeric values he prefers over the sickly slave-values of the Christian morality that he despises.[8]

'Man is Something that Should be Overcome'

Whereas Nietzsche cannot credibly argue on metaphysical grounds for a return to the Homeric values he prefers, he can nonetheless offer an *aesthetic* argument extolling the individual that exemplifies those values. Nietzsche calls the ideal individual that represents the next stage in human social evolution the *Übermensch*. Zarathustra's first speech begins: 'I teach you the *Übermensch*. Man is something that should be overcome' (Nietzsche 1883–5, §3). Unlike Christian saints with their sights set on another world, Nietzsche's *Übermensch* is a man of *this* world. He signifies the reestablishment of the self-creative, aristocratic values quashed by slave morality. He rejects all forms of weakness, including religion. By creating his own values he makes his own morality – the morality of a master, rather than that of a slave. Nietzsche (1888a, IX, 44; 1888b, p. 261) describes him as intrinsically valuable and explicitly contrasts the *Übermensch* as the embodiment of a type of supreme achievement with 'good men.' It is may be no accident that Roy Batty sarcastically applies that designation to Deckard and (with reference to killing Zhora and Pris) derisively asks him, 'Proud of yourself, little man?' Not without justification, Roy sees humans like Deckard as his inferior. He is so physically and mentally superior to the human beings that he fairly could be described as 'beyond-human.'

Drawing comparisons between Nietzsche's *Übermensch* and Roy Batty can illuminate additional aspects of *Blade Runner*.

Mulhall (1994, p. 95) notes that Nietzsche describes the *Übermensch* as one who dances through life, reveling in each moment while acknowledging its essential nature as transitory. This is just how Roy Batty approaches the final minutes of his life as he revels in his pursuit of Deckard. He is completely at home in his own element, enjoying and relishing every moment. Roy was designed as a combat model. To engage in a life and death struggle that pits his physical and mental attributes against a worthy opponent is to him the highest expression of his capacities, resulting in increased energy, excitement, and joy. This is evident as well when he briefly pauses in his pursuit of Deckard to feel the rain on his face. He is reveling in being alive. Walter Kaufmann (1974, p. 324) notes that, '*Amor fati*' [love of one's fate] is Nietzsche's 'formula for the greatness of a human being.... [T]he man who experiences this joy is the powerful man – and instead of relying on heavenly powers to redeem him, to give meaning to his life, and to justify the world, he gives meaning to his own life by achieving perfection and exulting in every moment.' In the last few minutes of his life, Batty comes close to achieving perfection in this sense by exulting in his physical and mental powers before they slip away.

In *Beyond Good and Evil*, Nietzsche writes, 'A man's maturity consists in having found again the seriousness one has as a child, at play' (Nietzsche 1886, §94). The waning moments of Roy's life become for him a joyful opportunity to play. After ramming his head through a tiled bathroom wall, Roy exhorts Deckard, 'You'd better get it up, or I'm gonna have to kill ya! Unless you're alive, you can't play, and if you don't play....' He does not finish the sentence, but its double meaning is clear. Unless Deckard agrees to play, Batty will kill him right then and there.[9] At a deeper level he is conveying that unless one approaches life with an attitude of play, one is not fully alive. Even those moments that involve pain and injury are occasions for joy.

The importance Roy places on approaching life as play is manifested in other ways as well. His accusation that Deckard's act of shooting at an unarmed opponent is 'unsportsmanlike' is just the first of several allusions to sport as they engage in a life-and-death struggle with one another. As his pursuit of Deckard begins in earnest, Roy lets loose a baleful wolf howl that reverberates through the building, signaling that the hunt is on. After Deckard hits him on the head with a metal pipe, Batty exhorts Deckard, 'Good, that's the spirit!' and then adds in a slightly bemused tone, 'That hurt. That was irrational. Not to mention, unsportsmanlike.' Mulhall (1994, p. 98) interprets Roy's behavior as 'a conjuration of the Nietzschean vision of revelry or play as the authentic mode of mortal existence: like Zarathustra's disciples, Roy is dancing on the edge of the abyss.'

Finally, the Nietzschean ideal of the individual who is a creator of values may be evident in the way that Roy Batty appropriates Christian symbols for his own non-Christian purposes. He drives a spike through his right hand to stave off his impending death, and then appears on the rooftop against a background of ventilation fans as rotating crosses. Later he becomes Deckard's savior by grasping him with his impaled hand. At the moment of his death, Roy releases a white dove, symbolic not only of his death of also of the Holy Spirit, thus completing his invocation of the Christian trinity of the Father (by addressing Tyrell as such), the Son (the mantle he assumes as he becomes Deckard's savior with his spiked hand), and the Holy Spirit. In each case, Roy mobilizes an important Christian symbol for his own non-Christian purposes. Mulhall (1994, p. 96) observes that, 'The Christian imagery which gradually collects around Roy in this sequence ... should thus be seen as part of a means of revealing the distance Roy has moved beyond the morality expressed in such symbols: they are available for him to use or discard as he sees fit, as tools for his own personal purposes.'[10]

A Nexus 6 *Übermensch*?

In Mulhall's (1994, p. 98) view, 'Roy's way of conducting his life-and-death duel with Deckard confirms his achievement of the status of Overman.' As we have seen, there are ample grounds for this identification. Yet it could be argued that Roy Batty is not quite the *self-disciplined* individual that Nietzsche envisions the *Übermensch* to be. The Overman is conceived by Nietzsche as both more passionate and more capable of controlling his passions than the slaves – indeed, the main difference between the old aristocrats and the new man would be a much higher degree of self-consciousness – the fruit of having passed through and overcome slave morality. Roy has extremely strong impulses, especially the impulse to live, but he has only partial control over his impulses. Having been denied 'more life,' he kills Tyrell in a fit of rage, and then kills Sebastian as well – a gratuitous act that serves no purpose.[11] Kaufmann (1974, p. 224) notes that, 'Nietzsche believed that a man without impulses could not do the good or create the beautiful any more than a castrated man could beget children. A man with strong impulses might be evil because he had not yet learned to sublimate his impulses, but if he should ever acquire self-control, he might achieve greatness.' We cannot know whether Roy would have achieved this greatness had he been granted more life. Consequently, at most we can conclude that Batty, if not exactly *the Übermensch*, is at least *übermenschlich*. The irony is that whereas Nietzsche conceives of the *Übermensch* as heralding the next phase of human moral evolution, Batty is not even considered *human* by the humans in the film, yet he still conveys something of what a Nietzschean vision of the beyond-man might look like.

'Is He Good?'

I have been suggesting that applying resources from Nietzsche's philosophy illuminates aspects of *Blade Runner* that might otherwise go unnoticed or simply remain puzzling. But how seriously should we take Nietzsche's philosophy in its own right? Presupposed in Nietzsche's meta-moral critique of Christian morality is the idea that moralities *themselves* can be subjected to moral evaluation, which in turn raises the question of where the values for this meta-moral evaluation of moralities are supposed to come from. Writing a meta-moral critique of a given morality, as Nietzsche aims to do, requires a privileged perspective from which to issue moral evaluation. It is not clear how this is possible given the philosophical resources at Nietzsche's disposal. On the one hand, any attempt to ground a critique of Christian morality or to endorse a return to a Homeric conception of morality in a metaphysical realm is, given Nietzsche's rejection of metaphysical justifications of morality, precluded in principle. On the other hand, why should one adopt a morality that does not have an objective metaphysical ground? Why, for instance, should one prefer the 'noble' morality that Nietzsche prefers to any other? Once one historicizes moralities, as Nietzsche attempts to do, it becomes difficult to recover an objective ground for values.

It can be argued in response that what we should prefer is not so much the values associated with any particular morality, but rather the transvaluation of values itself. Indeed, in Nietzsche's view the transvaluation of values itself represents the highest achievement of humanity. He thus appears to anticipate a time when the new aristocratic morality will be sufficiently internalized as a 'herd morality' that it, too, will need another transvaluation. It is not the achievement of a new moral view *per se* as much as the encouragement of a *process* of overcoming that Nietzsche takes as the character of a more fully human future – not some static set of values but the human capacity to overcome values and thus to create new worlds, new vistas, in a quasi-divine way.

But this raises serious performative problems for Nietzsche's view. Why should we consider the regular overcoming of values as itself worth valuing? On what ground? By what standard? Nietzsche can provide no objective standard for judging his preference as better. The best he can do is to describe it in such a way that we find it (aesthetically) appealing, too. The aristocratic morality he heralds assumes that there will always be a difference between the herd, which always follows, and the masters, who have the capacity to imagine, articulate, and persuade others to follow down new paths. But again, there is no ground, in Nietzsche's view, for the claim that the master/herd distinction and the preference for overcoming are really the best. Nietzsche prefers them, and hopes that we will, too. But any hope of grounding that preference in something more solid than personal preference is ultimately vain.

Conclusions

Michael Deely, *Blade Runner*'s producer, rightly observes that, 'The central problems in *Blade Runner* are essentially moral ones. Should the replicants kill to gain more life? Should Harrison Ford be killing them simply because they want to exist?' (Sammon 1996, p. 91).[12] These are excellent questions; variations on them are addressed elsewhere in this book. In this chapter we have considered the possibility that the film raises even deeper moral questions – not about whether any *particular* action is good, but more fundamentally about how we should understand what it might *mean* to judge someone or something as 'good' in the first place. Where do our notions of 'good' come from, anyway? Some commentators have suggested that *Blade Runner* addresses such questions by incorporating themes and images resonant with Nietzsche's critique of Christian morality and his endorsement of an alternative, life-affirming morality of nobility. As we have seen, there is substantial evidence in support of this suggestion, although it is also possible to push a 'Nietzschean reading' too far. The safest conclusion regarding this issue is that an understanding of Nietzsche's philosophy illuminates aspects of the film that might otherwise remain obscure, without thereby making *Blade Runner* a 'Nietzschean film' in all respects.[13]

We can perhaps learn as much from the failures of Nietzsche's project as from its successes. In his critique of Christian morality, Nietzsche takes for granted one of the key elements usually insisted upon by its advocates, namely, that in the absence of a God there can be no objective basis for preferring one set of values over another. He can give no argument for why one should prefer one set of values rather another apart from extolling them on aesthetic grounds. He thus teaches us that any attempt at an *ultimate* justification for morality necessarily already presupposes a set of values, and thus can never be truly ultimate. Nietzsche also provides a valuable service in calling us to examine the nature and source of our moralities, and to ask whether other, better moralities might be possible. Regardless of whether one finds Nietzsche's critique of Christian morality and his proposed alternative to it to be persuasive, it raises the important question of how one can motivate acceptance of a morality in the absence of an objective metaphysical ground for it, for example, in the will of a personal God who creates human beings and gives their lives a purpose. Examining issues related to *that* idea is our next task.

8 God

> 'It's not an easy thing to meet your maker.'
> (Roy Batty, to Eldon Tyrell)

Introduction

In a deleted scene, Rick Deckard visits Dave Holden, being kept alive in a life-support pod after his ill-fated interview of Leon, in order to pick up some clues that might help him to track down the replicants. His fellow blade runner's philosophical perspicacity startles Deckard:

Holden: Don't you see what they're after? Who they're looking for?
Deckard: What? Who?
Holden: God.
Deckard: God....

Meanwhile, Capt. Bryant and Gaff are eavesdropping on their conversation from another room:

Bryant: God?
Gaff: Metaphysics....
Bryant: It's pathetic, that's what it is. Two old blade runners trying to grapple with metaphysics. You gonna turn out like that, Gaff?
Gaff: I spit on metaphysics, sir.[1]

Gaff's dismissive attitude toward metaphysics notwithstanding, Holden is right on the mark. The replicants are on a quest is to confront *their* God, Dr Eldon Tyrell.[2] When Tyrell remarks to Batty that he is surprised that he did not find him sooner, Roy responds, 'It's not an easy thing to meet your maker.' That statement, of course, is true in more ways than one. As his creature, Roy has pointed questions for his creator about why he was made the way he was, and why he was not made differently. Implicit in his questions is Tyrell's ultimate moral responsibility as his creator.

Part of what makes *Blade Runner*'s treatment of the creature–creator relationship so potent is the ways that it draws upon and reconfigures classic literary treatments of this issue going back at least four centuries, including those of John Milton's seventeenth-century epic poem, *Paradise Lost* (1667), William Blake's eighteenth-century allegorical poem, 'America: A Prophecy' (1793), and Mary Shelley's nineteenth-century Gothic novel, *Frankenstein* (1818). Comparing *Blade Runner*'s treatment of the creature–creator relationship to these earlier treatments shines a brighter light on the film. In keeping with the philosophical focus of this book, however, we also need to consider not just how others *have* thought about these issues, but also how we *might* and perhaps even *ought* to think about them. How is creaturely rebellion possible in the first place? What might make such rebellion admirable? Jean-Paul Sartre's existentialism will once again supply rich philosophical resources for addressing these issues. Our concern in this chapter is not with the existence or non-existence of God, but rather with exploring the implications of thinking of oneself as having a creator and therefore of *being made*. Ultimately, what is at stake is the degree to which we can and should think of ourselves as capable of, and responsible for, *self-creation*.

'Fiery the Angels Fell'

Upon entering the Eye Works, Roy Batty informs a very startled Chew, 'Fiery the angels fell. Deep thunder rolled around their shores, burning with the fires of Orc.'[3] The words echo those in 'America: A Prophecy' (1793), an allegorical poem by William

Blake (1757–1827) that celebrates the struggle for personal freedom and independence using the American Revolution as its centerpiece. Roy's version, however, is intriguingly different from the original. In Blake's poem,

> Fiery the Angels rose, & as they rose deep thunder roll'd Around their shores: indignant burning with the fires of Orc....
> Down on the land of America, indignant they descended. Headlong from out their heav'nly heights, descending swift as fires....
> In flames as of a furnace on the land from North to South.

Blake tells us (twice) that the angels *rose*. In Roy Batty's version the angels *fell*. But like Blake's angels, the replicants too have descended from the heavenly heights (the Off-world colonies where they rose up against the indignity of enslavement) down on the land of America. One need only recall the opening scene of *Blade Runner* with its smokestacks belching fire and smoke to note the unmistakable thematic connection with the last line above.

There are other striking poem–film connections as well. In Blake's poem, Orc represents the spirit of freedom. He leads the revolt against tyrannical oppression, and is described as a

> Blasphemous Demon, Antichrist, hater of Dignities;
> Lover of wild rebellion, and transgressor of God's Law.

Roy Batty also transgresses *his* God's law by illegally trespassing on earth, blasphemously cursing his creator, and (if the analysis of the previous chapter is sound) co-opting Christian symbolism for his own anti-Christian purposes. In addition, when we read in Blake's poem,

> Loud howls the eternal Wolf! ... and my punishing Demons terrified.

it is hard not to be reminded of Batty's baleful wolf howl in his pursuit of Deckard, the demon that has already punished two of his close comrades, and the latter's evident terror in hearing it.

Blake's poem was first published with eighteen of his own original illustrations. One, titled 'A Breach in a City,' conveys the idea that rebellion is a natural struggle for freedom against oppression – an apt description of the replicants' Off-world rebellion and breach of Los Angeles.

'Rebel Angels from th' Ethereal Skie'

The main story arc of *Paradise Lost* (1667), by John Milton (1608–1674), begins after Satan and four other rebel angels have been banished to hell for waging an unsuccessful war in heaven against God and his obedient angels. Satan is presented as the most beautiful of all the angelic beings, but also as deeply arrogant, powerful, cunning, persuasive, deceptive, and charismatic. He is driven by the conviction that he ought to be regarded as equal to God. He is cast down to hell because of his unwillingness to be subservient to his creator. Of Satan we learn that,

> Of Rebel Angels, by whose aid aspiring
> To set himself in Glory above his Peers,
> He trusted to have equal'd the most High,
> If he oppos'd; and with ambitious aim
> Against the Throne and Monarchy of God
> Rais'd impious War in Heav'n and Battel proud
> With vain attempt. Him the Almighty Power
> Hurld headlong flaming from th' Ethereal Skie
> (Book I, lines 38–45)

Just as Satan and his rebel angels, 'Rais'd impious War in Heav'n and Battel proud,' before shifting their 'Battel' to earth (the realm of men), Roy Batty (a play on 'Battel'?) and his rebel replicants kill a shuttle crew in deep space before continuing their rampage on earth in an attempt to wrest from their creator a status equal to his own. But whereas Milton's rebel angels are 'Hurld headlong flaming from th' Ethereal Skie,' the place where immortal angels dwell, *Blade Runner*'s rebel angels hurl themselves into a flaming the City of Angels in *search* of immortality.

Consider as well Milton's description of hell:

> A Dungeon horrible, on all sides round
> As one great Furnace flam'd, yet from those flames
> No light, but rather darkness visible
> Serv'd only to discover sights of woe,
> Regions of sorrow, doleful shades, where peace
> And rest never dwell, hope never comes
> That comes to all; but torture without end
> Still urges, and a fiery Deluge, fed
> With ever-burning Sulphur unconsumed
> (Book I, lines 61–9)

With its fire-belching smokestacks, unrelenting darkness, incessant rain, fume-venting streets, and seething masses, Los Angeles 2019 is a striking facsimile of Milton's description of hell.[4]

The similarities between Satan and Roy are also striking. Both are charismatic and rhetorically gifted leaders that embrace adversarial roles in relation to their oppressors.[5] The association of Roy with Satan is further enhanced by their mutual association with light. The Gospel of Luke (10:18–19) tells us that Satan fell 'like lightning from the sky.' Satan is also known as Lucifer ('light-bearer'). Roy is likewise associated with light, a point Tyrell explicitly acknowledges when he effuses, 'The light that burns twice as bright burns half as long. And you have burned so very, very brightly, Roy!' Finally, Satan's and Roy's efforts to achieve a status equal to their creators each ultimately proves to be a 'vain attempt.' Having failed to achieve his goal of equality with his creator, Roy, like Satan, then becomes the implacable adversary of (a) man.[6]

'I Ought to be Thy Adam'

Blade Runner also conforms to the general 'arrogant scientist makes creature, creature goes berserk, justice is done to the scientist by the hands of his own creature' theme that has become a staple of science fiction since its debut in Mary Shelley's gothic novel, *Frankenstein; or, the Modern Prometheus* (1818). The specific parallels between the book and the film are numerous. Eldon Tyrell is the counterpart to Victor Frankenstein.[7] Both Frankenstein and Tyrell treat their creations cruelly – Frankenstein because he is disgusted by what he has created, and Tyrell because for him his creations are simply commercial products. Both works focus on 'the struggle with human facsimiles' (Strick 1982, p. 168) – that is, with creatures that are fascinating because they are human-like but, in the view of their creators and others, not quite human. Frankenstein creates a human-like monster (it is never given a name) from various human (and perhaps non-human) body parts stitched together. Tyrell creates replicants from body parts grown in various specialized labs like Chew's Eye Works. Both creatures are *synthetic humans*.

Like Frankenstein's monster, the replicants lack personal histories and are more concerned with the future than with the past. In both stories the creature finds itself forced to live apart from human society, either because of its hideous appearance or because it has been marked out for retirement. Both are emotionally vulnerable, abandoned in a hostile world, and existentially alone. Frankenstein's monster is physically powerful, intelligent and, thanks to considerable time spent reading and observing human beings, knowledgeable and articulate. Tyrell's Nexus 6 replicants are 'superior in strength and agility, and at least equal in intelligence, to the genetic engineers who created them.' Judging from his ability to creatively rework poetry as well as his detailed grasp of biochemistry, Roy Batty is also highly knowledgeable.

Both creatures deliver lyrical farewells. Before casting himself onto an ice raft in the Arctic, Frankenstein's monster's last

God

words are: 'I shall no longer see the sun or stars, or feel the winds play on my cheeks. Light, feeling, and sense, will pass away ... I shall die, and what I now feel be no longer felt.... My spirit will sleep in peace, or if it thinks, it will not surely think thus. Farewell' (Shelley 1818, p. 205). Moments before his death, Roy Batty laments his imminent extinction: 'I've seen things you people wouldn't believe.... All those moments will be lost in time, like tears in rain. Time to die.' But whereas Frankenstein's monster's anticipation of peace is merely a wish, Roy Batty achieves that peace with his release of a dove into the overcast sky.

Frankenstein and Tyrell both make synthetic humans that are tragically flawed, either in beauty or in longevity. Their creatures petition them to compensate for or to correct their perceived flaws. Frankenstein's monster demands a female companion as hideous as himself who therefore will not (he supposes) judge him for his own hideousness. Roy Batty feels short-changed by his creator because he has a less-than-human life span. The monster pursues and eventually finds Frankenstein atop an enormous glacier. Roy Batty confronts Tyrell atop his enormous neo-Mayan pyramid. After Frankenstein destroys the female companion he was creating, the monster vows to enact revenge on him. After Deckard (representing his human creators more generally) kills Roy's female companions, Roy enacts revenge by breaking Deckard's fingers.

In both stories the creatures are compared to, or are, slaves driven by desperation to turn on their human masters, Both enact a reversal of roles to convey to their oppressors a sense of what it feels like to be a slave. Frankenstein's monster commands his maker, 'Slave ... Remember that I have power ... You are my creator, but I am your master; obey!' (Shelley 1818, p. 152). When Batty gazes down at Deckard, clinging tenuously to a protruding girder, he triumphantly taunts him: 'Quite an experience to live in fear, isn't it? That's what it is to be a slave.'

Finally, both stories encourage us to sympathize with their *creatures* and to view their acts of rebellion as admirable and perhaps even justified. This raises further interesting questions. How is such creaturely rebellion possible in the first place? How does a creature acquire the ability to rebel against its maker? What might make such rebellion admirable or even justified? The existentialist philosophy of Jean-Paul Sartre provides resources useful for exploring these questions in more depth. To make use of these resources, however, we first need to understand his account of 'human reality.'

'Man is Nothing Else but What He Makes of Himself'

In describing what he calls 'human reality,' Sartre makes a fundamental distinction between *human beings* and *artifacts*. An artifact is any object made for a specific purpose. Its existence begins with a concept in the mind of an artisan. This concept is the artifact's *essence* – that is, what it essentially *is*. The artisan then makes the object according to the essence he has in mind. For example, a paper-cutter begins as an idea in the mind of an artisan who then makes it according to his idea. Once it is made, nothing can change its essence. Sartre (1946, p. 14) expresses this idea by saying that, 'for the paper-cutter, essence … precedes existence. Thus, the presence of the paper-cutter … is determined.' Sartre thinks that this is how *human beings* are viewed in theistic religions.[8] To think of God as 'the Creator' is to think of him as a superior artisan. According to this theistic religious conception, he thinks, 'God produces man, just as the artisan, following a definition and a technique, makes a paper-cutter. Thus, the individual man is the realization of a certain concept in the divine intelligence' (p. 14).

Sartre completely rejects this conception of human beings. In his view, artifacts and humans are two entirely different sorts of beings. The crucial issue is the presence or absence of *freedom*. If human beings are designed and created for a specific purpose, preconceived in the mind of a Creator, then their nature is determined in advance and they lack the freedom needed to continuously create themselves through their choices. Clearly, however, we *can* choose ourselves. The theistic view of human nature must be rejected, therefore, and the relationship between essence and existence characteristic of artifacts must be reversed. As Sartre explains, 'Atheistic existentialism ... states that if God does not exist, there is at least one being in whom existence precedes essence, a being who exists before he can be defined by any concept, and that this being is man, or ... human reality' (p. 15). In his view, 'there is no human nature, since there is no God to conceive it. Not only is man what he conceives himself to be, but he is also only what he wills himself to be after this thrust toward existence. Man is nothing else but what he makes of himself. Such is the first principle of existentialism' (p. 15).

'You Were Made as Well as We Could Make You'

Sartre's primary concern is to elaborate the implications of atheistic existentialism for 'human reality.' But his account nonetheless has implications for our understanding of the replicants. Like Sartre's paper-cutter, the replicants are artifacts made with specific attributes intended to make them well-suited for performing their specialized Off-world tasks. Indeed, Tyrell even boasts that the replicants were made as well as they could be made. Leon has the great strength and modest intelligence necessary to be a nuclear loader. Zhora has the mental and physical agility required to be an effective member of 'an Off-world kick-murder squad' specializing in political homicide. Pris has the attractive appearance and seduction skills befitting her job as 'a basic pleasure model – the standard item for military clubs in the outer colonies.' Roy Batty has the superb intelligence, athleticism, resourcefulness, and 'optimum self-sufficiency' of a combat model designed for the Colonization Defense Program. The replicants' purposes are made are determined for them before they are created. In Sartrean terms, the replicants' essence precedes their existence.[9] Hence, the replicants' essence as slaves is as inescapable for them as is the paper-cutter's essence as a tool for cutting paper. Sartre's analysis also places the replicants in an entirely different category than that of human beings whose existence precedes their essence, and hence who are free to create their own essence through their choices.

Despite the initial plausibility of this Sartrean analysis, three aspects of it should at least give us pause. First, it presupposes that whereas the replicants have a creator, human beings do not. If human beings *are* the products of a Creator, however, then we too are artifacts and the distinction between human beings and artifacts collapses. Of course, Sartre has reasons for rejecting the existence of such a Creator. He thinks that because human beings have radical freedom, and such freedom is incompatible with being made by a God, it follows that there is no God. The claim that humans have radical freedom is critically examined in the previous chapter where some of the problems with that notion are identified. The assumption that being created is incompatible with being free is at least equally problematic. The notion of God as understood in Judaism, Christianity, and Islam does not necessarily preclude the creation of free human beings. All teach that God creates human beings 'in God's image,' that is, as intelligent, free, and capable of love. There may or may not be such a God, but the key issue here is that the notion of creation operative in these religions is far from the idea of an artisan designing an artifact whose 'presence ... is determined.'

Second, without knowing *anything* except that they are manufactured beings, Sartre is committed to denying that the replicants could have anything like the sort of freedom possessed by human beings. This conclusion follows directly from the fact that they are *artifacts* conjoined with his claim that artifacts *necessarily* lack the freedom characteristic of human reality. The facts that the replicants are in almost all other respects virtually indistinguishable from human beings, and that it requires a sophisticated test to distinguish them from human beings, are apparently irrelevant. It would be natural to wonder, however, whether such a deductive *a priori* method is a reliable guide to the truth in matters that seem to depend on ascertaining facts about actual capacities.

Third, despite being artifacts, it seems clear that the replicants are able to reject the specific purposes for which they were made and to choose their own – at least to the same extent that human beings can. Deckard left behind his former life as a blade runner because he'd had 'a bellyful of killing.' Yet he is easily pressed back into service by Bryant, and seems trapped by the identity others have assigned to him. Apart from his reluctance to retire Rachael, Deckard demonstrates little inclination to reject the purposes others have chosen for him. By contrast, we never encounter the replicants when they are *not* rejecting the purposes for which they were created. How can Sartre accommodate these facts?

Of course, Sartre is concerned with understanding 'human reality,' not with robots, androids, cyborgs, clones, replicants, or other exotica of science fiction. His aim is to wake people up to their inescapable freedom and to make them realize that they must take full responsibility for their choices and their lives. His distinction between human beings and artifacts is accordingly intended to highlight an important difference between (human) beings that can choose their own purposes and mere 'things' that cannot.[10] Nonetheless, the mere *possibility* of beings such as the replicants poses a serious problem for his analysis. If *synthetic humans* that enjoy freedom comparable to that of human beings are even *possible*, then his fundamental distinction between human beings (whose existence necessarily precedes their essence), and artifacts (whose essence necessarily precedes their existence) is in danger of collapsing. Sartre, it seems, is wrong about human beings, wrong about artifacts, or wrong about both.

One response would be to reject the claim that artifacts are *necessarily* incapable of choosing their own purposes. Obviously, *some* artifacts, for example, paper-cutters, staplers, and can-openers, are incapable of choosing their own purposes. But this hardly seems true, much less *necessarily* true, of more complex artifacts that possess self-awareness and some degree of autonomy. What matters is *what one can do*, not *how one came to be*. The irrelevance of *having been made* can be seen by recognizing that it is *possible* that human beings *have* been made by a God and hence that we, too, *are* artifacts. Yet were this possibility to be actual it would make no difference to our ability to choose the purposes we will embrace and pursue. We could even choose purposes that do not coincide with any purposes a God might intend for us. Not only is this possibility countenanced by much traditional religious belief, it is taken granted by it (for example, by the concept of *sin*). By the same token, we know that the replicants were created by an intelligent being to serve specific purposes. As such, their purposes are assigned to them prior to their existence. But because they are conscious beings that are aware of themselves as agents with their own interests, they have the ability to reject the purposes for which they were made and to embrace purposes of their own choosing. It follows that *being made* (or not) is not decisive for a being's ability to choose its own purposes.

A second response would be to question the identification of a thing's *essence* with its *purpose*. In Sartre's view, if an object is created to serve a specific purpose, that purpose just *is* that object's essence. Because essences as such are *unchanging*, it follows that nothing could ever change an artifact's purpose. Once an artifact has been created its purpose is necessarily forever fixed. But this is false even for simple artifacts like paper-cutters which can be used for many other purposes besides opening envelopes – for example, for buttering toast, as a tool for drawing straight lines, and as a weapon. Its essence as a paper-cutter does not preclude it from being re-purposed for other tasks. It is therefore important to distinguish between a thing's essence and its purpose. An *essence* in this context refers to the sort of thing a thing most basically is. A 'circle' is a two-dimensional closed figure all the points of which are equidistant from a central point. That is just what a circle *is*.

A *purpose*, by contrast, is either the function for which something was initially created, *or* the goal that guides its continuing existence. A circular shape can be used for any number of purposes – to draw a peace sign, to represent the Chinese concept of yin/yang, to practice calligraphy, and so on. A circle's essence determines its basic characteristics but leaves entirely open the purposes for which such a shape might be used.

If this is true for objects such as paper-cutters and circles, it should be no less true for beings that possess self-awareness and some degree of personal autonomy. The replicants were created to be slaves; there is nothing anyone can do to change this fact about their creation. But purposes of this sort can be rejected, modified, or replaced, by others or by themselves. (We know that Zhora was re-trained from 'hot pleasure model' to 'political assassination.') Having been made to be slaves is no doubt an impediment to the replicants' self-determination. It need not be an insuperable obstacle. Of course, such a view does not entail that a replicant or a human being can become *anything* it chooses to be. A replicant cannot cease being a replicant any more than a paper-cutter can cease being a paper-cutter, or a human being (while remaining alive) can cease being human. In this sense a human being, a replicant, and a paper-cutter are all on a par. What differentiates the replicant and the human, on the one hand, from the paper-cutter, on the other, is that the former can accept or reject the purposes (if any) for which they were made and can embrace new purposes of their own. By refusing to live as the slaves they were created to be, the replicants demonstrate that being an artifact is not incompatible with meaningful self-determination.

'Man is the Being Whose Project is to be God'

Creaturely rebellion is sometimes possible because some creatures are created such that they are capable of conceiving of purposes for themselves other than those for which they were designed. What makes creaturely rebellion admirable is the same thing that makes a creator's creative acts admirable, namely, the freedom to direct oneself according to one's own freely chosen ideals. The latter claim, at least, is how Sartre understands the fundamental nature of *human* reality. Human freedom, in Sartre's view, follows from the fact that there is *no human nature* to determine our existence: 'If existence really does precede essence, there is no ... fixed and given human nature' (Sartre 1946, pp. 22–3). There is no human nature because there is no *God* to create human beings according to a preconceived idea of what they should be. Therefore, we cannot turn either to a God or to human nature to discover *objective commands or values* to legitimize our choices: 'all possibility of finding values in a heaven of ideas disappears along with Him; there can no longer be an *a priori* Good, since there is no infinite and perfect consciousness to think it' (p. 22).

With no human nature or God to provide objective values by which to guide our lives, we are forced to take on the role of God ourselves. Indeed, Sartre says, 'The best way to conceive of the fundamental project of human reality is to say that man is the being whose project is to be God' (p. 63). 'Being God' in this sense might seem like an unqualified good, but it imposes a heavy cost. Being unable to rely upon any external source of values, we must invent our own: 'We are alone.... man, with no support and no aid, is condemned every moment to invent man' (p. 23). Sartre takes this notion of being 'condemned' quite seriously: 'Man is condemned to be free. Condemned, because he did not create himself, yet ... responsible for everything he does' (p. 23). Yet such freedom presents possibilities for self-creation that would otherwise be impossible.

Sartre thinks that he can say with confidence that there is no God. We might not be so confident. One of the enviable advantages the replicants have over human beings is that they can *know* with complete certainty that their God exists (or that he existed). They can even know where to find him and, with a little deception, manipulation, and luck, they can meet with him to demand a personal accounting for his creative decisions.

God

This is the proximate purpose of their quest. But the ultimate purpose of their quest is to acquire a status equal to that of their God. In this sense, their quest is to become (like) God. Tyrell, however, refuses (or is unable) to alter what he takes to be their essential nature as slaves with a predetermined life span – a nature that he himself created. Realizing that the quest to become like his God is doomed to failure, Roy kills Tyrell. By doing so, he *symbolically* negates his status as an artifact with a predetermined purpose.

Roy's failure to achieve the replicants' ultimate goal paves the way for the achievement of an even greater accomplishment made possible by making it clear that he must now freely choose his own values, purposes, and actions. Initially this newfound freedom engenders a profound sense of abandonment and disorientation, as evidenced by the confusion transfiguring his face as he descends the Tyrell Corporation pyramid.[11] Alone and abandoned, he now has to make his own way without any guarantees. No longer laboring under the illusion that if only he had 'more life' his most important problems would be solved, he comes to understand that the amount of life he has left is sufficient – if he makes good use of it. Rather than focusing on what is no longer in his power, his attention shifts to those things that are still within his control. Liberated from the possibility of gaining *more* life from his creator, he finally becomes free to revel in his time.

Conclusions

In his play, *The Flies*, Sartre writes: 'Once freedom has exploded in the soul of man, the gods no longer have any power over him.' Roy's experience suggests that the converse may be true as well. Once his God no longer has any power over him, his soul explodes with freedom. His final minutes of life are infused with the joy of self-expression. He spends the final minutes of his life expressing the physical and mental attributes of a combat model. This description might suggest that Roy is merely executing his programming and hence has reverted to his status as an artifact whose purposes are determined by his creator. But not only would this interpretation fail to take into account the evident *joy* with which he pursues Deckard, it would also fail to explain how he is able to act against that programming. He arrives at the Bradbury building too late to share his newfound wisdom with Pris, who moments before had been killed by Deckard. But he can still express his newfound understanding by manifesting it concretely in his actions, and attempting to convey something of his discovery to Deckard. One might have expected that he would kill Deckard or at least let him die. Instead, he uses the situation as an opportunity to impart a lesson to his adversary. As Judith Barad (2009, p. 32) notes, 'At last, he has freely chosen his essence by choosing to be a life giver rather than the life-taking combat model he was programmed to be.' In that moment his freedom and autonomy are complete. Rather than killing Deckard or letting Deckard die, he saves him, showing that even in the waning moments of his life he is still free to act against his 'essence.' The fact that he still has a choice makes all the difference. This is a lesson that Deckard appears to have learned, because he subsequently acts against his own programming to spirit Rachael away so that Gaff or another blade runner cannot kill her. An artifact has taught a human being how to create himself and to be free.

9 Death

> 'What seems to be the problem?'
>
> (Eldon Tyrell, to Roy Batty)

Introduction

The replicants consider death to be the most important problem they face – even greater than their slavery in the Off-world colonies. Their dangerous and difficult quest to meet their creator makes no sense without this belief. Although there are many previous hints in the film, this fact is finally made explicit in the tense scene in which Roy Batty finally confronts Tyrell:

Tyrell: What ... What seems to be the problem?
Roy: Death.
Tyrell: Death. Well, I'm afraid that's a little out of my jurisdiction, you ...
Roy: *I want more life*, father!
Tyrell: ... you were made as well as we could make you.
Roy: But not to last.

Batty and Tyrell share the belief that death is a *serious problem*. They are in good company. Most people dread death and go to great lengths to postpone it for as long as possible. But *why*, exactly, should death thought of as a problem? Death is unquestionably often bad for people *other than* the person who dies, for example, for loved ones. Hence, often it makes sense to do one's best to postpone one's own death as long as possible for *others'* sakes. But how can the replicants be harmed by their own deaths? How can *anyone* be harmed by one's own death? What does one really gain by having a few more years added to one's life? These might seem like ridiculous questions. After all, if *death* does not count as harming the one who dies, what could? Besides, if some life is good, then more must be better, right? The fact that such beliefs are so seldom questioned is itself a good reason to examine them more closely, but such an examination is especially important for understanding the replicants' desperate quest. My aim in this chapter is thus to examine the replicants' belief that death is a problem. As we will see, this belief is on shakier ground than is often supposed. Perhaps it is not even true – *not* because one can expect a beatific afterlife, but just because in an important sense, *death is nothing*.[1]

'Can the Maker Repair What He Makes?'

Before examining philosophical responses to the problem of death, it is worthwhile trying to disambiguate the problem that Roy lays at the feet of his creator, because getting a clearer understanding of the problem is essential to assessing proposed solutions to it. Roy's specific complaint – that he was made 'not to last' – lends itself to two interpretations. On the one hand, his complaint might be that he was *made not to last*, that is, that he was *designed to expire* after just four years. Accordingly, he is upset because he has *a predetermined life span* and wants the mechanism responsible for that limit to be disabled. Having that mechanism disabled would not *guarantee* him any specific additional number of years, but it might at least allow him to have a life span on a par with that of human beings. On the other hand, Roy's complaint might be that he was *not made to last*, that is, that he was not made such that he could reasonably expect to live longer than just four years. In this case he would be complaining about his *poor design* rather than (as in the former case) about his *unfair design*.[2] A better design presumably would be one that permits him to live much longer than the meager four years that his current body can last.

Roy might insist that both limitations are problems. It might be a problem to have a predetermined life span because no one else, not even one's creator, should be in a position to decide how long one will live, even if that turns out to be very long indeed. Batty's demand for 'more life' suggests at least that this was not his *primary* concern. Rather, he is upset because he was made such that his life will run out prematurely. That is, he is deeply upset because he believes that his life will run before it *should*. But this raises further questions. What sort of modification would satisfy his demand for 'more life'? How long 'should' he live? It seems unlikely that he would be satisfied with a mere *doubling* of his expected life span. There is nothing special about having a four-year life span, so doubling that to eight years seems equally arbitrary. The same would be true of a *tenfold* increase in his expected life span to forty years, or indeed any other similar increase.

It might be supposed that the only truly *non-arbitrary life span* would be one equivalent to that of *the average human being*. Many commentators assume that this is what Roy wants.[3] Perhaps he does. But a little reflection makes clear that this standard is no less arbitrary. Some organisms tend to live fewer years than the average human being; others tend to live more years. Individual human being's lives vary tremendously from less than a minute to over a century. The fact that human beings tend *on average* to live a certain number of years is a function of our evolutionary history and whatever cultural advances we have so far managed to achieve. Both could be, and historically have been, otherwise. Some have even suggested that given continued advances in medicine of the sort that we have seen in the last hundred years, it may someday seem like a profound disability to not be able to run an ultra-marathon at the age of 500 (Harris 2010).

If *death* really is a problem, the only solution to *that* problem is to never die, and hence the only *truly* non-arbitrary life span is one that *has no end*. Roy is thus not exaggerating when he says that what he has in mind is 'a little more radical' than mere modification. It is no wonder that Tyrell, despite his considerable intelligence (and arrogance), considers solving *that* problem to be a little out of his jurisdiction. Philosophers, too, are in no position to solve Roy's problem in the way that he *desires*. They cannot confer immortality. But they offer other solutions to the problem of death which, if sound, might provide just the solution that Roy actually *needs*.

'I'm Afraid That's a Little Out of My Jurisdiction'

Arguments that one ought not to consider death bad or to fear it go back at least to Socrates (469–399 BCE). Facing execution stemming from charges of corrupting the youth of Athens and denying the gods of the city, Socrates offers a stunningly simple argument that no one should fear death or consider it an evil: 'To fear death is to think oneself wise when one is not, and to think that one knows what one does not know' (Plato 2000, p. 32). People generally fear death as if they knew it to be the greatest of evils. But for all anyone knows, it might be the greatest of blessings. We simply do not know. Like Tyrell denying any authority to speak to this ultimate issue, Socrates can be interpreted as reminding us that pronouncing on what comes after death is just a little out of his cognitive jurisdiction, and ours.

Apparently forgetting this plea for intellectual humility, Socrates then offers a second argument that takes for granted the truth of a premise that was entertained merely as a possibility in the first one, namely, that death might be the greatest of blessings. Death, he argues, is one of two things: 'Either the dead are nothing and have no perception of anything, or it is ... a change and a relocating for the soul from here to another place' (Plato 2000, p. 41). In the former case, being dead entails a complete lack of perception, 'like a dreamless sleep.' Who wouldn't look forward to restful slumber like that? In the latter case, death means entering a pleasant afterlife. That would be an even greater blessing inasmuch as one could then spend eternity in the company of great men of ages past. In light of these two possibilities, Socrates confidently concludes that, 'a good man cannot be harmed either in life or in death' (Plato 2000, p. 42).

Setting aside the question of whether a good man can be harmed in this *life*, the argument implies that the two post-mortem fates mentioned – total unconsciousness or hob-knobbing with great men of ages past – exhaust the range of possible fates that could befall one after death. It ignores the unpleasant prospect that one might find oneself spending eternity in the company of really annoying people, or worse. Presumably Socrates dismisses those possibilities because, being a good man himself, the gods would be sure to treat *him* well in the afterworld. Perhaps, but then the argument ceases to be generally applicable insofar as few of us can be equally confident that our own good qualities will be viewed by the gods in a comparably appreciative way. The argument also overlooks the fact that the 'dreamless sleep' Socrates extols is one from which one never awakens. What that state really amounts to is the total extinction of one's consciousness. Such a state cannot be experienced as *pleasant*. In fact, it cannot be experienced at all.

'How Long Do I Live?'

According to Epicurus (341–270 BCE), Socrates was right to deny that death harms the person whose death it is – not because one can look forward to pleasant experiences in an afterlife, but rather because by no longer existing one will no longer be in a state in which one can suffer any harm. As a materialist, he held that we *are* our bodies. Our souls, if they exist at all, are material as well. Hence, when one's body dies one ceases to exist. Being dead is not a state that anyone will, or can, experience.[4] One is either alive or one is dead. If one is alive, then (obviously) one has not been harmed by death. If one is dead, then one no longer exists (and hence can suffer no harm). Therefore, whether one is alive or dead, one cannot be harmed by death. There is no reason to fear that which cannot harm one. Consequently, there is no reason to fear death.

Epicurus' argument depends on a number of presuppositions, including: *materialism* (all that exists is material, so death entails personal annihilation); *egoistic hedonism* (one's own pleasure is the only intrinsic good, and one's own pain is the only intrinsic evil); *experientialism* (only that which can be *experienced* by an individual can be good or evil for that individual); and *non-deprivationism* (if one cannot be harmed in *being dead*, one also cannot be harmed by *becoming dead*). Materialism and egoistic hedonism are controversial philosophical views; a critical examination of them would take us too far afield. We can assume their truth for the sake of argument and focus here on a critical evaluation of experientialism and non-deprivationism.

Critics of experientialism think that it is relatively easy to imagine situations in which one might be harmed despite having no experience of being harmed. I can be harmed by malicious slander that prevents me from getting a desired promotion at work even if I remain completely unaware of this slander or its effect on my career. An individual may be harmed by being exposed to a radioactive substance despite being completely unaware of the cause of his mysteriously declining health. In response, the defender of experientialism can point out that in such cases the person is harmed only if they *experience* in some way a negative consequence of the events in question. Being slandered behind my back only harms me if it contributes to events that *do* involve a painful experience – for example, the emotional pain I feel in being passed over for a promotion. Being exposed to radioactivity only harms one if unpleasant health problems result. Such events have to culminate in unpleasant or painful *experiences* for them to constitute harm.[5]

Consequently, critics of experientialism have to show that it is possible to be harmed by death even if one does not and indeed cannot experience any of its harmful effects. They attempt to do this by challenging non-deprivationism. They argue that death harms one by depriving one of knowing, doing, and experiencing all the things that one *could* know, do,

Death

and experience were one to continue living. Marilyn Gwaltney (1997, p. 36) expresses this deprivationist perspective with regard to *Blade Runner* when she writes:

> The genius of the movie ... is that it makes us feel the pain Roy Batty feels when faced with the knowledge of his approaching death in conjunction with his consciousness of his potentiality for knowledge and accomplishment. We are aware with him of all the valuable things he will never know or do. This is the same pain we feel when confronted with the death of a child or adolescent: it is a profound sense of loss of potentiality.

Thus, death harms Roy by depriving him of his potentiality for additional knowledge and accomplishments. That may sound plausible enough. The problem, however, is that *potentialities are promiscuous*. There are indefinitely many things that Roy *could* in principle know, do, or experience by living longer; yet the vast majority of these are not things that he would *in fact* come to know, do, or experience even if he *did* live longer. If Tyrell had been able and willing to grant Roy's request for more life, he could have gone on to become a professional flower arranger, perhaps creating beautiful floral arrangements for Deckard and Rachael's wedding, for Tyrell Corporation Christmas parties, and so on. His death precluded this blossomy career trajectory from efflorescing. Yet it is difficult to see how he is *harmed* by being deprived of this and by indefinitely many other *possible* experiences. How can one be harmed by being deprived of an experience one would never have no matter how long one lives?

In response, critics can argue that death harms one by depriving one of the valuable knowledge, worthwhile actions, and positive experiences that one *would* have had were one to not die when one does. In this view, death does not harm Roy by preventing him from becoming a florist, a ladies' handbag designer, or the proprietor of a petting zoo, but it does harm him by preventing him from doing any number of other things that he *would* have gone on to do were he to not die when he does. The problem with this suggestion, however, is that it is impossible to specify in advance in anything but the most general terms what these possibilities would be.[6] Given a full pardon and assured of a longer life, Roy might have chosen to pursue any number of activities and experiences that not even he could have imagined. If one continues to live, necessarily there will be additional knowledge, actions, and experiences of *some* sort. But, for all one knows, they might be additions that make a longer life miserable and even one which is not worth living at all.

The critic of non-deprivationism need not concede defeat. She can argue that even if it is difficult to identify the specific experiences one is deprived of by one's death, nonetheless we can be sure that death deprives one of *some* positive experiences. If the act of making choices is valuable, then by becoming dead one is harmed by losing the ability to choose with respect to *any* of the positive experiences that would become available in the future. (As Rachael reminds us, 'The great advantage to being alive is having a choice.')[7] But even if one supposes that death harms Roy by cutting off the possibility of him choosing which experiences to pursue, it is still not evident that he is thereby harmed. For all anyone knows, the life Roy would have were he to live longer might be one in which intense suffering exceeds any fleeting moments of joy, making a longer life one which, by his own lights, is worse than death.

Common to the foregoing critiques of non-deprivationism is the idea that one can be harmed by losing something that does not now and never will exist. Death harms one because *it robs one of one's future*. But this idea generates its own puzzles. By definition, the future does not now exist. That claim is equally true for every 'now' there has ever been and ever will be. In what sense, then, can one really be said to *lose* something – a future – that does not now and never will exist?

Mark Rowlands attempts to solve this puzzle by arguing that there is a sense in which one's future *does* exist now, thus making it the *sort* of thing that one *could* lose. Using terminology from the philosopher Martin Heidegger (1889–1976), he characterizes a human being as a *being-towards-a-future* and writes that 'a person has a future, in a minimal sense, if he or she possesses certain *future-directed states*' (Rowlands 2003, p. 247). If one merely has desires one has a future in a weak, non-conceptual sense. But if in addition to desires one has explicit goals and projects that one *conceives of* as being realized in the future, one has a future in a strong, conceptual sense. Rowlands' specific claim is that, 'The more you have invested in the future, judged in terms of the organization, orientation, disciplining and regimentation of your present behavior and desires, then the more you lose when you lose that future.... This, and only this, is why death can harm us when we are no longer around to be harmed' (p. 254).

This is a valiant attempt to make sense of how one can be robbed of a future that does not exist. Unfortunately, this argument faces at least three serious criticisms. First, it is far from obvious that the more one has invested in the future, judged in terms of the organization, orientation, disciplining and regimentation of one's present behavior and desires, the more one loses when one dies. Consider a 94-year-old woman fully invested in the future in all these ways, and a 2-year-old toddler with no investment in the future of that sort whatsoever. If we presume an average human life span, then by dying the elderly woman loses at most a few years of life, whereas the toddler is deprived of at least half a century of additional life. By dying has the elderly woman lost more and suffered a greater harm than the 2-year-old toddler?

Second, a troubling consequence of Rowlands' solution is that it is narrowly human-centered. To the best of our knowledge no other living things can organize, discipline, and regiment their present behavior and desires in the service of explicit plans and projects whose realization lies in the future. Hence, whereas death can harm human beings by robbing them of a future, oddly it cannot harm other living things in this way. But even some human beings are incapable of these impressive cognitive feats due to damage to their pre-frontal cortex that prevents them from formulating future-oriented goals and plans. Death would not harm any of these people by robbing them of a future, either. One way to avoid being harmed by death, therefore, would be to intentionally incur damage to one's pre-frontal cortex so that one is unable to formulate any future-oriented plans. One could thereby become invulnerable to being harmed by death. This seems like a steep price to pay.[8] Moreover, not even all human beings that *are* capable of organizing, disciplining, and regimenting their present behavior and desires in the service of explicit plans and projects whose realization lies in the future actually do so. Some people seem perfectly content to live day to day. It is far from clear that Roy Batty would be interested in organizing, disciplining, and regimenting his behavior and desires in the service of explicit plans and projects whose realization lies in the future. He *was* interested in doing that at some point, otherwise he would not have succeeded in returning to earth to confront his maker. But we can never know what plans he would have formulated had Tyrell been able and willing to comply with his demand for 'more life.' Perhaps he had not thought that far ahead. Perhaps he could not.

Third, Rowlands' proposal fails to solve our original puzzle of how one can be harmed by losing something that does not exist. The *being-towards-a-future* of which he writes consists entirely of one's explicit desires, goals, and projects – that is, of cognitive states that exist in the *present* if they exist at all. It is true that with one's death these presently existing cognitive states will disappear along with *all* one's cognitive states. To describe this as 'losing a future,' however, is at best figurative.

Consequently, the basic puzzle of how death can harm the one who dies remains.

'I Want More Life'

Titus Lucretius Carus (c. 99 – c. 55 BCE) advances another striking Epicurean, materialist argument intended to show that death is nothing, and hence is nothing to be feared:

> Death is nothing to us, of no concern whatsoever, once it is appreciated that the mind is mortal. Just as in the past we had no sensation of discomfort when the Carthaginians were converging to attack ... so too, when we will no longer exist ... nothing at all will be able to affect us and to stir our sensation – not if the earth collapses into sea, and sea into sky.... Look back, then, at how the unending stretch of time before we were born is nothing to us. Nature, therefore, offers this mirror to us of the future time after our eventual death. Do you see anything there to dread?[9]

Lucretius' 'Symmetry Argument,' as it is known, aims to show that the *ontological symmetry* between one's prenatal and postmortem nonexistence warrants an *attitudinal symmetry* toward them as well. The eternity before one's birth and the eternity after one's death are like mirror images of one another. If one is not harmed by not existing before one was born, then by parity of reasoning one is also not harmed by not existing after one dies. But where there is no possibility for harm there are no grounds for fear and no cause for lament. No one fears or laments his *prenatal* nonexistence. So too, no one *ought* to fear or lament his *postmortem* nonexistence.[10]

A critic can respond that perhaps he should. There is a strong temptation to begin itemizing personal benefits and harms at one's birth (or even at conception) and to extend this accounting for however long one continues to live. It hardly occurs to most of us to consider ourselves harmed by the fact that there was a vast period of time before we were born during which we failed to accumulate benefits. But by being born when one was rather than at some earlier time, one will (or at least may) have missed out on a quantity of life that one *could* have enjoyed *had* one been born earlier. As Stephen E. Rosenbaum (1993, p. 128) points out, 'A living person can live longer not only by dying later but also by being born earlier' (presuming, of course, that one does not have a predetermined life span, like the rogue replicants). Thus, if life is good, by not being born earlier one will have missed out on something valuable just as surely as one would by dying prematurely. To miss out on a good is to be harmed. Consequently, it seems that one may be harmed after all by not existing before one was, in fact, born.

In response, it could be objected that the foregoing criticism begs the question against the experientialist who denies that someone can be harmed without them having any *experience* of such harm. Moreover, this criticism presumes that a particular person *could* have come into existence prior to the moment when they *did* come into existence. But if the existence of any human being depends on a particular human sperm fertilizing a particular human egg at a never-to-be-repeated time in never-to-be-repeated circumstances, then any particular person could *not* have begun to exist at any other moment in time than when they *did* begin to exist.

Ironically, this defense of the Symmetry Argument invites yet another criticism of it. If there is an asymmetry in the nature of one's existence inasmuch as one could *not* have begun to exist at any time earlier than one did, but one *could* have continued to exist beyond the moment at which one does, in fact, cease to exist, then it looks like prenatal and postmortem non-existence are *asymmetrical* in this respect. Does this asymmetry spell trouble for the Symmetry Argument?

Some philosophers conclude that it does. The fundamental difference between prenatal and postmortem nonexistence, they argue, is that whereas the former does not *deprive* one of anything, the latter does. One *loses* nothing by not yet being born because one *could not* have been born earlier than one was. One cannot be harmed by missing out on something that was never even possible in the first place. But death involves losing something that is both possible and actual, namely, one's life. Thus, we are harmed by dying but not by not yet being born.

The proponent of the Symmetry Argument cannot respond by reminding us of the difficulty of making sense of how one can lose something that does not exist, namely, one's *future*, because the objection being considered turns on losing something *present* and *actual*, namely, one's life. At best, the proponent of the Symmetry Argument can point out that even if death does involve losing something present and actual that should be no cause for concern because one will still not be in a position to have any experience of that loss. Experientialism blunts the objection. Anthony J. Brueckner and John Martin Fischer argue that the Symmetry Argument fails even if one grants experientialism because, 'Death deprives us of something we care about, whereas prenatal nonexistence deprives us of something to which we are indifferent.' It follows, they say, that 'if we have asymmetric attitudes toward past and future experienced goods, then death is a bad thing in a way in which prenatal nonexistence is not' (Brueckner and Fischer 1986, p. 219).

Brueckner and Fischer avoid begging the question against the Symmetry Argument by denying experientialism, but they are in danger of begging the question in another way. Rather than attempting to *justify* our present mostly unreflective attitudes toward death, the Symmetry Argument *challenges* our usual blindness to the symmetry of our prenatal and postmortem nonexistence and thereby counsels us to rethink our unreflective attitudes toward death. The point of the argument is to address our anxiety about death by assuring us that postmortem nonexistence should be no more worrisome than prenatal nonexistence. The fact that a certain myopic perspective on our lives happens to be our natural, unreflective default view does not make it normative. Besides, we are not necessarily as indifferent to past pleasures as Brueckner and Martin assume. Not only do we often enjoy remembering past pleasures, we sometimes find ourselves regretting that we did not take advantage of some opportunities for greater pleasures. There are even circumstances in which knowing that one has *already* experienced some good in the past can be considered preferable to being assured of some good in the future. The future is never guaranteed; hence, anxiety about hoped-for future goods will be hard to avoid. Already-experienced goods, by contrast, are completely secure. That can be a great source of consolation.

It is time to take stock. Roy Batty's demand for 'more life' is a demand for an alteration that would permit him to *continue* living. Presumably it never crosses his mind to criticize his maker for not creating him *sooner*. It was obviously too late to do anything about *that*, and so long as the replicants are made with a predetermined four-year life span, it does not matter *when* they are made – they will have (at most) four years of life regardless of their incept dates. But these contingent facts about the replicants do not negate Lucretius' argument. If the replicants had been made without a predetermined life span, then it would have made sense for Roy to wonder whether the fact that his life would eventually come to an end should have been of any greater concern to him than the fact that he had not always existed. It is not clear that it should.

'Four, Five. How to Stay Alive'

Deckard goes to the Bradbury building to find and kill Batty and Pris. After he kills Pris, Batty turns the tables on him. Deckard now becomes the hunted. In a self-congratulatory display of sportsmanship intended to contrast with Deckard's evident lack of a sense of fair play, Batty decides to give Deckard a head-start before he comes after him: 'I'm gonna give you a few seconds before I come. One, two, three, four.... I'm coming. Four, five. How to stay alive.' In that context those last four words are marvelous because they can be interpreted in so many different ways. Batty is encouraging Deckard to draw upon all of his resources to try to stay alive. He is also saying aloud what Deckard must surely be thinking now that he knows first-hand what sort of formidable adversary he is dealing with. With his own body shutting down, Roy is also wondering how he will stay alive long enough to bring his life to a fitting conclusion. Perhaps most importantly, he is reminding himself that treating matters of life and death lightly, as a game to be played with gusto, is *how one remains fully alive* to the many possibilities that being alive makes possible. It is as if he is saying to himself and to Deckard, *this* is how one stays alive! Later, as Deckard witnesses Roy's death and tries to understand why he saved him, he reflects, 'Maybe in those last moments he loved life more than he ever had before. Not just his life, anybody's life, my life.' Evidently, the replicants found life to be good.

This fact helps to explain the replicants' quest for more life but thereby poses another problem for the Epicurean arguments discussed above. The replicants consider death to be a serious problem – so serious, in fact, that its solution merits killing anyone that stands in their way of acquiring more life. If the Epicurean arguments we have been considering are sound, however, then not only are the replicants profoundly mistaken to view death as the *most important* problem, they are mistaken to view death as a *problem* at all. According to Epicurus and Lucretius, one should regard one's own death as *nothing*, as of no concern whatsoever. Once one comes to appreciate this insight, they think, one can then go about enjoying one's life, free from anxiety concerning death and from the need to try to extend one's life. But a corollary of considering *death* to be 'nothing' may be that *life* becomes 'nothing' as well. After all, if death should *not* be 'regarded as an evil' (Epicurus), but rather as 'of no concern whatsoever'

(Lucretius), then life itself seems to be devalued to such an extent that it literally makes no difference whether one lives or dies. Why bother?[11]

This is a serious concern, and one that Epicurus himself takes seriously. What matters to him is not the duration of one's life but rather its quality. In his view, 'just as [the wise man] chooses the pleasantest food, not simply the greater quantity, so too he enjoys the pleasantest time, not the longest' (Long and Sedley 1987, p. 150). The quality of one's experiences trump the quantity of one's experiences. Hence, it literally makes no difference whether one's life is long or short. From the perspective of eternity, a 'long life' is indistinguishable from a short one. All that matters is its quality. The point of life, he thinks, is to enjoy it to the fullest possible extent, and this does not require amassing more and more pleasant experiences. One of the greatest obstacles to fully enjoying life is a fear of death. By putting death in perspective as an event that cannot harm one, one's life will be more pleasant than it would be if one feared death, and thus one will have no reason not to continue living, so long as one's life is good.

Conclusions

'When we are, death is not; when death is, we are not.' Epicurus believes that accepting this simple insight can lift a great burden from one's life. Rather than struggling to add a few more years to one's brief life or living in fear of one's inevitable death, understanding that death is *nothing* makes one's life enjoyable, 'not by adding to life an unlimited time, but by taking away the yearning after immortality. For there is nothing fearful in living for those who thoroughly grasp that there is nothing fearful in not living.' People shun and fear death as the greatest of all evils. But the wise person, Epicurus thinks, neither deprecates life nor fears its ending: 'The thought of life is no offense to him, nor is death regarded by him as an evil' (Hicks 1910, p. 169).

Death

    This insight remains as powerful now as it was when he articulated it over two millennia ago. But that is not the replicants' view. They believe that death is a serious problem. Ironically, by seeking more life all but Roy die sooner than they otherwise would.[12] But the film also provides a glimpse of another possible attitude toward death. Rachael naturally would presume that as a young woman she has many years of life ahead of her. When she discovers that she is a replicant designed (so far as she knows) with a four-year life span, she is at first understandably upset, but then appears to accept this harsh fact with remarkable equanimity. We do not know how she accomplishes this feat. Perhaps she chooses to value the life she has rather than longing and struggling for one that she can never have. That is an important lesson.

10 Time and Meaning

'Time enough'

(Roy Batty, to Leon)

Introduction

There are many clues that the replicants are obsessed with *time*. 'Time' is the first word we hear from Roy Batty as he emerges from a phone booth to assure Leon: 'Time enough.' At that point his declaration is still utterly mysterious. Time enough for what? As later becomes clear, the replicants are obsessed with time as it relates to their 'morphology, longevity, incept dates' – that is, to the amount of life they have left, and how they might acquire more of it. When Leon drags Deckard into an alley after witnessing Zhora's retirement, time is clearly on his mind as well:

Leon: How old am I?
Deckard: I don't know.
Leon: My birthday is April 10, 2017. How long do I live?
Deckard: Four years.
Leon: More than you! ... Wake up! Time to die.

Deckard is saved in the nick of time by Rachael who shoots Leon in the head with Deckard's blaster. Back in Deckard's apartment, time is on Rachael's mind as well: 'Deckard? You know those files on me – the incept date, the longevity, those things. You saw them?' Deckard unconvincingly replies, 'I didn't look at them.' Later, time is still on Roy Batty's mind when he finally meets his maker. His demand for *more life* is simply a demand for *more time*. Having reviewed for him the supposedly insurmountable technological obstacles to extending Roy's life,

Time and Meaning

Tyrell attempts to appease his dangerous visitor by suggesting that the brevity of his life is counter-balanced by its brilliant intensity: 'The light that burns twice as bright burns half as long. And you have burned so very, very brightly, Roy.... Revel in your time!' This is not the response Roy wants to hear. Angered by Tyrell's refusal to grant him more time, he kills him in a fit of violent rage. Soon thereafter, however, he joyfully embraces Tyrell's advice to revel in his time by bringing all combative skills to bear in his pursuit of Deckard.[1] When his death is imminent, he chooses to spend his last few precious moments reflecting on his most memorable times. It cannot be a coincidence that Roy's last words – 'Time to die' – are also Leon's last words. Both are acutely aware that time imposes a limit on life and that death cannot be postponed indefinitely.

Simply acquiring more time, however, cannot be the replicants' *ultimate* goal. Their chances for living the full four years allotted to them were greater had they chosen to remain slaves in the Off-world colonies. They seek more *time* because they believe that the brevity of their lives prevents them from living more *meaningful* lives. They believe that with *more time* their lives would be *more meaningful*. They are in good company. Hardly any important belief is less questioned than the belief that a longer life is better and more meaningful than a shorter one.[2] A consistent application of this logic entails that the most meaningful life of all would be one that never ends.[3] My aim in this chapter is to assess this belief in order to apply any lessons learned to the replicants' quest for 'more life' – and perhaps to our lives, as well. Doing so requires first assembling some philosophical resources to assist us in that assessment.

'All Those Moments Will Be Lost in Time'

Some thinkers maintain that living forever is necessary for life to have any meaning at all. For example, the Spanish philosopher Miguel de Unamuno (1864–1936) declares, 'Whatever is not eternal is also not real.... We must needs believe in the other life, in the eternal life beyond the grave ... in order that we may live this life, and endure it, and give it meaning and finality' (Unamuno 1972, pp. 45, 258). Such a view is not restricted to religious believers. Jean-Paul Sartre categorically rejects belief in a God and an afterlife, but nonetheless expresses a very similar view: 'Death is ... that which on principle removes all meanings from life. If we must die, then our life has no meaning because its problems receive no solution and because the very meaning of the problems remains undetermined' (Sartre 1943, p. 690). Such a view *may* be correct; but to be persuaded that it is we need a cogent *argument* in its support. What might such an argument look like?

The Russian novelist Leo Tolstoy (1828–1910) presents his own life as providing such an argument. In an autobiographical essay he relates how at about the age of 50 he experienced a profound personal crisis during which he realized that everything he had achieved in his life would eventually disappear completely. But if so, he wondered, what was the *point* of doing anything? When he realized that he had no answer, the foundations on which he had been living collapsed. His life came to a standstill and he was forced to acknowledge an awful truth: 'The truth was that life was meaningless.... [I]t was impossible to shut my eyes so as not to see that there was nothing before me but suffering and actual death – absolute annihilation' (Tolstoy 1882, p. 14). The solution to this terrible problem came to him as he was reflecting on how the ordinary, uneducated peasants solved it. He concluded that only by embracing their simple religious belief could he, too, find a solution. Hence, 'Whatever answers faith may give, every one of these answers gives an infinite meaning to the finite life of man, a meaning which is not destroyed by suffering, privation, and death. In faith alone, therefore, is found the possibility of living and a meaning in life' (p. 44). Only by living forever, he thinks, can his life have any meaning at all.

Tolstoy's solution to the problem of the meaning of life relies on two questionable assumptions that should give us pause.

First, he appears to take for granted that one can and should adopt whatever beliefs one deems necessary to view one's life as meaningful. But if beliefs, by their very nature, represent one's best judgments about what is *true*, they are not the sorts of things that one can responsibly adopt irrespective of logic and the evidence, no matter how convenient it might be to do so. To *intentionally* (attempt to) acquire a belief *solely* because one judges that it would be beneficial to do so is to engage in an act of self-deception.

Second, Tolstoy's argument depends on what we might dub 'the Permanence Principle,' that is, the principle that declares that an experience, an activity, an accomplishment, or a life can be meaningful *only if* it lasts forever. The truth of this principle is far from self-evident. Indeed, there are good reasons for rejecting it. We do not demand that every experience *in* life (for example, a book, a concert, a film) must last forever for it to be meaningful. We tend to think that each has whatever meaning it has for us despite the fact that it eventually ends. Tolstoy has given us no reason to think that one's life as a whole is any different.

'All the Time, Pal'

Tolstoy is so concerned with finding a way to prevent the *loss* of the things he has worked so hard to achieve that he seems not to consider the possibility that merely living forever might not be sufficient to deliver the meaning he craves. This truth is strikingly conveyed by the French/Algerian writer and philosopher Albert Camus (1913–60) in his retelling of the ancient Myth of Sisyphus. According to one version of the myth, through his defiance Sisyphus displeased the gods. As punishment, 'The gods had condemned Sisyphus to ceaselessly rolling a rock to the top of a mountain, whence the stone would fall back of its own weight. They had thought with some reason that there is no more dreadful punishment than futile and hopeless labor' (Camus 1955, p. 119). Sisyphus labors at his task day and night, forever. One day is just like the next. Absolutely nothing ever comes from all his effort. Despite the bleakness of his life, Sisyphus continues to roll his rock up the mountain, pausing only to scorn the gods for their excessive cruelty.

Camus finds inspiration in Sisyphus' attitude and concludes rather incongruously on a cheerful note: 'Sisyphus teaches the higher fidelity that negates the gods and raises rocks.... The universe henceforth without a master seems to him neither sterile nor futile.... The struggle itself toward the heights is enough to fill a man's heart. One must imagine Sisyphus happy' (p. 123). Setting aside this surprising conclusion, Camus' retelling of the Myth of Sisyphus is important because it provides a vivid picture of a life that *never ends* yet remains *meaningless*. Living forever adds nothing to the meaningfulness of Sisyphus' life but only makes it even more absurd. The lesson seems inescapable: living forever is *not* by itself sufficient to render one's life meaningful.

'Time to Die'

Bernard Williams goes even further by arguing that living forever may even be *incompatible* with finding one's life meaningful. In his view, 'Immortality, or a state without death, would be meaningless ... so, in a sense, death gives the meaning to life' (Williams 1973, p. 82). He arrives at this provocative conclusion by reflecting on a play by Karel Čapek that tells of a woman named Elina Makropulos (or EM). Her father is a sixteenth-century physician who gives her an elixir of life that arrests the normal aging process. Although she continues to live year after year, and hence grows older in a chronological sense, her body does not age and she comes no closer to death. In the play we meet her when she is 42 years old – an age she has been for three centuries. Rather than rejoicing in her remarkable longevity, however, she is despondent. As Williams explains, 'Her unending life has come to a state of boredom, indifference and coldness. Everything is joyless' (p. 82). She refuses to take the elixir again, and finally dies.

In Williams' view, this strange story conveys an important lesson. EM discovers after a mere 300 years that she has already had all the life she can stand. Her problem is not due to some personal deficiency. Instead, it is one that would afflict *anyone* in her situation: 'Her trouble was ... boredom: a boredom connected with the fact that everything that could happen and make sense to one particular human being of 42 had already happened to her' (p. 90). Others might sustain the desire to live a bit longer than that, but *eventually* everyone would arrive at the same truth: 'an endless life would be a meaningless one; and ... we could have no reason for living eternally a human life' (p. 89). We should therefore be grateful that our lives eventually come to an end with death, because the alternative *literally* would be a fate worse than death. Immortality would be no blessing; indeed, it would eventually become an intolerable curse. In Williams' view, therefore, we should therefore consider ourselves *'felix opportunitate mortis'* – fortunate to have the chance to die (p. 100).

Not everyone is persuaded by Williams' argument. John Martin Fischer, for example, takes issue with Williams' claim that a never-ending life would necessarily become intolerably boring for the person whose life it is just because there is no *single* utterly absorbing state or activity that would make boredom unthinkable. He thinks that there is no reason why a never-ending life could not consist in a mix of activities, possibly including friendship, love, family, intellectual, artistic and athletic activity, sensual delights, and so forth. By repeating such activities, perhaps with substantial time elapsing before returning to any given activity, one need never succumb to boredom. Consequently, Fischer concludes, 'Given the appropriate distribution of such pleasures, it seems that an endless life that included ... repeatable pleasures would *not* necessarily be boring or unattractive' (Fischer 2010, p. 370).

Williams is unlikely to be moved by Fischer's argument insofar as he already considers and rejects that possibility. The problem that EM encounters, he says, is not a peculiar feature of her particularly limited personality or interests but is instead an inescapable feature of *any* human life. The problem resides in our finite capacities as human beings. Our characters necessarily limit what we can experience, absorb, and find interesting; and eternity is a long time. The profound difficulty, therefore, is that of 'providing any model of an unending, supposedly satisfying, state or activity which would not rightly prove boring to anyone who remained conscious of himself and who had acquired a character, interests, [and] tastes ... in the course of living, already, a finite life' (Williams 1973, pp. 94–5). 'Nothing less will do for eternity,' Williams thinks, 'than something that makes boredom *unthinkable*' (p. 95). But there is no reason to suppose that there is any such thing or even any such *collection* of things, even if activities are periodically changed. Consequently, he concludes, '[F]rom facts about human desire and happiness and what a human life is, it follows ... that immortality would be, where conceivable at all, intolerable' (p. 82).

'Time Enough'

If Camus and Williams are right, living forever is not *sufficient* to render one's life meaningful, although it might be sufficient to render one's life meaningless. If Richard Taylor is right, living forever is not *necessary* to render one's life meaningful, either. To show this, he invites us to reconsider the Myth of Sisyphus, this time treating it like a thought experiment whose features can be altered systematically until the crucial factor enabling Sisyphus' pointless life to become meaningful is identified.

Suppose, then, that instead of struggling to roll an enormous boulder up the hill, Sisyphus merely has to carry a small *pebble* to the top of the hill, letting it roll back down each time, and that he has to repeat this task forever. His task has become considerably easier, but his life is no less meaningless. Hence, it is not the *difficulty* of his task that makes Sisyphus' life meaningless.

Next, suppose that Sisyphus rolls a *different* rock to the top of the hill with each ascent, where each is incorporated into a

Time and Meaning

beautiful and enduring temple. In a sense his life has now acquired a meaning because his labors have a point: something of value is being created by his efforts. But if Sisyphus is essentially a slave laboring to create something that *others* value but that *he* does not, then his life still lacks meaningfulness in an important sense.

Suppose, however, that the construction of such a temple is *his* greatest desire. In this case his life has a meaning that it formerly lacked because his *will* is importantly engaged in his labors. But if his *only* interest is in seeing the temple completed, then upon its completion another problem intrudes: infinite boredom. Having achieved his goal, he will have nothing else for which to live. He could begin a new project, but that, too, would eventually come to an end, and the process would have to begin again, essentially replicating the repetitive act of rolling one rock after another up the hill. Boredom and meaninglessness will reappear.

Suppose, however, that the gods mercifully implant in Sisyphus an insatiable desire to roll rocks. In this case what was an awful punishment has become his obsession and greatest joy. Indeed, 'he seems to himself to have been given an entry to heaven' (Taylor 1970, p. 259). The key point to notice in this final permutation of the story is that nothing has changed in Sisyphus' life except his *attitude* toward his task. From an external observer's perspective *nothing* about his life is any different. From Sisyphus' internal perspective, however, *everything* is different. In this way, Taylor concludes, 'an existence that is objectively meaningless [may] nonetheless acquire a meaning for him whose existence it is' (p. 260). Indeed, it is the only sort of *bona fide* meaning that his life *can* have. What is true of Sisyphus' life, Taylor thinks, is equally true of our own: '[T]he meaning of life is from within us, it is not bestowed from without, and it far exceeds in both its beauty and permanence any heaven of which men have ever dreamed or yearned for' (p. 268).

Taylor's view is attractive insofar as it makes clear the necessary and sufficient conditions for a meaningful life and, potentially at least, makes such a life available to all – provided, of course, that one is able to act on one's deepest desires. But by making meaningfulness so accessible it may make it *too* accessible. A consequence of Taylor's view is that the drug addict who succeeds in satisfying his deep desire for drugs has a more meaningful life than the humanitarian who deeply desires to eradicate malaria in third-world countries but whose desire is thwarted by an inability to raise the needed funds. Taylor could respond that this objection simply begs the question. If the meaningfulness of one's life just *is* a matter of satisfying one's deepest desires, then the drug addict's life *is* the more meaningful of the two. That is just how *meaning* works. We might judge the humanitarian's life to be better on other grounds, but that is precisely the point: those would be *other* grounds. A meaningful life need not be 'best' in every respect.

A more worrying criticism concerns the seemingly *arbitrary nature* of one's desires. Many of our desires are induced in us by others (parents, the media, advertisers, religious authorities, and so on) that wish us to act in ways that satisfy *their* desires – which, ironically, may be induced in them in the same way by still others. In devoting one's life to satisfying such artificially induced desires, one essentially becomes a *slave*, albeit perhaps a happy one. Taylor perhaps recognizes this danger when he hints that it may not be enough to act on just *any* set of desires with which one happens to find oneself. Rather, 'the point of living is simply to be living, in the manner that it is [one's] nature to be living' (p. 267). Talk of one's 'nature' suggests that it is possible to distinguish artificially induced, superficial desires from deeper, more authentic desires. Presumably the key to a meaningful life is thus to identify and satisfy those desires that are constitutive of one's nature. Those desires will still be arbitrary in the sense that they were not chosen and could conceivably have been different. But they might still seem more truly one's own than those imposed upon one by the contingent circumstances of one's environment.

That recognition, however, gives rise to another concern, namely, that even one's deepest desires have no objective justification beyond the fact that one simply *finds oneself* with one set of deep desires rather than another. We do not choose our deepest desires any more than we choose any of our desires. In a sense we exercise even *less* choice with regard to (or have less control over) those desires. Ironically, therefore, truly *understanding* what makes one's life meaningful (in Taylor's sense) threatens to undermine that very meaningfulness. One might consider one's life to be perfectly meaningful *so long as* one is fully engaged in pursuing one's deepest desires, but it might come to seem much less so when one stops to ask oneself *why* one has *those* specific desires rather than others. At that point the house of cards could collapse.[4]

'Four Years Was a Short Time or a Long Time'[5]

According to Thomas Nagel (1986), this problem is virtually inevitable for beings constituted as we are. The problem of the meaning of life arises directly from our ability to view our lives from two entirely distinct perspectives. On the one hand, I can view my life from an internal, subjective, first-person perspective. From this point of view, my existence in the world seems inevitable, my projects seem vitally important, and my eventual annihilation in death seems inconceivable. On the other hand, I can also occupy an objective, third-person perspective on my life. From this point of view, I recognize that I did not have to exist at all, the success or failure of my personal projects is ultimately of no significance whatsoever, and upon my death the world will continue as if I had never existed. The two views could not be more different.

By itself, however, that recognition does not generate serious problems. Problems arise because I can shift from one perspective to the other, and it is impossible to *integrate* the two distinct perspectives into a single, consistent, unified vision of my life. This is precisely where problems about the meaning of life typically arise: 'The same person who is subjectively committed to a personal life in all its rich detail finds himself in another aspect simultaneously detached; this detachment undermines his commitment without destroying it – leaving him divided' (p. 210). Consequently, Nagel says, 'In seeing ourselves from the outside we find it difficult to take our lives seriously. This loss of conviction, and the attempt to regain it, is the problem of the meaning of life' (p. 214).

Nagel notes that our ability to occupy these two divergent perspectives can lead to the feeling that our lives have been profoundly *undermined*: 'The external standpoint and the contemplation of death lead to a loss of equilibrium in life' and can impel us to feel 'a constant undertow of absurdity in the projects and ambitions that give our lives their forward drive' (pp. 210–11). At times the problem can become acute: 'Finding my life objectively insignificant, I am nevertheless unable to extricate myself from an unqualified commitment to it – to my aspirations and ambitions, my wishes for fulfillment, recognition, understanding, and so forth. The sense of the absurd is the result of this juxtaposition' (p. 218).

As we saw, Tolstoy felt this problem acutely. His solution was to take refuge in religious belief. Nagel's suggested response is to adopt an attitude of *humility*: 'Humility falls between nihilistic detachment and blind self-importance. It doesn't require reflection on the cosmic arbitrariness of the sense of taste every time you eat a hamburger' (p. 222). It encourages us to accept our momentary existence in time: 'The present is where we are, and we cannot see it only in timeless perspective. But we can forget about it now and then, even if it won't forget about us' (p. 222). Such an attitude will not banish the sense of the absurd from human life. Our ability to occupy two quite different perspectives on our lives guarantees that the absurd will always be a part of it. But in the end, Nagel thinks, 'It is better to be simultaneously engaged and detached, and therefore absurd, for this is the opposite of self-denial and the result of full awareness' (p. 223).

'It's Too Bad She Won't Live'

This brief survey of philosophical responses to the problem of the meaning of life provides a set of perspectives that can be used to understand and assess the replicants' quest for 'more life.'

Like Tolstoy, the replicants assume that *death* poses the most serious obstacle to viewing their lives as meaningful. There are two aspects to this problem: one that looks forward to the future, the other that looks back to the past. Leon articulates the forward-looking aspect when he complains that the replicants have 'potential with no way to use it' because for them 'the future is sealed off.'[6] Because of their severely curtailed life spans the replicants are precluded from some of the experiences that give meaning to human life, for example, 'Sex, reproduction, security, the simple things.' Roy Batty articulates the backward-looking aspect of this problem in his lament to Deckard: 'I've seen things you people wouldn't believe.... All those moments will be lost in time, like tears in rain.' Roy laments the loss of a set of valuable experiences that will disappear from the world when he draws his last breath. Like Tolstoy, the replicants believe that the only solution to these problems is to secure *more time*. How *much* more time is necessary remains unclear. If the replicants *do* have the potentials that Leon identifies, being granted an average human life span (along with the freedom to pursue human lives) would presumably be sufficient. By contrast, living a few more years would not solve the problem with which Roy struggles. Only a life that never ends could satisfy Roy's desire that his experiences never disappear.

Camus teaches us that a life that never ends is not necessarily a meaningful life. Even if Tyrell granted Roy additional years of life, there is no guarantee that his life would necessarily become more meaningful as a result. A longer life may provide *opportunities* for him to engage in activities that enhance the meaning of his life. But in that case it is those activities, not the longer life *per se*, that is the source of meaning. A life that is lacking in meaning cannot become more meaningful *simply* by extending its length any more than a piece of music, a film, or a book can become *better* simply by making it *longer*. Indeed, the danger is that the opposite will occur. Roy seems not to have considered this danger, or if he did, he did not take it seriously.

Williams *does* consider this danger. He argues that a life that never ends necessarily would eventually become intolerable. At that point, death would be welcome. Roy, Zhora, Leon, and Pris never have to face this prospect. All of them are killed or expire months shy of their expected termination dates. Rachael may be different. In the Theatrical Release as Deckard and Rachael are driving away from Los Angeles, Deckard informs us that, 'Tyrell had told me Rachael was special: no termination date. I didn't know how long we had together. Who does?' Although Deckard's voice-over narration was removed for later versions of the film, we cannot assume that Rachael is like the other replicants in having a four-year life span. After all, as Tyrell explains, Rachael is an experiment. Without a termination date, Rachael might live as long as the average human being. However, as an experimental synthetic human, she might live even longer, perhaps even considerably longer. Given her intense concern with 'incept date ... longevity, those things,' she might be delighted to learn that unlike the other replicants she has no termination date. How much more so might she be if she learns that she can live *forever*? If Williams is right, however, there would eventually come a time when she concludes that she has already lived too long. At that point she would understand that a longer life can be a blessing *or* a curse.

Taylor's retelling of the Myth of Sisyphus shows why Tolstoy's profound existential crisis and Roy Batty's wistful end-of-life lament stem from a misunderstanding of the nature of meaning. If the meaning of life is found within, then a meaningful life, no matter how long it lasts, is available to the replicants no less than to Tolstoy despite their equally finite life spans.[7] Were the replicants able to engage in those activities they most deeply desire to pursue, regardless of what those desires are and regardless of where they came from, their lives would *seem* to them – and indeed in Taylor's view would *be* – as meaningful as they could be. What those activities would be for the replicants is hard to say. Perhaps they did not even dare to think that far ahead. In this respect as in so many others, the replicants are not much different than many of us.

However, even if they were able to pursue what are for them deeply satisfying activities, then like us they could eventually find themselves reflecting on their lives and asking why they should attach importance to the particular desires with which they happen to find themselves. They might then experience the clash between the subjective and objective perspectives on their lives that Nagel says is the inescapable consequence of the ability stand outside of one's life while simultaneously occupying it. The replicants would then find themselves in the very same existential dilemma that all reflective beings face. In this regard, at least, they would not be 'more human than human,' as Tyrell bragged, but they would at least be equal to human beings in their capacity for being be simultaneously engaged and detached from their own lives, and also in their need to find a way to continue to live and flourish in the bright light of this realization.

Conclusions

It is no accident that the culmination of Deckard's battle with Roy Batty takes place high above the streets of the city. As Roy chases Deckard through the dilapidated building, they continually ascend higher, as if striving for some higher truth, until they finally arrive on the roof. When Deckard attempts to leap from one rooftop to another, he falls short. By contrast, Roy leaps from one rooftop to another with ease, even clutching a dove as he does so. Their respective leaps are symbolic of one of the central themes of the film. At that point, Deckard has still not quite made the leap to understanding that the replicants stand in the same relationship to life and death and meaning as do humans. That understanding has to await his observance of

Roy's poignant death. Roy's successful leap symbolizes his nascent understanding that the fact of one's inevitable death does not distinguish replicants from human beings, and that Tyrell was right to counsel him that the value of life resides in its quality rather than in its mere quantity. This hard-won insight is on display, not when he relates to Deckard some of the remarkable things he has seen – attack ships on fire off the shoulder of Orion, C-beams glittering in the darkness at Tannhäuser Gate – remembered experiences that will disappear forever with his death, but rather in his acceptance that it is 'Time to die.' In the end, Roy faces his own death wistfully, smiling and at peace. He crossed a great chasm that few succeed in crossing. In the final moments of his life, he began to understand what makes life, any life, worth living. As Deckard (in a deleted scene) reflects on the replicants, 'Four years was all they had. Four years was a short time or a long time, depending on how you looked at it, what you had in mind.' Whatever meaning our lives can have is available to us right now, in the present moment. Thus like Pindar we might exclaim, 'O my soul, do not aspire to immortal life, but exhaust the limits of the possible.'[8] Or, like Tyrell, we might choose to exhort ourselves just as he exhorts his proudest creation: 'Revel in your time!'

Epilogue

'I've seen things you people wouldn't believe.'
(Roy Batty, to Deckard)

In the Preface I noted that despite the occasional recognition that *Blade Runner* is a thought-provoking film, its potential for eliciting and exploring philosophical issues had so far not been fully appreciated. I have attempted to remedy that situation by examining how issues of universal human concern arise and are addressed within the film. I have argued not only that the film *raises* philosophical questions, but also that it suggests *answers* to at least some of them. I do not expect to have convinced the reader of all my specific interpretations and conclusions. But I *do* hope to have convinced the reader that *Blade Runner* is, indeed, 'a philosophical film.'[1]

Nonetheless, that basic claim could be challenged, and in fact *is* challenged – by the film's director, no less. Ridley Scott explicitly *denies* that the film is philosophical at all, declaring that, 'this film does not have any deep messages' (Peary 1984, p. 55). According to him, not only are there no *deep* messages in the film, but apparently there are no intentional messages of *any* sort in it: 'There is simply no intentional message in this picture, although people will probably read all sorts of things into any film. Basically, I see moviemaking as creating entertainment' (Sammon 1982, p. 140). The legendary studio head Samuel Goldwyn reportedly said of movies, 'Pictures are for entertainment; messages should be delivered by Western Union.' Scott apparently concurs: 'After all, movies are a form of entertainment, not education' (Knapp and Kulas 2005, p. xv).

If Ridley Scott is right, the present book would seem to be fundamentally misguided. If Rutger Hauer is right, however, the situation appears even worse. In his view, not only should we not expect a film like *Blade Runner* to convey important *truths*, but like other films it should be seen as promulgating *falsehoods* – as illustrated by Deckard's use of the Esper machine to explore the three-dimensional depths of Leon's photograph. Is there one Roy Batty in the photo or are there two? Is that Zhora with a snake tattoo, or a stand-in? According to Hauer, ultimately the answers do not matter because 'that whole Esper sequence shows how you can play with images and tell a story and, at the same time, completely bullshit someone. Which is just like making a motion picture, come to think of it. But the truth of that photo is – there is no truth' (Sammon 1996, p. 146). Movies may entertain, but they do not and cannot enlighten.

Scott's and Hauer's remarks suggest that it is a fundamental misunderstanding of the nature and purpose of movies to look to them for insights into the real world. Movies are entertainment. They are not, and by their very nature cannot be, vehicles for philosophic insight. After all, how could *fictional characters* interacting in a *fictional world* convey important truths about *the real world*? Worse still, how could careful thinking about *synthetic humans* that do not and may never exist possibly help us to understand *real* human beings and their deepest concerns? Confusing entertainment with enlightenment, it seems, is a serious mistake.

It will come as no surprise to learn that I do not think that the views expressed by Scott and Hauer entail these implications. Even if a film is not intended by its director or actors to convey any deep messages, the final product may end up doing so nonetheless because the meaning and significance of any work of art is not entirely within the control of the artist. As we saw in our discussion of creatures in Chapter 8, artifacts are capable of serving purposes other than those for intended by their creator. What matters is not *why they were made* but *what they are*. In addition, 'truth' or 'lies' hardly exhausts the epistemic value of a film like *Blade Runner*. A more potent epistemic value of the film is its remarkable ability to prompt philosophical reflection and to suggest a range of philosophical perspectives that might

Epilogue

otherwise remain disembodied abstractions. Moving pictures can serve as *vehicles* for philosophic insight.

Some philosophers deeply distrust moving images and thus would categorically reject that claim. We owe to Plato (c. 429–347 BCE) the most famous and influential account of the relationship between moving images and reality. In *The Republic* he invites us to imagine people sitting in the darkness of an underground cave, chained in place from birth, facing a wall with a fire burning on a platform behind them. In front of the fire is a path along which others carry statues of various objects that cast shadows on the wall of the cave. Unbeknownst to the prisoners, sounds that appear to emanate from the cave wall are merely echoes coming from the people carrying the statues. The prisoners, being completely unaware of the source of the shadows and sounds, attempt to find order and meaning in them. Occasionally one of the prisoners manages to escape from his bondage and to ascend to the world outside the cave. He then realizes that what he had before taken to be reality was merely a faint copy of a copy of it. But when he returns to the cave to tell his former friends, 'I've seen things you people wouldn't believe,' not only do his friends not believe him, but having spent their entire lives listening to distorted echoes reflected from the cave wall, they cannot even understand him. To them his in-sights are unintelligible babbling.

The similarities between the experience of the prisoners in Plato's Cave and our experience as film-goers are obvious. In both cases we find ourselves seated in a darkened space, listening to sounds and trying to make sense of the images projected by a light above and behind us. The differences are equally noteworthy. Unlike Plato's fettered prisoners, we are willing spectators. We are able to move freely between the 'reel world' of fictional images projected onto the screen and the real world outside the movie theater projected through our senses into our minds. Most importantly, in viewing a movie we gladly *allow* ourselves to be deceived; we *voluntarily* suspend our disbelief so that we can *play* with our sense of what is real. At some level we retain awareness of the film-induced nature of our experiences so that when we emerge we can ask ourselves what the images represent (or could represent). Whereas in Plato's Cave the prisoner's ascent to enlightenment is a one-way journey in which the prisoner escapes from the world of images to the real world, in viewing movies we can travel back and forth between the world of images and the real world, using the former to enhance our understanding of the latter.

What Philip K. Dick said about science fiction (SF) is thus equally true of some films: 'SF makes what would otherwise be an intellectual abstraction concrete; it does this by locating the idea in a specific time and place, which requires the inventing of that time and place' (Dick 1980, p. 44). By situating ideas within specific contexts, films allow us to explore the implications of those ideas in ways that are difficult to do with words alone. Through engagement with images we are able to imagine a world other than our own. This act of imagination can be remarkably fruitful. Whether or not the film represents the world as it is, we can learn from the film. If the film is *like* the real world, we can learn ways of viewing and interpreting our world from the film, or new ways of dealing with the world. If the film world is *not* like the real world, we can contrast the two in order to understand the possible versus the actual, as well as the boundaries of the possible. Imagination – assisted through viewing and reflecting on films – is a form of release from our cave-prison – a chance to imaginatively alter the constraints of our experienced world a little or a lot, and to work out the consequences for matters of universal human concern.

Notes

Preface

1. The foregoing description comes from the back cover of Paul M. Sammon's invaluable book, *Future Noir: The Making of Blade Runner* (1996). In 1993 *Blade Runner* was selected by the Library of Congress for preservation in the United States National Film Registry as being 'culturally, historically, or aesthetically significant.' In 2007 it was named the second most visually influential film of all time by the Visual Effects Society. In 2012 in a poll with over 10,000 votes cast it was ranked by *SFX* magazine as the greatest science fiction film of all time.
2. Sammon's comments appear in his audio commentary on the Workprint version of the film (included in the Five-Disc Ultimate Collector's Edition).
3. Bukatman is here referring specifically to the film's *visual* density, but his subsequent remarks make clear that he intends this judgment to apply to the film's thematic elements as well.

1 Introduction

1. Although we are told in the film's opening crawl that blade runner units are special police squads created to hunt down trespassing replicants, 'blade runner' nowhere appears in Philip K. Dick's novel and its significance is never explained in the film. *Blade Runner* was suggested as a title for the film by Hampton Fancher, who wrote the original screenplay, after he came across it in his library as the title of a script by William Burroughs based on a novel by Alan E. Nourse about smugglers of medical supplies. Despite the absence of any thematic connection between the Nourse novel and Dick's book, the title nonetheless proved to be perfect for the film. 'Blade runner' conjures up an image of someone whose job it is to make split-second decisions along a razor-thin line. In the film this means distinguishing humans from replicants, and right from wrong, in situations that are fraught with uncertainty and moral dangers. Scott liked the 'edgy' sound of 'blade

Notes

runner' over the more conventional term 'detective.' Rights to its use were purchased from Burroughs and Nourse (Sammon 1996, pp. 53–4).

2. The novel's interest in animals is reflected in more subtle ways in the film as well. For example, each major character in the film is linked to an animal (or animals): Leon – tortoise; Tyrell – owl; Zhora – snake; Rachael – spider; Sebastian – rat; Deckard – chicken; Gaff – unicorn; Bryant – cape buffalo; Pris – raccoon; Roy – wolf (and dove) (see Sammon 1996, p. 172).

3. Dick's comments are included in the Enhancement Archive DVD (included in the Five-Disk Ultimate Collector's Edition).

4. Source: http://www.philipkdick.com/new_letters-laddcompany.html. Accessed 7 May 2012.

5. Sammon (1996, pp. 394–408) painstakingly catalogues every difference among these versions, except for the Final Cut, which appeared after his book was published.

6. Voice-over narration was apparently always a part of the movie's conception. It is present in the 24 July 1980 script by Hampton Fancher (hereafter, BR 7-80). It was subsequently reduced to just a few lines toward the end of the 23 February 1981 script by Fancher and David Peoples (hereafter, BR 2-81). The final script reintroduces considerable voice-over narration, albeit entirely different from the narration that appears in the previous scripts.

7. Contrary to a common belief among fans who lament the addition of this tacked-on happy ending, a happy ending (of sorts) was planned for the film until shortly before shooting ended. The scenes were scripted but not shot due to falling behind schedule and cost overruns. But after negative audience reactions at the Denver and Dallas sneak previews, additional scenes were shot after all and added to the film (Sammon 1996, pp. 299–300, 307–8). BR 2-81 has Deckard whisking Rachael away from the city, as Gaff gives pursuit. BR 7-80 also ends with Deckard whisking Rachael out of the city so that Rachael can see snow and trees … before he shoots her.

8. Even these changes were not enough to satisfy some people. Rutger Hauer (Roy Batty in the film) dislikes the Deckard–Rachael relationship at the end of all versions of the film even more than he dislikes the happy ending of the Theatrical Release: 'Forget the happy ending. I didn't even like the fact that Deckard ran off with Rachael at the end. Deckard loving replicants didn't make any sense to me. Frankly, I thought Deckard was a little sick, because he ran away with a vibrator that *looked* like a woman. Some people get angry with me when I tell them that. They say, "Rutger, you missed the point. You really should read Philip K. Dick's book." Well, they don't know that I read the book. Whose whole moral, I thought,

boiled down to this: "Does a computer love you? No, a computer does not." End of story' (Sammon 1996, p. 201, n. 15).

9. See, for example, the many 'clues' identified by Byron (2008), although in the end he concludes that resolving the question of whether or not Deckard is a replicant is unimportant.

10. Scott Bukatman (2012, p. 92) observes that, 'sometimes it seems that the question, "Is Deckard a replicant?" has generated more discussion on the Internet than the existence of God.' Judging by the urgency with which this issue is debated, to some people the answer is even more critical than its theological counterpart.

11. I take the question at issue to be whether Deckard is a *replicant*, not whether he is *human* because, as the discussion in Chapter 2 suggests, being human and being a replicant are not necessarily mutually exclusive: it is possible to be both. Nonetheless, to avoid cumbersome circumlocution I will adopt the convention of asking whether Deckard is a replicant *or* human.

12. There is no end to the clues viewers have detected in the film suggesting to them that Deckard is a replicant. For example, it has been noted that Deckard's job is to *retire* replicants, and he is a *retired* blade runner (Mawby 2001, pp. 147–8). Durham (2013, p. 4) takes for granted that Deckard is an even more advanced Nexus 7 replicant, and suggests that it is possible that the selection of Deckard to retire the rogue replicants 'indicates an experiment on the part of the maker to test the limitations of his invention.' This is, indeed, *possible*. But there is no evidence to support such speculations and they will not be considered here.

13. This interpretation is bolstered by the final scenes as scripted in BR 2-81 where Deckard describes the tinfoil unicorn as 'Gaff's gauntlet.' Shortly thereafter he places it on the dash of his car as he and Rachael speed past birch trees at 160 mph with Gaff in his spinner racing after them in hot pursuit.

14. Reported by Paul M. Sammon in his audio commentary on the Workprint version (available in the Five-Disk Ultimate Collector's Edition).

15. The unicorn motif lends itself to many other interpretations as well. According to Nick Lacey (2000, p. 44), 'The unicorn is a mythical beast that can only be tamed by a virgin, the single horn being an obviously phallic symbol. Rachael is a virgin and she tames the hunter Deckard, giving meaning to his alienated life.' According to Philip Strick (1992, p. 8), by contrast, the unicorn scene was 'lifted' from *Legend* (Scott's next film after 1982's *Blade Runner*), whose opening titles explain that 'precious light ... is harboured in the souls of Unicorns, the most mystical of all creatures.... they can only be found by the purest of mortals.' From this observation Strick

Notes

(inexplicably) concludes that, 'In the *Blade Runner* context, its main implication is that Deckard, who has hitherto shown little inclination towards the poetic, is again drinking too hard or has taken leave of his senses.' Alternatively, Peter Brooker (2005, p. 222) proposes that, 'The appearance of a fabulous beast from the borderland realm of myth or fable reinforces the film's underlying interest in a new hybrid, posthuman type.' We also have the testimony of Ridley Scott, who explains that, 'while so much has been made by critics of the unicorn, they've actually missed the wider issue. It is not the unicorn itself which is important. It's the landscape around it – the green landscape – they should be noticing' (Sammon 1996, p. 377). Picking up on this remark, Gerblinger (2002, pp. 26–7) opines that, 'Deckard's and, to a lesser degree, Gaff's unicorns take on the function of the "nature" construct and its multiple meanings. Since the unicorn's mythological framework is built upon the symbolism of folklore and Christianity, its correspondence to nature in *Blade Runner* implies that the concept of nature may be assigned a similar metaphorical implication.' Still other interpretations are possible. In a deleted scene Deckard explains that after administering the Voight-Kampff test to Rachael, 'Tyrell ... ran scans of her memory implants for me, a proud father showing off the insides of his kid's brain.' If one of those implants had included unicorn imagery, then Deckard's daydream could signify that he was thinking about Rachael. I include this small sampling of interpretations to underscore the point that there are *many* interpretations of this scene besides the one that views it as conclusive evidence that Deckard is a replicant.

16. Scott's comments appear in the Enhancement Archive DVD (included in the Five-Disk Ultimate Collector's Edition).
17. This interpretation gains some support from considering earlier scripts and deleted or alternative scenes in which the possibility that Deckard is a replicant is more pronounced than it is in any released version of the film. In BR 2-81, after Deckard survives his life-and-death battle with Roy Batty, Gaff shouts to him across the rooftop: 'You did a man's work. But are you a man? It's hard to be sure of who's who around here.' (In an alternate scene available in the Five-Disk Ultimate Collector's Edition Gaff says: 'You've done a man's job, sir. But are you sure you are a man? It's hard to tell who's who around here.') In an unused scene that would have appeared last in the film as Deckard and Rachael drive through a forest, she looks at him and says, 'You and I were made for each other.' The look on Deckard's face shows that he understands the significance of her comment.
18. Sammon is reporting a common sentiment expressed by fans who view Deckard as human. His own judicious view is that the only

correct answer to the question of whether Deckard is a replicant is: 'Maybe.'
19. In the documentary DVD *Dangerous Days: Making Blade Runner* (included in the Five-Disk Ultimate Collector's Edition), Hampton Fancher remarks, 'My interpretation [of the unicorn scene] had *nothing* to do with, oh, that shows that Deckard is a replicant. I don't think that *anything* should show that Deckard is a replicant. If you think that you're already wrong. It's just a question mark that is interesting. The answer is stupid.'

2 Being Human

1. Likewise, fellow blade runner Dave Holden derisively refers to Zhora as 'a washing machine.' His comment appears in a deleted scene available in the Five-Disc Ultimate Collector's Edition.
2. See, for example: Barad (2009), Bukatman (2012), Kolb (1997), Mulhall (1994, 2008), and Redmond (2008).
3. In BR 7-80 Deckard (a play on 'Descartes'?) expresses to Rachael a similar view: 'Andies [that is, androids] only simulate suffering – if they're programmed for it,' to which Rachael pointedly responds, '[S]ome of the folks around here are more programmed than me.'
4. In BR 7-80, Holden expresses a somewhat similar view to Deckard: 'Believe me, take it from an old pro, no matter how good we get we're never gonna make an artificial anything that can feel. It's a contradiction.'
5. We learn from Leon's file, being read by Deckard in a deleted scene, that 'Leon had been an ammunition loader on intergalactic runs. He could lift 400 lb atomic loads all day and night. They jacked his pain threshold up so high the only way you could hurt him was to kill him.' But that does not mean that he lacked intelligence, or a sense of humor. Brion James (Leon Kowalski in the film) explains: 'But even though Leon had only a C-level mental capacity, I always thought C-Mental was still about fifty percent above anything that was human. I think that comes across during Leon's interrogation; in that scene, I'm fucking with Holden, playing mind games with him' (Sammon 1996, p. 107). In BR 7-80, after he shoots Holden with a laser pistol, for good measure he shoots the Voight-Kampff machine Holden was using as well.
6. Or not – perhaps this mismatch was left uncorrected in order to further convey the inherent uncertainty in matters of life and death that is a major motif in the film. That alley scene is crucial because a moment after Leon names the moment of Deckard's death, his own

Notes

moment of death arrives, thereby illustrating an ancient truth: *Mors certa, hora incerta.* ('Death is certain, the hour uncertain.')

7. Perhaps to underscore one of the film's themes that nothing is quite as it seems, Pris's and Zhora's appearances and abilities seem to be switched in relation to their respective Off-world functions. Zhora, whose Off-world job description is 'political homicide,' attempts to conceal her identity on earth by posing as an erotic entertainer, whereas Pris, whose Off-world function is as a 'basic pleasure model,' displays impressive hand-to-hand combat skills in her attempt to kill Deckard. A clue is provided in a deleted scene in which Deckard, reading from Zhora's file, says: 'Zhora – originally turned out as a hot pleasure model, had been re-trained for assassination. Her psychological profile looked like a combination porno tape and a very serious traffic accident.'

8. In BR 7-80, Deckard's (talking) Esper machine informs him that the replicants are 'third generation Nexus Sixes, constructed of skin-flesh culture, selected enogenic transfer conversion capable of self-perpetuating thought, paraphysical abilities and developed for emigration program.'

9. The final 1982 script says 'man' and 'police-man,' but BR 2-81 says 'men' and 'Police men.' The fact that Deckard and Gaff are both in Leon's room, and that the spoken words (inflected by Rutger Hauer's slight accent) could be heard either way, favors the plural construal.

10. We learn from Roy's file, being read by Deckard in a deleted scene, that 'Military tests had thrown him into every Off-World battle from the fighting at Tannhäuser Gates to the massacre on the Menezualen moons. Consistent excellence. Top performance, it said.'

11. We also have the testimony of the director himself. According to Ridley Scott, 'Certainly because the replicants are highly sophisticated machines one starts to relate to them as human beings. But one must remember that they are *not* human beings' (Peary 1984, p. 53).

12. In BR 2-81 Bryant tells Deckard that they did an autopsy on the replicant fried trying to break into the Tyrell Corporation. They did not realize that it was a replicant until three hours into the autopsy, suggesting that the replicants' internal anatomy is similar to that of humans. That they are physically nearly indistinguishable is a given, although it takes some of the characters a while to realize this. In a deleted scene Dave Holden warns Deckard what he is up against: 'It ain't like it used to be, Deck, it's tough now. These replicants are not just a bunch of muscle-miners anymore. They're no damn different than you or me... They're almost us, Deck.'

13. The owl is a traditional symbol of wisdom; so perhaps Tyrell's artificial owl symbolizes his false wisdom (Sammon 1996, p. 171).

Notes

He certainly seems to lack common sense. Rather than telling Roy, 'Sure, we'll fix you up,' while secretly calling for security, he gives him an academic answer and explains to him why his request cannot be granted – then gets his head crushed.

14. In *Electric Sheep* (Dick 1968a, p. 26) PKD presents the androids as utterly *lacking* this distinctive human characteristic. As Deckard there reflects, 'Empathy, evidently, existed only within the human community, whereas intelligence to some degree could be found throughout every phylum and order including the arachnida.' A page later, PKD has Deckard conclude that, 'Evidently the humanoid robot constituted a solitary predator' (Dick 1968a, p. 27). The humanoid robot, like a spider, lacks empathic capacities. By contrast, all normal human beings have this characteristic. Consequently, the humanoid robots of the novel are decidedly *less* than human.

15. In BR 7-80 this scene conveys a very different sense of Batty and what he values. There he says sarcastically, without even looking at Leon, 'Did you get your precious "things"?'

16. Joseph Francavilla (1997, p. 9) writes, 'not only [does] the contrast and opposition between the human and the android [sic] become blurred, but also ... the contrasting characteristics of each life form ... switch sides.' To be more precise, the contrasting characteristics do not really *switch sides* – as if the humans and replicants in the film come to *acquire* characteristics of one another that they previously lacked. The change to which Francavilla refers takes place (if the film is successful) in the *audience* rather than in the characters. As the story unfolds it becomes progressively clearer that some of the characteristics typically associated with human beings are possessed by the replicants, and vice versa. Rachael might be an exception. As Rushing and Frenz (1995, p. 158) point out, so long as Rachael believes herself to be human, she acts with cold, mechanical indifference, just like the people around her. When she begins to suspect that she is a replicant, and even more so once she fully accepts that she *is* one, she drops her cold demeanor and begins to more freely express her emotions – just like the other replicants.

17. Leonard Heldreth (1997, p. 48) observes that, 'Holden ... looks more like our traditional view of an android than Leon does.' Rachela Morrison (1990, p. 3) goes even farther: 'The scene sets up the dichotomy of replicant vs. human, and blurs the distinction between the two.... [T]he blade runner cop is emotionless and perfectly groomed and the suspected replicant is round-shouldered, scruffy, and unshaven with a receding chin and protruding midriff. Immediately the spectator's expectations are frustrated in trying to differentiate the human from the nonhuman.'

Notes

18. According to Marilyn Gwaltney (1997, p. 33), 'Since these androids [that is, the replicants] are biologically human, even if they are not sexually reproduced, they must be considered human beings in the sense of being *homo sapiens*' [*sic*]. This is not self-evident. According to the most commonly accepted scientific understanding of 'species,' the replicants would *not* be *Homo sapiens* because they are not sexually produced beings in our evolutionary lineage. According to this view, simply being a living thing 'produced' by humans is not sufficient for membership in our species – otherwise thoroughbred racehorses and transgenic mice would qualify as members of our species. By contrast, we probably would consider human clones to be *human beings*, despite not being produced by sexual processes. Replicants might be *Homo sapiens* in *this* sense.
19. Judith Barad (2009, p. 32) writes: 'In the end, it's not Tyrell or any genetic engineer who can make Batty human – he must create this in himself.' In her view, what *Blade Runner* teaches us is that 'what it means to be human' is simply to be recognized as such by oneself and others.
20. As Stephen Mulhall (1994, p. 89) writes, '[W]e know all there is to know about the replicants which is relevant to their claim for human status; there is no further fact of the matter being kept from us. Nothing counts *against* their being treated as human … except the unwillingness or refusal of other human beings to do so.'
21. This is less clear in some deleted scenes in which Deckard is reviewing the 'poop sheets' on the rogue replicants and reflecting, 'You could call it [that is, Tyrell's business] commerce, or you could call it growing slaves, depending on whether you were polite or not.… For all practical purposes, they were people.'
22. Ironically (since in *Electric Sheep* Deckard becomes *dehumanized* by killing androids), Philip K. Dick glimpsed something of this when he expressed what he took to be another element (in addition to empathy) that struck him as an essential feature of the authentically human: 'It is not only an intrinsic property of the organism but the situation in which it finds itself. That which happens to it, that which it is confronted by, pierced by, and must deal with – certain agonizing situations create, on the spot, a human where a moment before, there was only, as the Bible says, clay' (Dick 1972, p. 202).
23. This issue is treated very differently in *Electric Sheep*. As Dick explains, 'In the novel, [J. R.] Isidore has a naïve love directed toward the androids; Rick Deckard's view is that the androids are vicious machines that must be destroyed. These two different (and mutually exclusive) views, running parallel to each other in a twin-plot scheme, merge toward the end of the work, when Isidore is confronted by

Notes

the cruelty of the androids as they cut the legs off the spider. Rick Deckard's view has won out, and the proof of this is that Isidore tells the bounty hunter where the androids are [hiding] within the decayed apartment building' (Dick 1968b, p. 155). In fact, however, in the book Isidore *refuses* to tell Deckard where the androids are hiding (Dick 1968a, p. 194). Perhaps Dick meant to underscore the idea that memory is a fallible guide to reality.

3 Persons

1. Judith B. Kerman (1997, p. 22) observes that, 'As the film builds our empathy with the replicants, it strongly suggests that they have the rights of humans, and the contradiction of the replicant industry becomes clear.'
2. In BR 7-80, Roy Batty cryptically remarks, 'The world doesn't minimize his omnipotence, just makes it more malignant.'
3. As neuroscientist Michael Gazzaniga (2005, p. 120) wryly observes, 'Of all the things we remember, the truly amazing fact is that some of them are true.'
4. Persons in this view are worthy of moral consideration, not because each *individual* person is capable of exercising reason but because persons are the *sort of being* that is capable of exercising reason. Some individual persons may have a negligible capacity for rational thought.
5. In BR 7-80 Rachael asks Deckard, 'Don't you think anything that can suffer deserves to be considered?'
6. Interestingly, in BR 7-80 Batty facetiously apologizes to Deckard for *his own* irrationality and unsportsmanlike conduct after bashing Deckard's head into the wall several times.
7. Stephen Mulhall (1994, p. 88) notes that the violence inflicted upon the replicants, and the pain and suffering they exhibit in response, 'drives home the fact that they are embodied, and hence capable of manifesting the range and complexity of behavior open to any human being.' He concludes that, 'The empathic claim exerted upon us by those scenes ... is what grounds the film's assumption that it is in this aspect of the replicants' embodiment which is pertinent to their candidature for human status.' This is not quite right. Pain-behavior *per se* is not sufficient to warrant an ascription of human status, otherwise any living thing with a complex nervous system might qualify as human. It *is* sufficient, however, to give the replicants, and any other beings capable of suffering, moral standing, and thereby to make them worthy of moral consideration.

Notes

8. Martin (2005, pp. 113–14) adopts a similar view with regard to the replicants: '[A]s we condescend to accept Roy's *ersatz* humanity, we compromise the value of our own. The problem here ... is in ascribing human attributes – compassion, feeling, morality – to the non-human, while at the same time denigrating humanity itself.... We compromise our dearest possession, our humanity, in letting ourselves be lured into Roy's trap.' Of course, this presupposes that the replicants are *non-human*, and thus begs the question considered in the previous chapter.
9. In the film Leon's remark about 'having an itch you can never scratch' is obscure. A clue to what he means is provided in BR 2-81 where he explains more fully: 'Sex, reproduction, security, the simple things. But no way to satisfy them. To be homesick with no place to go. Potential with no way to use it. Lots of little oversights in the Nexus 6. I tell you, nothing is worse than having an itch you can never scratch.'
10. Susana P. Tosca (2005, p. 92) describes Pris as 'a prostitute.' Suppose that description is correct. Is there anything wrong with Pris's design and use for this purpose? David Levy (2010, p. 229) asks: 'Should [robot prostitutes] ... be considered to have legal rights and ethical status, and therefore worthy of society's concern for their well-being and behavior, just as our view of sex workers is very much influenced by our concern for *their* well-being and behavior?' Levy does not answer this question, but it is worth asking. Besides, can a humanoid robot even *be* a 'prostitute' in the first place? Pris may be more like a robot sex slave – a description that carries its own load of perplexing moral quandaries.

4 Identity

1. In Descartes' philosophy 'soul' and 'mind' signify the same thing, namely, an immaterial thinking substance (*res cogitans*). In this chapter I use the word 'soul' to contrast it with other views of personal identity that focus on particular aspects of *minds* (memories, for example).
2. In *Electric Sheep* (Dick 1968a, p. 118), Rick Deckard asks fellow bounty hunter Phil Resch, 'Do you think androids have souls?' By that point in the novel Resch knows that he is himself an android. He doesn't answer Deckard's question: 'Cocking his head on one side, Phil Resch gazed at him in even greater puzzlement.'
3. Debbora Battaglia (2001, p. 507) asserts that, '*Blade Runner*'s replicants ... [by] clinging to ersatz photographs of families of origin that never

existed ... achieve a willed forgetting of the lie of their heredity.' This may be true of Leon, who values his photos while knowing full well that he is a replicant. In BR 7-80 his photos are even described as, 'The kind of anonymous stuff sold by the bunch in dusty junk shops.' But this does not seem equally true of Rachael who is sincere when she shows to Deckard the photo ostensibly of her as a young girl with her mother, and who then disgustedly discards this photo once her replicant status is confirmed.

4. In a technical sense this claim is not quite right, because there remains the logical possibility that Rachael had the experiences represented in the memories, had her memory erased, and then received memory implants which are the immediate cause of her present recollections. In the present context we can safely ignore bizarre logical possibilities like this.

5. In BR 7-80 Rachael remarks, 'It's strange to suddenly realize that what you thought was your life is actually someone else's fabrication.' Deckard then clumsily attempts to sympathize: 'I can imagine,' to which Rachael retorts, 'Can you? I couldn't.'

6. Abrams (2009, p. 13) interprets Rachael's situation prior to learning that she is a replicant as follows: 'She doesn't know her entire cognitive groundwork is artificial: her memories aren't real.' This description is not quite right. Rachael's 'cognitive groundwork' consists in more than just her memories; and presumably *all* of her memories are not implants. For example, her recollection of introducing herself to Deckard would be a genuine memory if anything is.

7. In BR 2-81 in response to Deckard's question about where Tyrell acquired the memories for Rachael, Tyrell explains: 'I simply copied and regenerated cells from the brain of my sixteen-year-old niece. Rachael remembers what my little niece remembers.'

8. This point can be reinforced by considering an addendum to the foregoing thought-experiment. Let all of the parts removed from my car during its extensive repair work be brought together and reassembled into a vehicle that is materially identical to the car prior to replacement of the first part. There would then be *two* candidates for being 'identical' to the car with which we began: one that has come about through a gradual replacement of each of its parts and one that was reassembled from all the original parts. Which one is *really* 'the same car' as the original? Is there some *fact* of the matter that makes one answer correct and the other incorrect? Depending on one's specific interests, either one might just as well be considered 'the same car,' or one might simply reject that question as presupposing a metaphysical view that need not be embraced. Metaphysically speaking that may be all there is to say about it.

Notes

9. In BR 7-80 Rachael reports, 'A part of me is glad [to know the truth]. I think I feel more. I don't like who I was before.'

5 Consciousness

1. In the previous chapter we considered Descartes' view that each of us is a *soul* for the purpose of understanding a popular view of personal identity. In this chapter I use the word 'mind' to better compare his view with competing views and explanations of consciousness.
2. Among his many accomplishments, Descartes invented analytic geometry, including the coordinate system named after him.
3. The 'location' problem seems irresolvable. But subsequent thinkers influenced by Descartes propose a number of ingenious solutions to the interaction problem. Gottfried Wilhelm von Leibniz (1646–1716) proposes that God designed the universe so that minds and bodies operate like two pre-synchronized clocks that never interact but only give the appearance of doing so. Nicolas Malebranche (1638–1715) suggests that perhaps at the moment a person decides to move his arm, God moves his arm for him. Unfortunately, these proposed solutions (and others even more bizarre) invariably generate problems as serious as the ones they were designed to solve. Would not a preset clockwork universe preclude genuine human free will, and hence morality? If all human actions are really brought about by God's intervention, then is not God ultimately at fault when the murderer plunges his knife into his victim's chest?
4. The choice of a chess game to be the vehicle by which Batty seeks to meet his maker and to thereby extend his life cannot be accidental insofar as it naturally invites the viewer to relate *Blade Runner* to another classic cinematic meditation on life, death, God, and meaning: Ingmar Bergman's *The Seventh Seal*. Both stories take place in worlds ravaged (it is suggested) by the consequences of human sin (the Black Death of the fourteenth century, nuclear fallout in the twenty-first century). In both films a warrior with short-cropped blond hair (the knight Antonius Block, the Nexus 6 combat model Roy Batty) embarks on a journey home, along the way playing chess with an individual (Death, Tyrell) who holds the key to extending his life. Both are told that the salvation they seek is unobtainable. Both are consequently forced to work out the problem of the meaning of their lives for themselves. Both are intent on saving others even as they attempt to fend off death themselves. Both achieve a kind of personal redemption by doing so just before dying. Significantly, the configuration of pieces on the chessboard is similar (though not

identical) to that of 'The Immortal Game' – a brilliant chess match played on 21 June 1851, in London, between Adolf Anderssen and Lionel Kieseritzky. Anderssen made bold sacrifices, giving up both rooks, a bishop, and finally his queen in order to checkmate Kieseritzky with just three remaining minor pieces. Roy Batty is playing chess to extend his life. Like pawns, replicants are considered to be of such little individual value that they can be sacrificed for the sake of those like Tyrell who dwell in kingly splendor far from ordinary people.

5. In 1997 an IBM computer system nicknamed 'Deep Blue' won a six-game chess match against then world champion chess grandmaster Garry Kasparov, suggesting to some that a mere machine had bested a human at an activity that is (or at least was thought to be) distinctively human. Nine years later another computer program, Deep Fritz, defeated then reigning world champion chess grandmaster Vladimir Kramnik, suggesting that to some that it was only a matter of time before computers would be surpassing humans in other ways as well.

6. Software programs may not be physical in the strict sense (it is unclear what the ontological status of 'rules' might be), but arguably they are not part of the computer *per se* anyway. One can have a perfectly good, albeit not very useful, computer prior to loading any software on it.

6 Freedom

1. Tosca's primary interest is in exploring implanted memories and freedom in the *Blade Runner* PC game (a commercial spin-off of the film), but her comments quoted here are meant to apply to *Blade Runner* (the film) and *Electric Sheep* as well inasmuch as 'free will [is] an important topic in both Ridley Scott's film and Philip K. Dick's source novel' (Tosca 2005, p. 92).

2. Mulhall (1994, p. 95) attributes this line to *Tyrell*, which is clearly in error. Martin (2005, p. 110) interprets Roy's words as posing a *question*: 'Nothing the god of biomechanics wouldn't let you into heaven for?' thereby making him ask Tyrell whether his own misdeeds are forgivable. This seems implausible, not only because Roy does not utter those words as a question, but because as the rest of his actions demonstrate he is utterly unapologetic about his deeds, conveying no sense of needing to be forgiven and no faith in an afterlife.

3. As I will use this term, 'Determinism' here refers to the view more precisely known as *Hard Determinism*. Shortly we will consider other views that either embrace causal determinism but deny that it precludes free will (e.g. *Soft Determinism*) or remain agnostic with regard

Notes

to determinism (*Compatibilism*), arguing that we can be free in a significant sense whether or not causal determinism obtains.
4. This line appears in BR 7-80. After driving out of the city, Deckard shoots Rachael – presumably at her request to deny Gaff or another blade runner the satisfaction of doing so.
5. In *The Last Samurai* (2003), the samurai leader Katsumoto Moritsugu (Ken Watanabe), reflecting on whether to array his men against an overwhelmingly superior military force, asks his American friend, Capt. Nathan Algren (Tom Cruise), 'Do you believe a man can change his destiny?' Algren responds, 'I believe a man does what he can until his destiny is revealed.' *The Last Samurai* is not the philosophical masterpiece that *Blade Runner* is, but Algren's response may still be the most sagacious response a film can offer to this philosophical problem.

7 Being Good

1. The analysis here is indebted to that of David Owen (2007, pp. 23ff.) but does not attempt to follow Owen's analysis in all respects.
2. In words reminiscent of Pierre-Simon Laplace's, Nietzsche (1878–80, §106) writes: 'When we see a waterfall, we think we see freedom of will and choice in the innumerable turnings, windings, breakings of the waves; but everything is necessary; each movement can be calculated mathematically. Thus it is with human actions; if one were omniscient, one would be able to calculate each individual action in advance, each step in the progress of knowledge, each error, each act of malice. To be sure the acting man is caught in his illusion of volition; if the wheel of the world were to stand still for a moment and an omniscient, calculating mind were there to take advantage of this interruption, he would be able to tell into the farthest future of each being and describe every rut that wheel will roll upon. The acting man's delusion about himself, his assumption that free will exists, is also part of the calculable mechanism.'
3. In *The Twilight of the Idols*, Nietzsche (1888a, §5) makes it clear that he thinks that Christian morality stands or falls with a belief in God: 'When one gives up Christian belief one thereby deprives oneself of the *right* to Christian morality. For the latter is absolutely *not* self-evident.... Christianity is a system, a consistently thought out and *complete* view of things. If one breaks out of it a fundamental idea, the belief in God, one thereby breaks the whole thing to pieces: one has nothing of any consequence left in one's hands.... it stands or falls with the belief in God.'

Notes

4. Roy Batty experiences this moral disorientation as he rides the elevator down the side of the Tyrell Corporation pyramid. He knows that his God is dead because he has killed him. With 'distant suns' clearly visible above him, his face registers the profound disorientation of someone who finds himself divested of any stable ground for values. With the death of his God went any hope of realizing the goal of acquiring 'more life' that had structured his decisions. Roy is now forced to confront the fact that he is without any fixed points upon which to anchor his choices and actions. His face shows that this prospect is both terrifying and exhilarating.
5. An indication of the importance of these lines is that they appear, *verbatim*, in BR 7-80, BR 2-81, and in the final *Blade Runner* script.
6. Robin Wood (2003, p. 165) interprets Batty's line as 'contemptuously ironic' inasmuch as 'hero and villain change places, all moral certainties based upon the status quo collapse.' Alexis Harley (2005, pp. 70–1) writes: 'Roy's ironic rendering of "good" calls into question its diffuse meanings: Christlike and virtuous, promoting happiness, competent, sporting, legitimate. Deckard's violent ... execution of Zhora and Pris contradicts the first two; his physical inferiority to Roy, the third; and his now desperate scramble to dispatch Roy however he can, the fourth. The only sense in which Deckard could possibly be "good" is in his legitimacy – his being legitimately human and so on the side of the law.' Byron (2008, pp. 52–3) goes further in interpreting this scene as providing clues that Roy is also challenging Deckard's status as a *man*, that is, as a human being – an interpretation which seems to me to be a stretch.
7. The brutality of the replicants is accentuated in BR 7-80 as they are considering what to do about Deckard as he approaches the building in which they are hiding. Pris offers to intercept him. Roy gives his blessing while conveying terrifying malice – 'Okay, but don't kill him. Save a little for everybody. A masterpiece.' A moment later he throws their 'best and only friend' Sebastian through a next-to-top floor window, sending him hurtling to the pavement thirty feet below (presumably as a message to Deckard) where his body explodes upon impact.
8. It may be no accident that the principal human characters in the film exhibit many of the sickly qualities characteristic (in Nietzsche's view) of slave-morals, such as weakness, impotence, cowardice, and meekness. Dave Holden conducts a spectacularly inept Voight-Kampff test on Leon, which results in his ending up on life support. Gaff limps along with the aid of a cane, and seems careful to stay out of harm's way, only showing up *after* replicants are retired or expire. Bryant comes across as someone more comfortable strong-arming others to

Notes

pursue dangerous assignments than in placing himself in the thick of things. Rick Deckard has a tendency to numb his feelings with booze, and seems to suffer from chronic *ennui*. Sebastian, who suffers from accelerated decrepitude and is so lonely that he has to create mechanical friends, appears weak and meek. In short, the humans in the film seem more like Nietzsche's 'last man' – spiritually exhausted – than the next stage of human social-philosophical evolution.

9. This is the sense conveyed in BR 7-80 where Roy *does* complete the couplet: 'Unless you're alive you can't play. And if don't play, you don't get to be alive.'
10. Less plausibly, Mulhall (1994, pp. 95–6) also suggests that Batty affirms Nietzsche's idea of eternal recurrence. The comparison *is* apt insofar as Roy eventually rejects any external guarantor of his the values. However, this doctrine does not sit well with Batty's soliloquy moments before his death which only makes sense on the assumption that he believes that those experiences could be his only *once*, and that once he dies they are necessarily lost forever.
11. As Rutger Hauer acknowledges, 'Sebastian's just a pawn, and a nice guy. I didn't need to kill him' (Sammon 1996, p. 176).
12. Obviously, Deely meant to refer to *Rick Deckard*, the character *played by* actor Harrison Ford! The tendency to conflate characters and actors when discussing a film sometimes reaches comic proportions, as when *Blade Runner*'s Associate Producer Ivor Powell, commenting on the final scene of the Director's Cut, opines that, 'Gaff was letting Deckard know that Eddie Olmos knew Ford's private thoughts' (Sammon 1996, p. 357).
13. In the documentary DVD *Dangerous Days: Making Blade Runner* (included in the Five-Disk Ultimate Collector's Edition), Jake Scott (Ridley Scott's son) describes *Blade Runner* as 'this Nietzschean, sort of dystopic, philosophical and dark existential film.' That seems about right.

8 God

1. This scene is available in the Five-Disk Ultimate Collector's Edition.
2. As Roy is killing Tyrell, we catch a brief glimpse of Sebastian, cowering in the shadows, soundlessly mouthing 'Oh my God!,' thereby reinforcing Tyrell's divine status.
3. In BR 2-81, Roy's improvised rendition of Blake seems somewhat less apropos of nothing. There it is in response to Chew's outrage at having two replicants standing in his lab: 'You illegal. Can't come here! Illegal. You not belong here. Up there!'

Notes

4. As W. Russel Gray (1997, p. 66) puts it, '*Blade Runner*'s Los Angeles resembles Hell on a good day (or night).' Philip K. Dick, drawing upon another classic depiction of hell, described it this way: 'It's like everything you hate about urban life now, escalated to the level of Dante's inferno…. You can't even run in the future, there's so many people milling around, doing nothing' (Rickman 1997, p. 106). The fire-belching smokestacks of the film's opening scene were inspired by the Chevron oil refinery in El Segundo, California, where I lived for five years, and which I still see on almost a daily basis.
5. David Desser (1997, p. 54) notes that, 'Satan is known as the Great Antagonist, the Adversary, who vows to bring down, first, God, and finding that impossible, Man, God's proudest creation. In *Blade Runner*, the antagonist of God and Man is clearly the character of Roy Batty, proudest creation of *Blade Runner*'s God-Figure, Eldon Tyrell.' Desser (1997, p. 54) also notes that, 'Batty's greatest Satanic characteristic is his willingness and desire to confront his creator, a creator who, god-like, dwells in Heaven – the penthouse of the 700-story pyramid that houses the Tyrell Corp…. Batty negotiates his way through hell before rising to Heaven's penthouse to confront his maker and kill him.' Interestingly, this trajectory is just the opposite of Satan's, who first confronts God in heaven, but being less powerful must pursue his diabolical plans in hell.
6. The poem's second story arc, centering on Adam and Eve, is concerned with their relationship to one another, their disobeying of God's command not to eat from the Tree of the Knowledge of Good and Evil, and their consequent expulsion from paradise. Eve is presented as deferring to Adam's greater knowledge and authority. Adam is presented as a heroic figure, but at the same time as a greater sinner than Eve because he is aware that what he is doing is wrong. This second story arc also has resonances in *Blade Runner* although they are less pronounced and detecting them requires taking greater interpretive liberties. Rachael defers to Deckard's greater knowledge and authority. Deckard is a heroic figure in protecting Rachael, but is a greater sinner because he comes to realize that what he has been doing, namely killing synthetic people, is wrong. David Desser (1997, p. 56) observes that, 'Milton's *Paradise Lost* ends with the promise of redemption to come for future generations of Mankind; *Blade Runner* ends with the redemption of one man who will perhaps, like Adam, bring forth a new race upon the Earth.' There is some merit in this interpretation. At the end of the Theatrical Version Deckard flees Los Angeles with Rachael to a sunny, verdant landscape that seems like paradise compared to the decaying squalor of the city. By rescuing rather than retiring Rachael, despite Bryant's

Notes

orders, Deckard *has* begun to redeem himself. Supposing that he and Rachael will literally bring forth a new race upon the earth, on the other hand, requires inferences that none of the versions of the film licenses us to make.

7. Sebastian, a deformed victim of premature aging, is the counter-part to Frankenstein's deformed assistant, 'Fritz,' in the 1931 film directed by James Whale. (There is no counter-part to Sebastian in Shelley's novel.) Sebastian meets the same fate as Fritz at the hands of the artificial life form he helped to create. Clayton (2006, p. 91) compares the slowly revolving fans on the roof of the Bradbury building to the windmills in Whale's film. The thematic connection is acknowledged in BR 2-81 when Deckard says to Tyrell: 'I saw an old movie once. The guy had bolts in his head' – an obvious reference to Frankenstein's monster in film versions of Shelley's story. That Tyrell is pleased by being compared to Frankenstein suggests that he did not grasp the moral of that story.

8. An almost opposite view is expressed in BR 7-80 in which Deckard in voice-over narration reports that the church backed the use of androids, or at least had no moral reservations about them: 'The big religious boys said that Androids, no matter how human, were objects; only God could make people. I'm not religious, but I was inclined to agree. Otherwise I'd be out of a job.' In Sartre's view, if people are made by God they are *objects* no less than are androids.

9. The idea of the replicants as manufactured objects whose essence has been stamped on them is underscored in *Electric Sheep* when Rachael explains, 'We *are* machines, stamped out like bottle caps. It's an illusion that I – I personally – really exist; I'm just a representation of a type' (Dick 1968a, p. 165).

10. In his longer and more demanding book, *Being and Nothingness* (1943), Sartre introduced a related distinction between 'being-in-itself' and 'being-for-itself.' An artifact (e.g. a stapler) is a 'being-in-itself.' Lacking consciousness, it cannot even conceive of itself, much less conceive of itself as different from what it is. A human being, by contrast, is a 'being-for-itself.' Through consciousness it is able to conceive of what is not, and hence can conceive of itself as different from what it is. Consciousness of what is not is the basis for the absolute freedom possessed by humans. Hence, according to Sartre, there is an absolute difference between an 'in-itself' and a 'for-itself.' It is in the gap between the self that is the subject and the object of awareness that human freedom is realized. As Sartre explains, this does not mean that human beings can *be* anything they wish to be simply by deciding, only that nothing external determines our choices.

11. *Blade Runner* screenwriter Hampton Fancher points out that this is 'the only shot in the whole movie where you see stars. And they're moving away from him, as if he's some kind of fallen angel' (Sammon 1996, p. 178) – a theme to be discussed later in this book. He also attributes to Roy the thoughts: 'What have I done? I'm going to die for this, but I'm going to be immortal for it, too' (Sammon 1996, p. 178). The attribution to Roy of the thought, 'What have I done?' seems plausible enough. Having staked everything on securing more life from his creator, he may not have had any backup plan. The attribution of the latter two thoughts, however, is rather implausible given that Roy knew that he was soon going to die soon anyway, and immortality (literally or figuratively) was precisely what was *not* available to him.

9 Death

1. As I will use the term, *death* is an event that stands between *dying* and *being dead*. It signifies the final cessation of vital processes in a body that was previously alive. But the word 'death' is also sometimes used to convey the idea of personal annihilation, that is, the end of the *person* in any form. 'Death' in the former sense need not entail a belief in 'death' in the latter sense. To see why, consider the perspectives of a Physicalist and a soul-body Dualist regarding their own deaths. For the Physicalist, application of the two meanings of 'death' will coincide perfectly. To her the final cessation of vital processes in her *body* (bracketing for now various science fiction scenarios) entails the complete annihilation of *herself*. For a soul-body Dualist, however, the cessation of vital processes in her body does not necessarily entail personal annihilation because she might believe that she will continue to exist in a disembodied form. In the discussions that follow the context should make clear which sense is intended.
2. In *Blade Runner* the replicants have been intentionally designed with a maximum four-year life span in order to better control them. In *Electric Sheep* the androids live only four years because no one could figure out a way to solve technical problems connected with cell renewal (Dick 1968a, p. 173). The latter idea is reflected twice in BR 7-80. The first is when Rachael remarks: 'I guess the date of your birth is important if you know you're not made to last.' The second is when Tyrell says to Batty: 'Rolls Royces are made to last – at least they were. But I'm afraid you're a Ferrari – a high-strung racing car – built to win, not to last.'

Notes

3. Mulhall (2008, p. 33) takes for granted that the replicants' quest is motivated by 'the desire to extend their allotted span of days until it matches that of a human being.' In his view, 'the leader of the replicants is obsessed in his quest for life, for a life which is on a par with that of human beings. To show that Roy Baty [sic] misconceives this quest as one for *more* life – as if a replicant might become human by living longer – is the goal of the film.' Of course, Roy *is* obsessed in his quest for more life. But Mulhall may have the motivation for Roy's quest backwards. It is not that he wants more life in order to become *more human*, as if that were intrinsically valuable. Rather, he wants to become more human only insofar as this means having *more life*, that is, to have more opportunities for the sorts of experiences that he relates to Deckard in the waning moments of his brief life.
4. As Ludwig Wittgenstein (1922, p. 185) observed many centuries later, 'In death the world does not change, but ceases. Death is not an event in life: We do not live to experience death.'
5. In defense of experientialism (in an entirely different context), Sam Harris insists that human well-being consists *entirely* in states of consciousness, which in turn depend entirely on states of the world and of the human brain: 'Let us begin with the fact of consciousness: I think that we can know, through reason alone, that consciousness is the only intelligible domain of value. What is the alternative? I invite you to try to think of a source of value that has absolutely nothing to do with the (actual or potential) experience of conscious beings. Take a moment to think about what this would entail: whatever this alternative is, it cannot affect the experience of any creature (in this life or in any other). Put this thing in a box and what you have in that box is – it would seem, *by definition* – the least interesting thing in the universe' (Harris 2010, p. 32). The fact that something is the 'least interesting thing in the universe' would not *ipso facto* guarantee that is it irrelevant for human well-being, but the burden would then be squarely on the opponent of experientialism to explain how it *could* matter.
6. Sartre articulates a potentially life-altering perspective. Contrary to people who complain that 'there remains within me a host of propensities, inclinations, possibilities, that one wouldn't have guessed from the mere series of things I've done,' Sartre (1946, p. 32) insists that, 'There is no reality except in action.... Man ... exists only to the extent that he fulfills himself; he is therefore nothing else ... than the ensemble of his acts, nothing else than his life.' Jean Racine was an acclaimed seventeenth-century playwright. Acknowledging Racine's considerable talents as a dramatist,

Notes

Sartre nonetheless insists: '[T]he genius of Racine is in his series of tragedies. Outside of that, there is nothing. Why say that Racine could have written another tragedy, when he didn't write it? A man is involved in life, leaves his impress on it, and outside of that there is nothing' (p. 33).

7. Steven Luper (1996, pp. 105–8) develops a similar argument focusing on *desires*. According to this argument, anything that thwarts one's desires is a misfortune. Because death thwarts all (or at least most) of one's desires, both those that one has at the moment of death as well as any that one would have acquired had one lived longer, it must be counted as the greatest misfortune of all. But this argument is vulnerable to the criticism that one only suffers a genuine misfortune if the desires that are thwarted are *ones that one would be better off having satisfied*. Some of the desires one has are such that, were they to be satisfied, they would bring more pain than pleasure. What matters are the positive experiences one would have had, not merely the satisfaction of one's desires. Consequently, we are back to the issue of whether by becoming dead Roy is harmed by missing out on whatever positive experiences that future might have included.

8. A somewhat less drastic way of making oneself relatively invulnerable to death on Rowlands' principles would be to limit oneself to goals whose achievement cannot be thwarted. For example, one could limit oneself to desiring only necessary truths, that is, facts or states of affairs that cannot fail to be or to be true, such as the desire that $2 + 2 = 4$, that all masses attract one another according to Newton's inverse square law, that the Berlin Wall fell in 1989, and the like. Such desires are satisfied regardless of when one dies, and thus are invulnerable to being thwarted by one's death. Obviously the cost of such a strategy would still be quite steep.

9. Titus Lucretius Carus, *On the Nature of Things*, 3.830–911 (Long and Sedley 1987, p. 151). '[T]he Carthaginians' probably refers Rome's adversary in the Punic Wars, a series of three wars fought between Rome and Carthage from 264 to 146 BCE – that is, to a period of time prior to Lucretius and his readers, and hence not something that any of them did or could experience.

10. Someone fascinated by imperial Rome at the height of its power who fancies that had he lived in that era he would have been among the political elite, might think himself unfortunate not to have been born in time for that experience. Even in cases like this, however, there will be still *earlier* times (for example, the Jurassic) for which he will not lament his absence, much less lament the fact that did not exist for the eternity prior to his actual birth.

Notes

11. Steven Luper (1996) calls attempts to 'death-proof' oneself as Epicureans propose 'thanatizing,' and those who engage in such an attempt, 'thanatics.' He rejects such attempts. The problem is that, 'Becoming dead to death requires becoming dead to life' (p. x). Thanatics are like physicians that propose a cure that is worse than the disease: 'To completely eliminate death's sting, we require an analgesic so powerful that it would numb us to *life*' (p. 104).
12. As Roy notes in BR 2-81, 'To act without understanding could lead to the very thing the act seeks to avoid.'

10 Time and Meaning

1. In BR 7-80 an ancestor of Tyrell's memorable line about 'the light that shines twice as bright' is spoken by Roy Batty to the fifth replicant, Mary: 'Think of yourself as a light, Mary. Shine before you're turned off.'
2. This assumption usually goes unquestioned. The cover of the US edition of *Time* magazine for 30 September 2013 asks, 'Can Google Solve Death? The search giant is launching a venture to extend the human life span' – thereby illustrating the common perception that death is a problem requiring a solution, and that the solution is and can only be a longer human life span.
3. Thomas Nagel (1986, p. 224) expresses such a view when he writes, '[G]iven the simple choice between living for another week and dying in five minutes I would always choose to live for another week; and by a version of mathematical induction I conclude that I would be glad to live forever.'
4. As Taylor (1970, p. 262) notes, 'we can in imagination disengage our wills from our lives' and for a few moments adopt a more objective perspective on them. We can note that we simply find ourselves in the world with one set of desires rather than another. But if so, what can quell the concern that at bottom acting on one's deepest desires is ultimately arbitrary?
5. Deckard, in a deleted scene. See the discussion below for the significance of this remark.
6. As Leon explains in BR 2-81, 'Sex, reproduction, security, the simple things. But no way to satisfy them. To be homesick with no place to go. Potential with no way to use it.'
7. As Ludwig Wittgenstein (1922, p. 185) rightly asks, 'Is some riddle solved by my surviving for ever? Is eternal life not as enigmatic as our present one?'
8. *Pythian Odes*, iii.

Epilogue

1. A related but distinct issue is whether or in what sense any film could be a genuine *work of philosophy* – a topic that constitutes a vigorous and ongoing debate within the philosophy of film. Among those who argue that films *cannot* constitute *bona fide* works of philosophy in any interesting sense are Andersen (2005), Livingston (2006), Russell (2000), and Smith (2006). Among those who counter that films *can* constitute *bona fide* works of philosophy are Carroll (2006), Cavell (1979), Mulhall (2008), and Wartenberg (2006). As my remarks here and throughout this book suggest, I am sympathetic to the latter perspective. *Blade Runner* is deeply philosophical in the way that it uses the replicants as mirrors for the human condition, thereby helping us to *see* the world through others' eyes and experiences and to thereby attain philosophical insights that might otherwise remain inaccessible to us. Whether or not one wants to describe this as an example of 'cinematic philosophy' seems to me less important.

Literature Cited

Abrams, J. J. (2009), 'Space, Time, and Subjectivity in Neo-Noir Cinema,' in M. T. Conard (ed.), *The Philosophy of Neo-Noir* (Lexington, KY: University of Kentucky Press), pp. 7–20.

Alessio, D. (2005), 'Redemption: "Race," Religion, Reality and the Far-Right: Science Fiction Film Adaptations of Philip K. Dick,' in W. Brooker (ed.), *The Blade Runner Experience: The Legacy of a Science Fiction Classic* (London: Wallflower Press), pp. 59–76.

Andersen, N. (2005), 'Is Film the Alien Other to Philosophy? Philosophy as Film in Mulhall's *On Film*,' *Film and Philosophy* 9:1–11.

Bahania, A. M. (1992), '1492: Conquest of Paradise,' in Laurence F. Knapp and Andrea F. Kulas (eds.), *Ridley Scott: Interviews* (Jackson, MS: University Press of Mississippi), pp. 81–8.

Barad, J. (2009), '*Blade Runner* and Sartre: The Boundaries of Humanity,' in M. T. Conard (ed.), *The Philosophy of Neo-Noir* (Lexington, KY: University of Kentucky Press), pp. 21–34.

Barlow, A. (1997), 'Philip K. Dick's Androids: Victimized Victimizers,' in J. B. Kerman (ed.), *Retrofitting* Blade Runner: *Issues in Ridley Scott's* Blade Runner *and Philip K. Dick's* Do Androids Dream of Electric Sheep, 2nd edition (Bowling Green, OH: Bowling Green University Press), pp. 76–89.

Battaglia, D. (2001), 'Multiplicities: An Anthropologist's Thoughts on Replicants and Clones in Popular Film,' *Critical Inquiry* 27(3):493–514.

Boozer, J. Jr. (1997), 'Crashing the Gates of Insight,' in J. B. Kerman (ed.), *Retrofitting* Blade Runner: *Issues in Ridley Scott's* Blade Runner *and Philip K. Dick's* Do Androids Dream of Electric Sheep?, 2nd edition (Bowling Green, OH: Bowling Green University Press), pp. 212–28.

Bray, H. (1982), Review of *Blade Runner*, *Christianity Today* 26(14):97.

Brooker, P. (2005), 'Imagining the Real: *Blade Runner* and Discourses on the Postmetropolis,' in W. Brooker (ed.), *The Blade Runner Experience: The Legacy of a Science Fiction Classic* (London: Wallflower Press), pp. 213–24.

Brueckner, A. J. and Fischer, J. M. (1986), 'Why is Death Bad?' *Philosophical Studies* 50(2):213–21.

Bryson, J. J. (2010), 'Robots Should Be Slaves,' in Y. Wilks (ed.), *Close Encounters with Artificial Companions: Key Social, Psychological, Ethical and Design Issues* (Amsterdam: John Benjamins), pp. 63–74.

Literature Cited

Bukatman, S. (2012), *Blade Runner*, 2nd edition (London: Palgrave Macmillan).

Byron, J. (2008), 'Replicants R Us: The Crisis of Authenticity in Blade Runner,' *Sydney Studies in English* 34:41–62.

Camus, A. (1955), *The Myth of Sisyphus and Other Essays* (New York: Vintage International).

Čapek, K. (1921), *Rossum's Universal Robots (R.U.R.)* (London: Penguin, 2004).

Carrère, E. (2004), *I Am Alive and You Are Dead: A Journey into the Mind of Philip K. Dick*, translated by T. Bent (New York: Metropolitan Books).

Carroll, N. (2006), 'Philosophizing Through the Moving Image: The Case of Serene Velocity,' *Journal of Aesthetics and Art Criticism* 64(1):173–85.

Cavell, S. (1979), *The World Viewed: Reflections on the Ontology of Film*, enlarged edition (Cambridge, MA: Harvard University Press).

Chalmers, D. (1996), *The Conscious Mind: In Search of a Fundamental Theory* (New York: Oxford University Press).

Churchland, P. M. (1981), 'Eliminative Materialism and the Propositional Attitudes,' *Journal of Philosophy* 78:67–90.

Clayton, J. (2006), 'Frankenstein's Futurity: Replicants and Robots,' in E. Schor (ed.), *The Cambridge Companion to Mary Shelley* (New York: Cambridge University Press), pp. 84–100.

de Waal, F. (2013), *The Bonobo and the Atheist: In Search of Humanism Among the Primates* (New York: W. W. Norton).

Descartes, R. (1998), *Discourse on Method*, and *Meditations on First Philosophy*, 4th edition (Indianapolis, IN: Hackett).

Desser, D. (1997), 'The New Eve: The Influence of *Paradise Lost* and *Frankenstein* on *Blade Runner*,' in J. B. Kerman (ed.), *Retrofitting* Blade Runner*: Issues in Ridley Scott's* Blade Runner *and Philip K. Dick's* Do Androids Dream of Electric Sheep?, 2nd edition (Bowling Green, OH: Bowling Green University Press), pp. 53–65.

Dick, P. K. (1968a), *Do Androids Dream of Electric Sheep?* (New York: Ballantine Books).

Dick, P. K. (1968b), 'Notes on Do Androids Dream of Electric Sheep?,' in L. Sutin (ed.), *The Shifting Realities of Philip K. Dick: Selected Literary and Philosophical Writings* (New York: Vintage Books, 1995), pp. 155–61.

Dick, P. K. (1972), 'The Android and the Human,' in L. Sutin (ed.), *The Shifting Realities of Philip K. Dick: Selected Literary and Philosophical Writings* (New York: Vintage Books, 1995), pp. 183–210.

Dick, P. K. (1978), 'How to Build a Universe That Doesn't Fall Apart Two Days Later,' in L. Sutin (ed.), *The Shifting Realities of Philip K. Dick: Selected Literary and Philosophical Writings* (New York: Vintage Books, 1995), pp. 259–80.

Literature Cited

Dick, P. K. (1980), 'Philip K. Dick on Philosophy: A Brief Interview,' in L. Sutin (ed.), *The Shifting Realities of Philip K. Dick: Selected Literary and Philosophical Writings* (New York: Vintage Books, 1995), pp. 44–7.

Dick, P. K. (1981), 'Universe Makers ... and Breakers,' *SelecTV Guide*, February 15 – March 28, in L. Sutin (ed.), *The Shifting Realities of Philip K. Dick: Selected Literary and Philosophical Writings* (New York: Vintage Books, 1995), pp. 103–5.

Durham, A. (2013), 'We *Have* Built You: On the Nature of Artificial Intelligence in *Blade Runner* and *Babylon Babies*,' *FORUM: University of Edinburgh Postgraduate Journal of Culture and the Arts* 16:1–13.

Fischer, J. M. (2010), 'Why Immortality is Not So Bad,' in D. Benatar (ed.), *Life, Death, & Meaning*, 2nd edition (Lanham, MD: Rowman & Littlefield), pp. 363–77.

Francavilla, J. (1997), 'The Android as Doppelgänger,' in J. B. Kerman (ed.), *Retrofitting* Blade Runner*: Issues in Ridley Scott's* Blade Runner *and Philip K. Dick's* Do Androids Dream of Electric Sheep?, 2nd edition (Bowling Green, OH: Bowling Green University Press), pp. 4–15.

Frankfurt, H. (1971), 'Freedom of the Will and the Concept of a Person,' *Journal of Philosophy* 68(1):5–20.

Gazzaniga, M. S. (2005), *The Ethical Brain: The Science of Our Moral Dilemmas* (New York: Harper Perennial).

Gerblinger, C. (2002), '"Fiery the Angels Fell": America, Regeneration, and Ridley Scott's *Blade Runner*,' *Australasian Journal of American Studies* 21(1):19–30.

Gray, W. R. (1997), 'Entropy, Energy, Empathy: Blade Runner and Detective Fiction,' in J. B. Kerman (ed.), *Retrofitting* Blade Runner*: Issues in Ridley Scott's* Blade Runner *and Philip K. Dick's* Do Androids Dream of Electric Sheep?, 2nd edition (Bowling Green, OH: Bowling Green University Press), pp. 66–75.

Gwaltney, M. (1997), 'Androids as a Device for Reflection on Personhood,' in J. B. Kerman (ed.), *Retrofitting* Blade Runner*: Issues in Ridley Scott's* Blade Runner *and Philip K. Dick's* Do Androids Dream of Electric Sheep?, 2nd edition (Bowling Green, OH: Bowling Green University Press), pp. 32–9.

Harley, A. (2005), 'America, a Prophecy: When Blake Meets *Blade Runner*,' *Sydney Studies in English* 31:62–76.

Harris, S. (2010), *The Moral Landscape: How Science Can Determine Human Values* (New York: Free Press).

Harris, S. (2012), *Free Will* (New York: Free Press).

Heldreth, L. G. (1997), 'The Cutting Edge of *Blade Runner*,' in J. B. Kerman (ed.), *Retrofitting* Blade Runner*: Issues in Ridley Scott's* Blade Runner *and Philip K. Dick's* Do Androids Dream of Electric Sheep?, 2nd edition (Bowling Green, OH: Bowling Green University Press), pp. 40–52.

Literature Cited

Hicks, R. D. (1910), *Stoic and Epicurean* (New York: Charles Scribner's Sons).

Hume, D. (1739–40), *A Treatise of Human Nature*, edited by D. F. Norton and M. J. Norton (Oxford: Oxford University Press, 2000).

Jackson, F. (1986), 'What Mary Didn't Know,' *Journal of Philosophy* 83(5):291–5.

James, W. (1897), *The Will to Believe and Other Essays in Popular Philosophy* (New York: Dover Publications, 1956).

Kant, I. (1785), *Groundwork of the Metaphysic of Morals*, translated by H. J. Patton (New York: Harper Torchbooks, 1964).

Kaufmann, W. (1974), *Nietzsche: Philosopher, Psychologist, Antichrist*, 4th edition (Princeton: Princeton University Press).

Kennedy, H. (1982), 'Twenty-First Century Nervous Breakdown,' in L. F. Knapp and A. F. Kulas (eds.), *Ridley Scott: Interviews* (Jackson, MS: University Press of Mississippi, 2005), pp. 32–41.

Kerman, J. B. (1997), 'Technology and Politics in the *Blade Runner* Dystopia,' in J. B. Kerman (ed.), *Retrofitting* Blade Runner: *Issues in Ridley Scott's* Blade Runner *and Philip K. Dick's* Do Androids Dream of Electric Sheep?, 2nd edition (Bowling Green, OH: Bowling Green University Press), pp. 16–24.

Knapp, L. F., and Kulas, A. F. (eds.) (2005), *Ridley Scott: Interviews* (Jackson, MS: University Press of Mississippi).

Kolb, W. M. (1997), 'Script to Screen: *Blade Runner* in Perspective,' in J. B. Kerman (ed.), *Retrofitting* Blade Runner: *Issues in Ridley Scott's* Blade Runner *and Philip K. Dick's* Do Androids Dream of Electric Sheep?, 2nd edition (Bowling Green, OH: Bowling Green University Press), pp. 132–53.

Lacey, N. (2000), *York Film Notes: Blade Runner* (London: York Press).

Laplace, P.-S. (1814), *A Philosophical Essay on Probabilities*, translated from the 6th edition by F. W. Truscott and F. L. Emory (New York: Dover Publications, 1951).

Levy, D. (2010), 'The Ethics of Robot Prostitutes,' in P. Lin, K. Abney, and G. A. Bekey (eds.), *Robot Ethics: The Ethical and Social Implications of Robotics* (Cambridge, MA: MIT Press), pp. 223–31.

Libet, B., Gleason, C. A., Wright, E. W., and Pearl, D. K. (1983), 'Time of Conscious Intention to Act in Relation to Onset of Cerebral Activity (Readiness Potential): The Unconscious Initiation of a Freely Voluntary Act,' *Brain* 106(3):623–42.

Livingston, P. (2006), 'Theses on Cinema as Philosophy,' *Journal of Aesthetics and Art Criticism* 64(1):11–18.

Locke, J. (1690), *An Essay Concerning Human Understanding*, 2 volumes (New York: Dover Publications, 1959).

Long, A. A., and Sedley, D. N. (eds.) (1987), *The Hellenistic Philosophers*, Vol. 1 (Cambridge: Cambridge University Press).

Literature Cited

Luper, S. (1996), *Invulnerability: On Securing Happiness* (Chicago: Open Court).

Martin, M. (2005), 'Meditations on *Blade Runner*,' *Journal of Interdisciplinary Studies* 17(1–2):105–22.

Mawby, P. (2001), 'The Kingdom is Within: Religious Themes and Postmodernity in Ridley Scott's *Blade Runner*,' in C. M. Cusack and P. Oldmeadow (eds.), *The End of Religions? Religion in an Age of Globalisation* (Sydney: University of Sydney), pp. 139–54.

McDonagh, M. (1991), 'Thelma and Louise Hit the Road for Ridley Scott,' in L. F. Knapp and A. F. Kulas (eds.), *Ridley Scott: Interviews* (Jackson, MS: University Press of Mississippi, 2005), pp. 70–4.

Morrison, R. (1990), '*Casablanca* Meets *Star Wars*: The Blakean Dialectics of *Blade Runner*,' *Literature Film Quarterly* 18(1):2–10.

Mulhall, S. (1994), 'Picturing the Human (Body and Soul): A Reading of *Blade Runner*,' *Film and Philosophy* 1:87–104.

Mulhall, S. (2008), *On Film*, 2nd edition (London and New York: Routledge).

Murphy, N. (2006), *Bodies and Souls, or Spirited Bodies?* (New York: Cambridge University Press.

Nagel, T. (1986), *The View from Nowhere* (Oxford: Oxford University Press).

Nietzsche, F. (1878–80), *Human, All Too Human*, translated by R. J. Hollingdale (Cambridge: Cambridge University Press, 1986).

Nietzsche, F. (1881), *Dawn: Thoughts on the Presumptions of Morality*, translated by B. Smith (Stanford, CA: Stanford University Press, 2011).

Nietzsche, F. (1882), *The Gay Science*, translated, and with a commentary, by W. Kaufmann (New York: Vintage Books, 1974).

Nietzsche, F. (1883–5), *Thus Spoke Zarathustra*, translated by R. J. Hollingdale (Baltimore, MD: Penguin Books, 1969).

Nietzsche, F. (1886), *Beyond Good and Evil*, translated, and with a commentary, by W. Kaufmann (New York: Vintage Books, 1966).

Nietzsche, F. (1887), *On the Genealogy of Morals*, translated by W. Kaufmann and R. J. Hollingdale (New York: Vintage Books, 1967).

Nietzsche, F. (1888a), *Twilight of the Idols*, translated by R. J. Hollingdale (Baltimore, MD: Penguin Books, 1968).

Nietzsche, F. (1888b), *Ecce Homo*, translated, and with a commentary, by W. Kaufmann (New York: Vintage Books, 1967).

Olson, E. T. (2003), 'An Argument for Animalism,' in R. Martin and J. Barresi (eds.), *Personal Identity* (Malden, MA: Wiley-Blackwell), pp. 318–34.

Owen, D. (2007), *Nietzsche's Genealogy of Morality* (Montreal and Kingston; Ithaca: McGill-Queen's University Press).

Pate, A. (2009), 'Nietzsche's *Übermensch* in the Hyperreal Flux: An Analysis of *Blade Runner*, *Fight Club*, and *Miami Vice*,' Master's Thesis, *Dissertations*

Literature Cited

and Graduate Research Overview, Paper 15. [http://digitalcommons.ric.edu/etd/15] Accessed 18 March 2011.

Peary, D. (1984), 'Directing *Alien* and *Blade Runner*: An Interview with Ridley Scott,' in L. F. Knapp and A. F. Kulas (eds.), *Ridley Scott: Interviews* (Jackson, MS: University Press of Mississippi, 2005), pp. 42–55.

Petersen, S. (2007), 'The Ethics of Robot Servitude,' *Journal of Experimental and Theoretical Artificial Intelligence* 19(1):43–54.

Petersen, S. (2012), 'Designing People to Serve,' in P. Lin, K. Abney, and G. A. Bekey (eds.), *Robot Ethics: The Ethical and Social Implications of Robotics* (Cambridge, MA: MIT Press), pp. 283–98.

Plato, *The Trial and Death of Socrates*, 3rd edition (Indianapolis, IN: Hackett, 2000).

Redmond, S. (2008), *Studying Blade Runner* (Leighton Buzzard: Auteur).

Reid, T. (1788), *Essays on the Active Powers of Man* (Cambridge: Cambridge University Press, 2011).

Rickman, G. (1997), 'Philip K. Dick on *Blade Runner*: "They Did Sight Stimulation on My Brain",' in J. B. Kerman (ed.), *Retrofitting* Blade Runner: *Issues in Ridley Scott's* Blade Runner *and Philip K. Dick's* Do Androids Dream of Electric Sheep?, 2nd edition (Bowling Green, OH: Bowling Green University Press), pp. 103–9.

Rosenbaum, S. E. (1993), 'How to Be Dead and Not Care: A Defense of Epicurus,' in J. M. Fischer (ed.), *The Metaphysics of Death* (Stanford: Stanford University Press), pp. 117–34.

Rowlands, M. (2003), *The Philosopher at the End of the Universe: Philosophy Explained Through Science Fiction Films* (London: Ebury Press).

Rushing, J. H., and Frentz, T. S. (1995), *Projecting the Shadow: The Cyborg Hero in American Film* (Chicago: University of Chicago Press).

Russell, B. (2000), 'The Philosophical Limits of Film,' *Film and Philosophy* (Special Interest Edition on the Films of Woody Allen):163–7.

Sammon, P. M. (1982), 'The Arts,' *Omni* 4(8):24, 140.

Sammon, P. M. (1996), *Future Noir: The Making of Blade Runner* (New York: HarperCollins).

Sartre, J-P. (1943), *Being and Nothingness: A Phenomenological Essay on Ontology*, translated by H. E. Barnes (New York: Washington Square Press, 1956).

Sartre, J-P. (1946), *Existentialism and Human Emotions* (Secaucus, NJ: Citadel Press, 1957).

Searle, J. (1990), 'Is the Brain's Mind a Computer Program?' *Scientific American* 262:26–31.

Shelley, M. (1818), *Frankenstein* (New York: Bantam Books, 1981).

Smith, M. (2006), 'Film, Art, Argument, and Ambiguity,' *Journal of Aesthetics and Art Criticism* 64(1):33–42.

Literature Cited

Strawson, G. (1994), 'The Impossibility of Moral Responsibility,' *Philosophical Studies* 75:5–24.

Strick, P. (1982), 'The Age of the Replicate,' *Sight & Sound* 51(3):168–72.

Strick, P. (1992), 'Blade Runner: Telling the Difference,' *Sight & Sound* 2(8):8–9.

Taylor, R. (1970), *Good and Evil: A New Direction* (New York: Macmillan).

Tolstoy, L. (1882), 'My Confession,' in *The Complete Works of Leo N. Tolstoy* (New York: Thomas Y. Cromwell & Co., 1899).

Tosca, S. P. (2005), 'Implanted Memories, or the Illusion of Free Action,' in W. Brooker (ed.), *The Blade Runner Experience: The Legacy of a Science Fiction Classic* (London: Wallflower Press), pp. 92–107.

Turing, A. (1950), 'Computing Machinery and Intelligence,' *Mind* 59:433–60.

Unamuno, M. (1972), *The Tragic Sense of Life in Men and Nations*, translated by A. Kerrigan (Princeton: Princeton University Press).

Vest, J. P. (2007), *Future Imperfect: Philip K. Dick at the Movies* (Westport, CT: Praeger).

Wartenberg, T. E. (2006), 'Beyond Mere Illustration: How Films Can Be Philosophy,' *Journal of Aesthetics and Art Criticism* 64(1):19–32.

Williams, B. (1973), 'The Makropulos Case: Reflections on the Tedium of Immortality,' in *Problems of the Self: Philosophical Papers 1956–1972* (Cambridge: Cambridge University Press), pp. 82–100.

Wittgenstein, L. (1922), *Tractatus Logico-Philosophicus* (New York: Harcourt, Brace & Company).

Wood, R. (2003), *Hollywood from Vietnam to Reagan ... and Beyond*, expanded and revised edition (New York: Columbia University Press).

Zunt, D. (2006), 'Who Did Actually Invent the Word 'Robot' and What Does it Mean?' [http://capek.misto.cz/english/robot.html] Accessed 22 December 2012.

Index

Abrams, J. J. 193
Adam and Eve 199–200
Alessio, D. 111
Allegory of the Cave, Plato's 181–2
'America: A Prophecy' 132–4
Andersen, N. 205
androids 2–7, 11, 14, 20, 29, 73, 141, 187, 189–92, 200, 201
animoids 1, 4, 12, 23, 24, 31, 60, 68, 188
Arick, Michael 9

Bahania, A. M. 10
Barad, J. 111, 146, 187, 190
Barlow, A. 48
Battaglia, D. 192
Batty, Roy 2, 12, 23, 32–7, 39, 42, 80, 86, 88, 89, 91, 92, 95, 101, 115, 132, 133, 134, 137, 145, 154, 161, 175–7, 184, 188, 191, 192, 195, 197–9, 201, 202, 204; and empathy 36–7, 111; and time 164, 175, 176; as Overman 118, 122, 124, 125–7; characteristics 26, 28, 30, 32, 57, 111–3, 123–5, 139, 177, 189; comparison with Frankenstein's monster 136–7; comparison with Satan 133–5, 199; demand for 'more life' 94, 147–9, 153, 156, 160, 194, 197
being human 22–42; definition problem 39–41; humans compared with replicants 37–8
Bergman, Ingmar 194
Blade runner units 1, 183
Blade Runner versions *see* Director's Cut; Theatrical (version); Workprint (version)
Boozer, J. Jr. 30
Bray, H. 9
Brooker, P. 186
Brueckner, A. J. 159, 160
Bryant, Harry 2, 12, 13, 16, 28, 38, 41, 45, 57, 72, 99, 100, 103, 104, 106, 115, 131, 184, 188, 197; as a bigot 37, 44
Bryson, J. J. 50–2
Bukatman, S. x, 183, 185, 187
Byron, J. 185, 197

Camus, A. 167–168, 170
Čapek, K. 31, 168
Carrère, E. 2
Carroll, N. 205
Cartesian Substance Dualism 81–6
Cavell, S. 205
Chalmers, D. 192
chess 35, 80, 86–7, 115, 194–5
Chew, Hannibal 8, 26, 29, 34, 35, 36, 63, 89, 90, 95, 132, 136, 198
Churchland, P. M. 93
Clayton, J. 200
compatibilism 105–10

Index

computers 23, 30, 78, 80, 100, 185, 195; replicants as 86–9
consciousness, as criterion of personal identity 67–8, 71–4, 79; explanations of 80–98

de Waal, F. 40
death 147–63; as a problem 147–50; Epicurus on 151–2; Socrates on 150–1
Deckard, Rick 2, 23, 35, 39, 43, 56, 60, 75, 78, 104, 106–8, 131, 161, 164, 178, 184, 190, 192, 197–200; as having or lacking free will 99–110, 113, 141; as Nietzschean Overman 116–8; as a replicant 11–21, 185, 186, 187, 197; characteristics 1, 5, 28, 38, 41–2, 59, 71, 146; in *Electric Sheep* 4–6, 197
Deck-a-Rep debate 11–20, 185–7
Deely, Michael 129, 198
deprivationism 152–6
Descartes, R. 24–7, 62, 81–4, 187, 192, 194
Desser, D. 199
determinism 101–3
Dick, Philip K. 2–7, 15, 34, 182–4, 189–92, 199–201
Director's Cut 10–12, 15, 198
Do Androids Dream of Electric Sheep? 2–6, 11, 14, 15, 24, 72–3, 189, 190, 192, 195, 200, 201
Durham, A. 185

eliminative physicalism 92–5
empathy 5, 6, 14, 19, 35–8, 45, 46, 111, 189, 190, 191
Epicurus 151, 161, 162
Esper machine 180, 188

experientialism 152, 159, 202
eyes 12–16, 34, 63, 86, 90, 95

Fancher, Hampton 112, 183, 184, 187, 201
Fischer, J. M. 159, 169
Francavilla, J. 42, 189
Frankenstein 136–8
Frankfurt, H. 108–10
freedom 99–114; Roy Batty's 110–13
Frentz, T. S. 189

Gaff (Inspector) 14, 15, 16, 38, 99, 115, 131, 146, 184, 185, 186, 188, 196, 197, 198
Gazzaniga, M. S. 191
Gerblinger, C. 186
God 131–46
Gray, W. R. 199
Gwaltney, M. 152–3, 190

Harley, A. 197
Harris, S. 112, 149, 202
Hauer, Rutger 2, 112, 179–80, 184, 188, 198
Heidegger, Martin 155
Heldreth, L. G. 189
Hicks, R. D. 162
Holden, Dave 4, 13, 26, 30, 37, 39, 115, 123, 131, 187, 188, 189, 197
Hume, D. 64–5

incept dates 28, 63, 85, 90, 160, 164, 176

Jackson, F. 94
James, W. 101–2

Kant, I. 48–50
Kaufmann, W. 125, 127
Kennedy, H. 29

Index

Kerman, J. B. 100, 191
Kolb, W. M. 187

Lacey, N. 185
Laplace, P.-S. 102, 196
Last Samurai, The 196
Leibniz, Gottfried Wilhelm von 194
Leon (Kowalski) 2, 4, 13, 26, 27, 30, 38, 72, 89, 115, 176, 184, 189, 204; and photos 33, 37, 180, 193; and time 164–5, 175; characteristics 28, 32, 34, 35, 36, 56–7, 123, 139, 187
Levy, D. 192
libertarianism 103–4
Libet, B. 112
Livingston, P. 205
Locke, J. 65–71
Lucretius 157, 160–2, 203, 212
Luper, S. 203, 204

Makropulos Case, The 168–70
Malebranche, Nicolas 194
Martin, M. 192, 195
Mawby, P. 185
memories 61–77, 191, 192, 193; genuine vs. pseudo 69–71; memory implants 12, 22, 60, 68, 69, 75, 186, 195
morality 115–30; Christian contrasted with Homeric 118–21; slave revolt in 120–4
Morrison, R. xi, 189
Mulhall, S. 187, 190, 191, 195, 198, 202, 205
Murphy, N. 96–8
Myth of Sisyphus 167–8, 170–3

Nagel, T. 173–4, 177, 204
Nexus 6 1, 28, 32, 43, 45, 46, 57, 80, 95, 136, 192

Nietzsche, F. 116–30, 196, 197, 198; critique of 127–9
Non-reductive physicalism 95–7

Off-world 1, 2, 4, 29, 44, 53, 57, 58, 100, 123, 133, 134, 139, 165, 188
Olson, E. T. 72–3
Owen, D. 196

Paradise Lost 132, 134–5
Pate, A. 116–18
Permanence Principle 167
Peoples, David 184
personal identity 60–79; body theory 71–4; consciousness theory 66–71; soul theory 62–6
persons 43–59; Kant's view 48–50
Petersen, S. 52–4, 58
photographs 13, 32, 33, 37, 60–1, 66, 77, 123, 180, 192–3
Pindar 178
Plato 62, 150, 181–2
Pris 2, 27, 35, 36, 37, 38, 73, 81, 84, 88, 115, 123, 176, 184, 197; characteristics 28, 30, 32, 34, 35, 57, 80, 89, 139, 188, 192

Rachael 2, 13, 22, 32, 36, 38, 117, 154, 163, 184–6, 189, 191, 193, 194, 196, 199–201; as a person 43–59; identity of 60–79; in *Electric Sheep* 5, 14, 200; no termination date 8, 176
Rawlings, Terry 21
Redmond, S. 111, 187
reductive physicalism 89–92
Reid, T. 104

215

Index

replicants: as having moral standing 44–52, 59, 191; as slaves 1, 31, 44, 50, 51, 52, 56, 58, 100, 137, 139, 143, 145, 147, 165, 190, 192; characteristics 1, 27–31; differences from human beings 32–3; similarities to human beings 33–7
Resch, Phil 11, 14, 192
Rickman, G. 199
robots 2–3, 30, 31, 37, 50–3, 72, 141, 189, 192
Rosenbaum, S. E. 158
Rowlands, M. 155–6, 203
Rushing, J. H. 189
Russell, B. 205

Sammon, P. M. xi, 3, 10, 15, 16, 20, 21, 34, 47, 112, 113, 129, 179, 180, 183, 184, 185, 186, 187, 188, 198, 201
Sartre, J.-P. 103–4, 107, 132, 143–5, 166, 200, 202–3; critique of 139–43; on human reality and artifacts 138–9
Scott, Jake 198
Scott, Ridley 2, 5–6, 8, 10, 15, 16, 17, 18, 21, 29, 34, 47, 111–12, 179, 180, 183, 185, 186, 188, 195
Searle, J. 88
Sebastian, J. F. 4, 8, 23, 32, 33, 35, 36, 37, 38, 42, 44, 63, 77, 80, 86, 87, 89, 115, 123, 127, 184, 197, 198, 200
sex 29, 30, 54, 59, 78, 175, 190, 192, 204
Shelley, M. 132
slave morality 120–4, 127, 197
Smith, M. 205
Socrates 62, 150–1
souls 150, 151; as constitutive of personal identity 62–7, 73, 74, 192, 194; as distinctive of human beings 40
spinner 185
sportsmanship 116, 122, 125, 126, 160, 191, 197
Strawson, G. 107
Strick, P. 136, 185–6
Symmetry Argument, The 157–60

Taylor, R. 170–3, 176–7, 204
Theatrical (version) 8, 10, 11, 12, 16, 19, 42, 100, 112, 176, 184, 199
time 34, 71–3, 137, 157, 158, 162; and meaning 164–78, 203
Tolstoy, L. 166–7, 174, 175, 176
Tosca, S. P. 100, 192, 195
Turing, A. M. 87–8
Tyrell, Eldon 2, 4, 5, 8, 22, 23, 26, 35, 37, 38, 39, 43, 60, 63, 77, 90, 94, 101, 123, 126, 135. 139, 147, 149, 165, 176, 177, 178, 184, 190, 193, 194, 195, 201; as a God-figure 131, 132, 145, 198, 199; comparison with Frankenstein 136–7, 200
Tyrell's niece 13, 22, 32, 60–3, 66–79, 193
Tyrell Corporation 1, 4, 12, 22, 23, 26, 27, 43, 57, 60, 61, 62, 68, 69, 71, 72, 85, 95, 115, 145, 153, 188, 197, 199

Unamuno, M. 165–6
unicorn 10, 15, 16, 184, 185, 186, 187

Vest, J. P. 17
voice-over narration 8, 10, 16, 44, 112, 176, 184, 200

Index

Voight-Kampff test 5, 12, 13, 19, 22, 23, 35, 36, 38, 43, 60, 63, 68, 69, 79, 111, 186, 187, 197

Wartenberg, T. E. 205
Williams, B. 168–70, 176
Wittgenstein, L. 202, 204
Wood, R. 9

Workprint (version) 7, 9, 10, 29, 30, 31, 183

Zhora 2, 5, 13, 14, 24, 26, 35, 38, 72, 85, 86, 176, 180, 184; characteristics 28, 30, 36, 57, 88, 139, 143, 187, 188
Zunt, D. 31

Printed in Great Britain
by Amazon